BACKPACKS FULL OF HOPE

Studies in International Governance is a research and policy analysis series from the Centre for International Governance Innovation (CIGI) and Wilfrid Laurier University Press. Titles in the series provide timely consideration of emerging trends and current challenges in the broad field of international governance. Representing diverse perspectives on important global issues, the series will be of interest to students and academics while serving also as a reference tool for policy-makers and experts engaged in policy discussion.

BACKPACKS
FULL OF HOPE

THE UN MISSION
IN HAITI

EDUARDO ALDUNATE

TRANSLATED BY
ALMA ROSA FLORES FERNANDEZ

CIGI The Centre for International
Governance Innovation
Centre pour l'innovation dans
la gouvernance internationale

Wilfrid Laurier University Press
[WLU]

Wilfrid Laurier University Press acknowledges the financial support of the Government of Canada through its Book Publishing Industry Development Program for its publishing activities. Wilfrid Laurier University Press acknowledges the financial support of the Centre for International Governance Innovation. The Centre for International Governance Innovation gratefully acknowledges support for its work program from the Government of Canada and the Government of Ontario.

Library and Archives Canada Cataloguing in Publication

Aldunate Herman, Eduardo, 1952–
      Backpacks full of hope : the UN mission in Haiti / Eduardo Aldunate Herman ; translated by Alma Flores.

Translation of: Misión en Haiti.
(Studies in International Governance Series)
Co-published by: Centre for International Governance Innovation.
Includes bibliographical references and index.
Issued also in electronic formats.
ISBN 978-1-55458-155-9

      1. Aldunate Herman, Eduardo, 1952–. 2. United Nations Stabilization Mission in Haiti. 3. Peacekeeping forces, Chilean—Haiti. 4. Peacekeeping forces—Haiti. 5. Haiti—History—1986–. 6. Generals—Chile—Biography. I. Flores, Alma II. Centre for International Governance Innovation III. Title.

F1928.2.A5413 2010   972.9407'3092   C2009-904998-8

ISBN 978-1-55458-160-3
Electronic format.

F1928.2.A5413 2010a   972.9407'3092   C2009-905621-6

Contents

About the Author

Brigadier General (R) Eduardo Aldunate Herman is an infantry officer in the Chilean Army.

He has commanded the Los Ángeles 17th Mountain Infantry Regiment, the Paratroopers and Special Forces School and the State National Mobilization Department, and served as Commander of the Army Schools Division.

He has specialized as a General Staff Officer and Expert Paratrooper, as well as in Military Intelligence, Commandos and Tactical Diving.

He holds master's degrees in Military History and Military Sciences and was Professor of Military Strategy and History at the Army War Academy.

He has written three books on leadership and military–civilian relationships, as well as several articles published in national and international magazines and newspapers.

He has received awards from Chile, Brazil, Honduras, the United States and the UN.

Between September 2005 and September 2006, he acted as Deputy Commander of the UN Military Forces in Haiti, MINUSTAH.

Foreword

In this book, General Eduardo Aldunate, of the Chilean Army, who was deputy commander (and, for a time, acting commander) of the UN peacekeeping forces in Haiti from September 2005 to September 2006, tells his story. At the time that the book was written, there was an increasing sense of promise for the country. In February 2006 Haiti's presidential elections took place, culminating in the election of former Prime Minister René Préval. The United Nations (UN), as well as the Organization of American States (OAS), played a critical role in making these elections happen. The Préval presidency provided a measure of stability and a window of opportunity for the Haitian people to regroup and relaunch their attempt to put Latin America and the Caribbean's first independent republic back on an even keel. After twenty years of intermittent transition to democracy, ever since the fall of Jean-Claude ("Baby Doc") Duvalier in 1986, the time following Préval's election has been the longest period of relative stability that Haiti has witnessed. This does not mean it has been an uneventful time.

The devastating earthquake that hit Haiti just outside the capital (Port-au-Prince), on 12 January 2010, is a tragedy that reminds the international community of the myriad problems facing the country (the poorest in the Western hemisphere), as General Aldunate recounts in the pages that follow. The earthquake caused great loss of life and the destruction of much formal assistance. At the time of writing, reliable estimates about the death toll are hard to come by (many well-informed groups estimate it to be approximately 110,000), and the UN has said that accurate numbers might never be known. What is clear is that the country will be scarred by this tragedy for years to come. Many places and people that General Aldunate refers to in this book are now gone, leaving immense gaps in the fabric of Haitian society.

In terms of this book, the most notable loss has been that of the headquarters of the UN's presence in the country. Colleagues and friends of General Aldunate were lost in this tragedy — people who were working hard to create a better situation for this impoverished nation. MINUSTAH, the United Nations Mission to Stabilize Haiti, was launched in 2004 and is the first UN peacekeeping operation to be made up primarily of Latin American troops. MINUSTAH has been in existence for five years, as of this writing, and has made a valiant effort to bring stability and order to the land of Dessalines and Duvalier, racked so long by conflict and strife.

Even before the earthquake, Haiti had been rattled by human and natural disasters. In the summer of 2008, two hurricanes (Gustav and Ike) and two tropical storms (Fay and Hanna) inflicted considerable damage, killing as many as 800 people and destroying substantial parts of Haiti's already precarious infrastructure. The 2010 earthquake has magnified these problems and brought them to another level. Haiti was also severely affected by the Great Recession of 2008, which hit the world economy with devastating consequences. The financial meltdown affected Haiti in a variety of ways, but mostly through a decline in remittances from the Haitian diaspora. It is estimated that the two million Haitians abroad sent US$1.83 billion in remittances to Haiti in 2007, of which some US$1.2 billion came from the United States. The former figure amounts to one-third of Haiti's GDP. The ensuing drop in remittances, caused by the economic slowdown in the US, Canada, France, and other countries that host the Haitian diaspora, thus hit the country severely.

These natural and man-made disasters have shown that the task of putting Haiti on a stable track is a long-term undertaking that demands an equally long-term commitment from the international community. Until recently, that commitment was seen as a duty to be shouldered by what people in Port-au-Prince refer to as the Big Three—the U.S., Canada, and France, the leading powers seen to have permanent interests in Haiti. Yet in a marked shift from that earlier scenario, the Big Three have increasingly been joined by the ABC—Argentina, Brazil, and Chile, South America's leading nations. Signalling an important change from an earlier, somewhat aloof position vis-à-vis Haiti's predicament, these latter three (as well as other Latin American nations like Bolivia, Ecuador, Guatemala, Peru, and Uruguay) stepped up, committing a large number of troops to MINUSTAH and indicating that they were in Haiti for as long as was deemed necessary to ensure the country is sufficiently stabilized and institutionalized to steer its own course. In the aftermath of the 2010 earthquake, this international commitment remains vital in treating the humanitarian crisis and restoring some semblance of stability.

The role played by Chile—and General Aldunate, of course, is of the Chilean Army—is worth noting, since Chile was at the forefront of Latin America's response to the February 2004 crisis in Haiti triggered by the fall of President Jean-Bertrand Aristide ("Titide," as he is known to his supporters). After Aristide left for the Central African Republic on a U.S. State Department plane, the United Nations Security Council unanimously approved Resolution 1529, authorizing the presence of a Provisional Multinational Force for a three-month period, to re-establish peace and security and provide humanitarian assistance.

U.S. Secretary of State Colin Powell called Chilean Foreign Minister Soledad Alvear to find out whether Chile would be willing to commit troops to this undertaking. Powell's question was by no means an easy one for Chile to answer. Some people argue to this day that Aristide did not fall but was toppled. This was CARICOM's position. Aristide had long been a darling of the left, and many organizations, including the Congressional Black Caucus in the United States, stood up for him.

Moreover, any commitment of troops would be the first time that Chilean troops had participated in what was to be, effectively, a peace-enforcement operation, as opposed to the peacekeeping operations with small contingents— as a rule, no more than fifty men— that the country had participated in until then. Latin American diplomacy has a strong herd instinct, and no one else, including Brazil (which said it would wait out the first three months "to see what happens"), was willing to send troops to Haiti.

The Chilean constitution did not make matters any easier. It states that the deployment of Chilean troops abroad must be approved by the Senate. Yet events in Haiti were moving so fast that there was not enough time for the sort of extended legislative deliberation and debate that such a momentous decision would require. In many ways, then, it would have been easier to say no to Powell or to follow the Brazilian example and wait and see.

Yet, as General Aldunate tells us in this gripping memoir of his Haitian sojourn, within twenty-four hours Chile accepted the invitation to deploy a sizeable military force, and within seventy-two hours some 329 Chilean military found themselves on their way to Port-au-Prince. They joined the U.S., French, and Canadian contingents for a mopping-up operation that went well. After the three-month period was over, the latter forces left the country; only the Chilean forces stayed on. By this time their number had increased to some 600 men and women from all three services as well as the national police, the *carabineros*. Argentina, Bolivia, Brazil, Ecuador, Guatemala, Peru, and Uruguay have all sent troops to what, as mentioned above, has become the first-ever United Nations peacekeeping operation manned mostly by Latin American forces. A Brazilian general, Augusto Heleno Ribeiro Pereira, was appointed as commander of the UN Blue Helmets, and from 2004 to 2006 a former Chilean foreign minister, Juan Gabriel Valdés, served as the UN Secretary General's Special Representative in Haiti.

That was the context when General Aldunate arrived in Haiti in September 2005 to take on his duties as deputy commander of the UN peacekeeping forces. In this book, his highly personal account of the challenges he faced, he brings to the fore the difficult choices the commanders of the Blue Helmets have to contend with, on the ground, in fragile and/or failing states.

In a single year, General Aldunate bore witness to and was part of an extraordinary series of events, which he narrates with passion and verve. It was during his tenure that Haiti's presidential elections took place, on 7 February 2006, the first in which Haitian voters could vote with a proper I.D. document. The drama surrounding that election—in some ways not unlike the Afghanistan presidential elections of September 2009 (though without the alleged fraud)—and whether and how a second round should be held according to the rules of the *ballottage*, was a key turning point in the efforts of the international community to stabilize the Haitian polity. In the run-up to the elections themselves, what stands out are the efforts of General Aldunate and his colleagues to strike a balance between maintaining law and order and not provoking unnecessary bloodshed, which might have derailed the critical democratic exercise. Clearly, the modern soldier-statesman in contemporary peacekeeping needs to have a good understanding not only of warfare but of the political dynamics of societies on the verge of breakdown.

A running thread throughout his story is the fate of Cité Soleil, where Haiti's leading gangs are found. How to cope with that Port-au-Prince neighborhood, where most of the casualties of the UN forces took place and where the Haitian National Police dared not set foot, was an ongoing challenge for the Blue Helmets. General Aldunate dwells in great detail on the constant dilemmas this posed to UN peacekeepers. With Port-au-Prince now levelled and MINUSTAH and Haitian police diverted elsewhere, this threat is increasingly real.

In today's media-driven societies, top military officers also have to deal with the false accusations that their public personas will sometimes trigger. While performing his duties in Haiti, General Aldunate had to deal with one such incident from back home in Chile. This book also tells the tale of how he came to terms with and disproved these unwarranted claims, which put such an enormous strain on him and his family.

Canada has always had a special relationship with Haiti. Along with Afghanistan, Haiti is, as of this writing, the single most important bilateral foreign policy priority in the Global South in terms of international cooperation. Canada has also developed over the years a special relationship with Chile, a "like-minded" country with which it signed, in 1996, the first Free Trade Agreement between any nation-state in the North and another in the Global South. Canada's Governor General, Michaëlle Jean, herself a native Haitian, delivered a tearful message to the Haitian people and the international community following the earthquake.

The translation from its original Spanish into English of this tale of a Chilean soldier in Haiti and its publication in the CIGI series on International Governance by Wilfrid Laurier University Press reflect not only Canada's ongoing traditional commitment to UN peacekeeping but also its more recent interest in the promotion of democracy and development in the Americas. Nowhere in the hemisphere is that imperative as urgent as it is in Haiti. This book provides eloquent testimony to the efforts of one soldier, hailing from a distant continental neighbour, who did his best to bring a measure of stability and peace to the people of that long-suffering half of Hispaniola.

With international attention now clearly focused on this fragile state, we hope that this book serves as a clear example of the immeasurable costs borne by those attempting to help Haiti. Hopefully, despite the brevity of the contemporary news cycle, sustained international attention will be given to the people of Haiti and their quest for a better life. The response of people across the world is encouraging; numerous telethons and charity drives have sprung up to help the people in the country. Governments from across the Western hemisphere and the world must maintain their commitments to this devastated country and work with the Haitian people to forge a better path. As General Aldunate highlights in this book, the Haitians are a proud and resilient people. In the face of yet another crippling crisis, it is time for the international community to devote significant resources and attention to rebuilding the country.

Jorge Heine
Distinguished Fellow, Centre for International Governance Innovation;
CIGI Chair in Global Governance, Balsillie School of International Affairs;
Professor of Political Science, Wilfrid Laurier University
Waterloo, Ontario

Acknowledgements

On 12 January 2010 the international community received news of a devastating earthquake that struck outside of Haiti's capital city, Port-au-Prince. Estimated to be a magnitude 7 earthquake, it caused the deaths of numerous Haitians, international aid workers, and the destruction of much of Haiti's fragile infrastructure. Many close friends died in this earthquake, and my thoughts go out to them.

This book is dedicated in their honour.

One of those who was lost is my dear friend Andrea Loi. She was an intelligent woman who dedicated herself to helping to rebuild the country. My thanks go out to Andrea for her valuable friendship. She was a great representative of our country, Chile, and I am thankful for her unwavering support during the hard moments of my time in Haiti.

I must also honour my friend Gerard Le Chevallier, a strong and enthusiastic person who was tasked with managing the electoral process that I detail in this book. Heddi Annabi, the special representative of the Secretary General of the UN, has also been lost. The last time we spoke, we discussed what we could do to help the situation in Haiti. To everyone who has been affected by this tragedy, my feelings of grief go out to you.

This earthquake, though, is both a chance to mourn the devastation that has been brought to the country and to also reflect on Haiti's future. Considering the pain caused by the earthquake, this will be no small feat. The immediate task is to respond to the crisis; we must then deal with its legacy. My hope is that the international community comes together and manages the crisis by coordinating its aid so that it addresses the problems of Haiti without contributing to them.

Success in Haiti will be achieved only if order is established. This will be facilitated through international funding and assistance that helps to rebuild the country and stabilize the country's political situation. Those who know the country, worry about its history of violence and hope that it does not return. I am afraid that it could return if the Haitian people do not feel that there is a timely solution to their most basic needs.

As I have attempted to show in this book, it is important that the redevelopment of the country creates solid institutions, sustainable development, and the conditions necessary for improving the condition of the Haitian people.

Perhaps now more than ever, Haiti is a country that has many problems, yet it also has much potential.

The earthquake tragedy highlights the need to revise the role of MINUS-TAH, establish the Haitian government, and develop the country's economy. The role of the international community in this is essential. It would be inexcusable not to use this moment as an opportunity to assist the country in its long-term development. Five UN missions have preceded MINUSTAH, and various countries have had a presence in Haiti. Unfortunately, these efforts have not led to the creation of the solid and stable institutions the country needs.

The first successful democratic election held in Haiti in recent memory is a significant milestones in the country's history. The event could not have happened without the hard work of the Haitian people and the international community. Their determination, enthusiasm, sacrifice, and bravery have been immeasurable. The election demonstrates that the international community's efforts in Haiti can lead to tangible results.

In the aftermath of the 2010 earthquake, we must not forget those who have given their lives to help Haiti. Specifically, I wish to acknowledge the sacrifices of the twelve UN soldiers who lost their lives during the Haiti mission, prior to 2010, and to the more than sixty Blue Helmets who were injured between July 2004 and September 2006, the month my mission as Deputy Commander of MINUSTAH ended. Everyone who has worn the blue helmet of the UN should feel proud to have contributed to the cause. The sacrifices made by those who worked in Haiti must not be in vain.

Special thanks are due to General Urano Bacellar. During his time as Force Commander he demonstrated great professionalism and humanity. He was succeeded by another remarkable commander, General Elito Siqueira. I also wish to thank Lieutenant Colonel Carlos Díaz Dogwood, noncommissioned Officer Alex Leiva, and my team of advisors, who were a great support in the many facets of this mission.

The mission in Haiti is a long-term commitment. It will demand extraordinary efforts from those involved. The needs of the country and of its people are immense and will be addressed only through time and effort. The Haitian people deserve this commitment and the international assistance necessary to create a better tomorrow. For Latin American countries, we must continue to support our regional neighbour.

One of the most important legacies we have left the Haitian people is that there is hope for a better tomorrow. While Haiti's future depends on the country's own government and society, the presence of the international community is crucial to ensure that what has been achieved does not crumble under the pressure of the enormous needs their nation faces.

Finally, I want to thank my wife and children, who had to worry about me during a year of their lives. They faced hard situations, and without their support I would not have been able to complete my mission.

I am also grateful to President Préval and his fine people, who deserve the best.

Brigadier General Eduardo Aldunate Herman (R)
Santiago, Chile

* * *

This English edition of General Aldunate's memoir of his Haitian sojourn was made possible by a great variety of people and institutions. It arose out of the commitment of the Centre for International Governance Innovation (CIGI) to global governance issues. Alma Flores did an outstanding job in translating the text from its original Spanish to the English language. Joe Turcotte shepherded the text from then on to its current version with admirable dedication and eye for detail. Max Brem, who heads CIGI's publications program, and Jessica Hanson, Publications Coordinator, were always there to break logjams, as was Rob Kohlmeier and the rest of the team from Wilfrid Laurier University Press.

As in other projects John English, the former executive director, and Daniel Schwanen, the deputy executive director of programs, created an environment amenable to productive research. CIGI was founded in 2002 by Jim Balsillie, co-CEO of RIM (Research In Motion), and collaborates with and gratefully acknowledges support from a number of strategic partners, in particular the Government of Canada and the Government of Ontario.

We hope this book will make it possible for General Aldunate's valuable insights and reflections — on MINUSTAH's experience in Haiti as well as on UN peacekeeping generally — to reach a wider reading public, not only in Canada (where peacekeeping was originally conceived) but around the world.

Jorge Heine
Waterloo, Ontario

List of Abbreviations

Note: French and Spanish names are given in parentheses.

AFC	Acting Force Commander
AOR	area of responsibility
APC	armored personnel carrier
CARICOM	Caribbean Community
CEP	Provisional Electoral Council (*Conseil Électoral Provisoire*)
CP	checkpoint
CSPN	Superior Council of the National Police of Haiti (*Conseil Supérieur de la Police Nationale*)
DDR	Disarmament, Demobilization and Reintegration Program (UN)
DFC	Deputy Force Commander
DGMN	Chile's State Department of National Mobilization (*Dirección General de Movilización Nacional*)
DPKO	Department of Peacekeeping Operations (UN)
EMDN	Chile's National Defence Chiefs of Staff (*Estado Mayor de la Defensa Nacional*)
FACH	Chilean Air Force (*Fuerza Aérea de Chile*)
FAd'H	Haitian Armed Forces (*Forces Armées d'Haïti*)
FC	Force Commander
FPU	Formed Police Unit (UNPol)
HQ	headquarters
ICG	International Crisis Group
IM	Marines
JMAC	Joint Mission Analysis Cell
JOC	Joint Operations Centre
LOA	letter of agreement
MIFH	Multinational Interim Force for Haiti
MINUSTAH	UN Stabilization Mission in Haiti
MOU	memorandum of understanding
NGO	non-governmental organization
OAS	Organization of American States
PAP	Port-au-Prince
PNH	Haitian National Police (*Police Nationale d'Haïti*)
ROE	Rules of Engagement (UN)

SONAPI	National Society of Industrial Parks (*Société Nationale des Parcs Industriels*)
SRSG	Special Representative of the UN Secretary General
UN	United Nations
UNPol	UN Police
UNSC	UN Security Council

Introduction

THIS BOOK IS THE STORY of my time in Haiti as Deputy Commander of the UN Stabilization Mission, known as MINUSTAH, between September 2005 and September 2006.

I will try to tell it as directly as possible, by relating events in the order they occurred, in other words, by providing a sort of journal of my experiences.

There is much more to Haiti than poverty and violence. In fact, nowadays there are many countries where the streets are more dangerous and other problems are more severe.

I do not want readers to think that I saw only problems during the mission in Haiti. I also got to know a proud people with a rich cultural heritage, whose country is beautiful in both its landscape and its inhabitants.

But neither can I forget that I was there on a UN mission. The international community had deemed it necessary to answer the Haitian authorities' call for help addressing the serious problems their country was facing. This book is an attempt to describe what I experienced in that context.

I will explain how I was appointed. Then I will sketch the political situation in Haiti that prompted — among other things — the presence of Chilean and multinational forces. Finally, I will provide a detailed account of the mission.

DURING THE TIME I was in the country, there was a military force of between 6,400 and 7,500 soldiers from 22 different nations, along with policemen, civilian advisers, and non-governmental organizations.

In March 2004, Chile sent soldiers to Haiti to join the Multinational Interim Force for Haiti (MIFH), which the UN Security Council (UNSC) had established to help stabilize the country during the insecure, chaotic environment of the months leading up to the abrupt departure of President Jean-Bertrand Aristide.[1]

Within 72 hours of being called, the Chilean Army had sent its Special Forces and other resources to the island — proof, if other countries needed it, that our Special Forces were thoroughly prepared and organized and that our country's defence policy was closely aligned with its foreign policy.

At that point in my career, I assumed it would be very difficult for me to join the mission, for I held a government position outside the army: head of the State National Mobilization Department (DGMN).

My immediate superior was the Minister of National Defence, Dr. Michelle Bachelet Jeria, who would later become President of Chile.

Something told me this situation might change. If a general were needed, I would be more than happy to raise my hand. But I realized this was wishful thinking, since it is rather unusual in the military for volunteers to be accepted–you have to wait to be called up. Besides, there were other very good candidates in the army.

To a certain extent I was misjudging my own situation. I was already participating indirectly in the Haiti operation, as the person in charge of arranging transportation of the troops' ordnance. At the DGMN, I was our country's authority in such procedures.

I followed the TV broadcasts about the dispatch of our troops to Haiti with a mixture of pride, interest, and envy. Many of those soldiers had been under my command. I had jumped out of planes with them.

As the days went by, with the Chilean troops already in Haiti, I contacted some of my comrades, who told me about the difficulties they were encountering: the extreme poverty, the shortages the country was suffering, and the enormous complexity of the task they were facing.

It seemed that a far greater effort — one that went well beyond military operations — would be required to ensure even minimal success in Haiti.

They told me that despite all the promises made by other countries, only half the assigned military forces had arrived so far (Chile was the exception: we had already sent our entire contingent).

They sounded extremely happy and proud to be serving in Haiti. But I also sensed they were being frustrated by the conditions there and by the slow progress they were making to overcome the country's problems.

Despite what they told me, I still longed to be with them.

PERHAPS 13 MONTHS is a mere a grain of sand, insignificant in the life of one person and even more so in the history of a country.

But having analyzed the conditions in Haiti as I found them on arrival, and having examined the country as I left it, I believe that the sacrifices of those who participated in the mission were not in vain. Each contingent, each soldier helped make that country a better place for its people — Haiti was much better off than before we arrived.

I hope to do justice to the blood spilled by our soldiers and to the efforts made by many men and women to foster a spirit of solidarity — a spirit that was reflected in those of us who served in MINUSTAH after 2004 and that will be, I am sure, reflected in those who follow in our steps.

For a professional soldier, the opportunity to lead an international mission in a situation where resources are used in real-life situations is extremely valuable — especially in peacetime, when soldiers can train only with charts and simulated exercises.

During this mission I encountered several situations I had not anticipated. Some of them reflected the dangerous environment, in which five of my comrades of different nationalities gave their lives. At the same time, I was able to experience the camaraderie that arises among a multitude of military contingents when they work together during times of conflict.

As commander of the force, I often had to make decisions in complex situations, to work with UN and Haitian authorities in politically restricted circumstances, and to interact with political figures from around the world. But the worst situation I had to deal with was undoubtedly the loss of my commander, General Urano Texeira Bacellar of the Brazilian Army, at a time when security in Haiti was reaching its tipping point.

How will I ever forget the marvellous opportunity to serve under General Elito Siqueira, an outstanding commander toward whom I can feel only gratitude and loyalty?

I also had the honour of working with the UN Secretary General's Special Representative, Ambassador Juan Gabriel Valdés Soublette, a prominent figure in Chile with whom I built a solid friendship based mainly on the difficult moments we shared; and later with Ambassador Edmond Mulet, his successor, whose support I deeply appreciate.

I was also able to observe the difficult but productive work of our diplomats, exemplified by Ambassador Marcel Young, who represents Chile so well in Haiti and whose continued optimism has been essential for me and for all the other Chileans on the mission.

Three months after starting my command, at a moment when the security situation was very delicate, I had to deal with a serious allegation made by a fellow countryman who, in the national and international media, accused me of having participated in a certain intelligence organization during Chile's military government. These accusations led to allegations that I had participated in human rights violations — allegations that were later refuted, as will be shown later in this book.

For an officer of my rank, representing his country in an organization such as the UN, these accusations were extremely serious. But owing to the strength of my arguments, I elicited the support of the Chilean government, the army, the MINUSTAH authorities, and my family, which helped me survive that torment. In the end, the accusations made against me only strengthened my convictions as a soldier and as a citizen.

The year I spent on the mission was not easy, but it was profoundly gratifying.

It was the first time I had been away from my family, who could only watch from a distance while I experienced many difficult months.

I hope this book will prove useful to those interested in defence topics, since it shows our soldiers' contributions to their country in this aspect of their calling and describes life as a peacekeeper. I hope this book will lead to initiatives that will streamline this aspect of military deployment as an integral part of our foreign policy.

Notes

1 Jean-Bertrand Aristide, President of the Republic of Haiti, 1991, 1994–96, and 2001–4.

CHAPTER ONE

A Self-Fulfilling Prophecy

IN LATE FEBRUARY 2004, the newspapers announced that Chile would be sending a military force to Haiti to help control the crisis there.

I was on holiday in southern Chile when I heard about this and started talking to my family about the difficulties Haiti was experiencing, how urgent it was to help, and how important it was for our country to have a presence there. I told them that as soldiers we *should* be there and that providing safety to Haitians was a contribution from our people to a sister nation. I even went so far as to say, "I'd like to be there with our boys."

As time went by, I often talked to my family about this, thinking deep down that there might be a chance that I would be able to participate in Haiti.

None of my children — Nicolás was 7, María José 11, Teresita 17 and Eduardo 19 at the time — paid much attention to the subject. Like most people in the country, they thought it was far removed from their interests.

Fortunately for my family, there was little news about Haiti. However, I knew that as far as security was concerned, the country was no easy assignment for our troops. E-mails I received from our personnel told me how difficult the situation was there.

I did some research and learned that in 2005 Haiti ranked 154th among the 177 countries on the Human Development Index, a measure employed by the UN Development Programme (UNDP). Also, Haiti was the second country in the Western Hemisphere to have achieved independence, after the United

States. Yet almost every source I consulted described Haiti as a place of cease-less chaos, corruption, poverty, and social upheaval.

Yet as I continued my research, instead of growing discouraged, I became convinced that in sending Chilean soldiers to Haiti, our government was acknowledging that the military was an appropriate tool in our foreign policy toolkit.

Besides that, our forces in Haiti were drawn mainly from the Special Forces. That meant two things: Chilean commandos were being entrusted with complex missions, and as a commando myself, I might have something to contribute.

On June 4, 2004, just as I was resigning myself to the idea of never being contacted, I received a phone call at my office from General Juan Emilio Cheyre, the Army Commander-in-Chief. I knew his voice right away.

"Alcamán" — my combat name in the commando units — "are you sitting or standing?"

"Standing," I answered, rather intrigued.

"Deputy Force Commander in Haiti," he continued. "What do you think?"

"Well, I am honoured," I answered quickly. "I deeply appreciate that you have considered me for this mission and I am ready and at your orders."

He told me he was about to go into a meeting with the Minister of National Defence — my direct superior — and the rest of the Armed Forces Commanders-in-Chief. The UN had asked the Chilean government to appoint an officer with the rank of general for the position. That would be the main item on the meeting's agenda, and he wanted to know whether I would be available.

The army, as a rule, never *asks* you whether you're available for a position or destination, but in this case, perhaps because of the complexity of the mission, it seemed logical to ask, and I thanked him for his consideration.

I continued working, saying nothing to my staff. General Cheyre had asked me to keep it a secret until the appointment was official.

At about 6 p.m., I left the office. I was driving home when I received a call on my cellphone from Colonel Jaime Beltramí, assistant to the Minister of Defence, Michelle Bachelet Jeria.

"General, the Defence Minister wants to talk to you."

Then Dr. Bachelet herself was on the line, and asked me bluntly: "General Aldunate, what would you say to being sent as Deputy Commander of the United Nations Forces in Haiti?"

"I am ready and at your orders, Madame Minister."

"Well," she continued, "the issue came up this evening at the Commanders-in-Chief Meeting, and I asked the Army Commander whether he had a candidate. He said he did. I told him I also had a potential candidate and that we should see if we agreed. He gave me your name and that's why I'm calling you, since both of us had you in mind for this appointment."

"Madame Minister," I replied, "it is an honour for me to be considered for the position. You know I belong to the Special Forces and I think one should always be ready for this type of mission, so of course I'm available."

"Well," she answered, "I expected nothing less from you, since I know you. But for the time being, we'll have to wait till the UN makes a decision. It seems that Argentina is also proposing a general, and now the matter will be decided in New York at the UN headquarters. In any case, congratulations! We'll talk about this later."

In August 2004 I went to New York for an interview at the UN headquarters with the head of the Department of Peacekeeping Operations (DPKO), a Dutch general. There, I was interviewed for almost an hour by eight officials.

During the meeting, the officials described several settings and asked me, among other things, what I would do in the event of offences by UN troops in my charge or human rights violations.

In my answers, I made it quite clear that standards should be applied and that compliance with the UN's own rules of engagement (ROEs) should be enforced, but that it was just as important to implement effective leadership and that I had no doubt about what should be done.

I also told them it was vital to win over the civilian population so that they would regard military force as legitimate, since it was only with the Haitian people's participation that a solution might be found to their problems.

The day before, the Chilean Ambassador to Argentina, Juan Gabriel Valdés, had been appointed Special Representative of the Secretary General of the United Nations in Haiti (SRSG), which made me think that another Chilean was unlikely to be appointed to the top UN leadership team there.

At that time, General Augusto Heleno of Brazil was in charge of the military forces. Brazil had about 1,200 men on the island, and established procedures required that the mission be in charge of a Brazilian general and that the second-in-command—the position for which I was being proposed by Chile—be a general from another country.

While I was in New York, I was told that the DPKO would also be interviewing General Eduardo Lugani of Argentina, the country with the second-largest contingent in Haiti.

After my interview, I was invited to lunch at a Lebanese restaurant with Heraldo Muñoz, Chile's UN Ambassador, and Ambassador Valdés.

When Valdés arrived, he told me: "General, congratulations on your interview. The UN staff was favourably impressed, but I must say I think you are unlikely to be nominated, since I myself have just been appointed to this position and the UN is trying to achieve a geographical balance of the countries involved in these missions."

He was well versed in the issue and in the codes of these international organizations, since he had recently served as Chile's UN Ambassador, where he had gained notoriety because of Chile's stance against the Second Iraq War.

I established an immediate rapport with Valdés, which suggested that if I were indeed appointed to the position, we would have a good working relationship.

On my return to Santiago, I received an e-mail informing me that General Lugani had been named to the position. The same document cited geographical reasons, then added that the UN hoped that at the end of General Lugani's commission, Chile would propose me as his replacement, for which I already had New York's approval.

Given the information I had, I was sure the mission would continue beyond a year. According to the press, though, a large number of Chileans wanted their country to pull out of Haiti, since the operation's financial costs were higher than first estimated and its political justification was questionable.

The issue of whether to keep our forces in Haiti was also affected by internal politics. People were discussing whether the Defence Minister was going to run for president in 2005. Both she and President Ricardo Lagos had been key supporters of Chilean participation. I was thinking, even then, that this would have implications for the presidential campaign.

Deep down, I thought that Chile would be involved in this mission for a long time. Beyond my personal views, this was based on the fact that Chile had been criticized in the region, accused of snubbing its neighbours. Because our economy was on the right track and the country had an orderly political situation — unlike other countries on the continent — some countries were suspicious of us.

I thought this suspicion had been partly offset by my country's determined effort to help Haiti, a sister nation, cope with its crisis. All of that led me to think that Chile would probably still be involved there a year from now.

Moreover, Chile had not taken part in the first Haiti mission, which had been composed entirely of Latin American countries and other UN members. That had not helped either our army or our foreign policy. According to Colonel Sánchez: "The main responsibility for this mission was taken by countries in the Southern Cone, which provided most of the troops and assumed the political and military leadership of one of the few UN missions that has unanimously been considered a success."[1]

It was clear to me that Chile's stature among nations could only grow if it participated in the mission.

In early March 2005, six months after my nomination, I met our Deputy Director of the Joint Chiefs of Staff, Air Force General Wolfram Celedón, who told me that the issue of Haiti was again being raised and that I should be prepared in case there was another opportunity for Chile. It seemed that again I would be a candidate for the position when General Lugani ended his tenure in late September.

I told him I was ready and that I only needed clear, timely information about the nomination, since we now knew the commission would be for one year.

Our country had organized a peacekeeping operations centre, with a Haiti office, and every so often the people there told me how our troops were doing. Once they even invited me to a videoconference with the Chilean battalion deployed at Cap Haïtien. Apparently the word was out that I might be appointed for this mission.

In May 2005 people started discussing the fact that General Lugani's command would end in September and that the UN had that position available for Chile. Moreover, my name had been submitted as Lugani's replacement.

By then I was in regular e-mail contact with Colonel Ricardo Toro Tassara of the Chilean Army, who at the time was MINUSTAH's Operations Officer in Haiti. I knew him well—he had been a student of mine in the strategy classes I taught at the War Academy, and later on we had attended the same High Command course at the National Academy for Strategic and Political Studies (ANEPE).

He told me that General Lugani's replacement was slated for September and that I was likely to succeed him.

Around the same time, Colonel Marcos López sent me an e-mail from New York saying that the subject of appointing a new Deputy Commander had arisen and that, as per the previous year's agreement, my name was definitely on the table.

But as always, nothing is that easy.

The situation in Haiti was difficult at the time, and various authorities were stating that, while the military force had arrived—with its problems and limitations—the economic aid promised by the main sponsor countries was nowhere to be seen. In Port-au-Prince the security problems were enormous. When a leader of one of the local criminal gangs was captured, he was immediately replaced.

General Heleno was to end his commission in July 2005, and General Lugani on September 22. That meant Ambassador Valdés would have to cope with the November elections at a time when MINUSTAH's two top commanders had only recently been assigned.

Ambassador Valdés tried to have General Heleno's commission extended by Brazil. If that was not possible, he hoped to have Lugani's commission extended by Argentina. He wanted to be able to count on one of them to achieve the mission's political objectives. Besides, on-the-ground experience was needed to cope with the violence in the capital.

Negotiations at UN headquarters continued with the goal of ensuring that either Heleno or Lugani, or both, would remain with the mission. As a result, my appointment was postponed until the situation of the military commanders was clarified.

In late April 2005 a National Congress delegation flew to Port-au-Prince to gather the information required to rule on the Chilean president's request that Chile's participation in MINUSTAH be extended. Under Chilean statutes, it was the Senate that authorized the deployment abroad of the country's forces.

This process is repeated every six months. Some people question it, thinking that it might be more appropriate to authorize the mission once, at the outset, instead of having to arrange an extension every six months. This was especially important because the Armed Forces had to be able to plan their personnel allocations and logistical support. In the event, it was decided that by May 2007, a four-year plan for the mission would be established.

The UN's request to the Chilean government to fill the position of Deputy Commander for MINUSTAH eventually arrived, and the Joint Chiefs of Staff sent a document to the Chilean Army requesting the name of a candidate for the position.

On Friday, May 5, I again received a call from the Army Commander-in-Chief, General Cheyre, who told me he had sent a document to the Joint Chiefs in which he stated that I was available.

Knowing that my appointment for the mission was going ahead, I took French lessons and began preparing my military gear.

On Friday, June 18, at 9:30 a.m., I received a call from the Director of the Joint Chiefs, Vice Admiral Jorge Huerta Dunsmore, who told me that the UN had accepted my nomination as Deputy Commander of MINUSTAH. I would serve in that position for one year, beginning in September.

I thanked him for his call and went to report the situation to the Director of the Joint Chiefs of Staff for the Army, General Javier Urbina. He and I were old friends, as were our families.

At the meeting, General Urbina told me I should not forget that my actions would represent my country and that a wrong decision on my part would eventually cause trouble both for the army and for Chile. He also suggested that I not be tempted to believe that good tactical actions would solve Haiti's serious problems.

He stressed that I would be representing our country and that caution should always guide my decisions. And he added that he trusted my ability to meet the challenge.

Though he didn't know it, General Urbina was telling me what General Heleno would tell me again later.

On June 25 I received my written orders from the army, declaring that I had been assigned to the position of MINUSTAH Deputy Commander.

In the months between my nomination and my arrival, the security situation deteriorated in Haiti. A Brazilian lieutenant and a Bolivian major had been injured, and two Jordanian soldiers had been shot by snipers. MINUSTAH's casualties now included 5 dead and about 60 wounded.

Before leaving, I talked to Colonel Rodrigo Bisbal and Major Fabián Mecklenburg. Both were well-known helicopter pilots who had served with international missions in Haiti and East Timor. Bisbal had served as commander in the MINUSTAH Joint Helicopter Unit. Both of them told me that security in the country was tenuous, that aircraft were being shot at, and that the situation was deteriorating.

For reasons that have yet to be explained to me, there was little discussion in Chile about the actual situation in Haiti, especially in Port-au-Prince, where most of the violence was. People in our country thought that our troops were safe in Cap Haïtien and that they were engaged mainly in humanitarian aid.

That was a half-truth: Our troops in the northern zone were encountering danger. Furthermore, people had forgotten that Chilean troops were also present in Port-au-Prince, where the situation was worse than in the north. Yet for some reason, only the Chilean battalion in Cap Haïtien was being reported on in the media, and little was being said about the other Chileans on the mission — about the helicopter pilots and the engineers and the headquarters staff. I wondered how Chileans would respond to the death or wounding of a Chilean soldier in Haiti.

I also wondered whether Chileans knew what we were actually doing in Haiti. I asked myself whether that country was too far away for our society to care what our soldiers were going through. I would have the answer later on.

I continued to prepare for my departure. Thinking that visiting Haiti would help me do that, I arranged a flight to Haiti on a military resupply plane. Before my tenure began, I needed to learn at first hand what the mission would involve.

CHAPTER TWO

First Contact with Haiti: Exploring the Paratroopers' Landing Area

WE LEFT ON THE EVENING of Wednesday, June 29, and were due to return to Chile on Thursday night. That gave me less than a day to make the contacts I needed before starting the mission itself. My schedule was going to be tight.

I traveled with Major Carlos Díaz, whom I had nominated as my assistant for this mission. The UN allowed me to choose my own.

We took off at 10 p.m. in a Boeing 737. The same flight was airlifting part of an infantry battalion — replacements for our troops at Cap Haïtien, which is in the north of Haiti and is the country's second-largest city. My fellow soldiers were happy to be going and optimistic about their work. Seeing that, and remembering that their departure had gone almost unnoticed in the Chilean media, I could only bristle that the Chilean people seemed to care so little that these men were risking their lives.

Around 8 p.m. we landed at Toussaint L'Ouverture Airport in Port-au-Prince. It took us around 20 minutes to disembark. The passenger stairs were not ready when we arrived, and it was rather comical to watch the pilots telling a Haitian who was driving an old truck with a staircase how to avoid bumping into the aircraft fuselage. Something told me this was a good introduction to what the country was going through.

I got off the plane, where several Chilean officers were waiting for me on the tarmac. Among them was Commander Carlos Zavala, better known as "Charly," the Military Attaché to the Chilean Ambassador to Haiti. I had served with him on the National Defence General Staff.

Charly was a highly seasoned army officer known for his diligence, leadership skills, and constant high spirits. It was a pleasure to meet him again. He was accompanied by Colonel Rodrigo Bisbal, commander of the Joint Chilean Army and Air Force Unit, one of our most experienced helicopter pilots.

When I got off the plane, a four-man unit from the FACH Parasar Group was waiting for me. This unit had been trained for crew rescue missions, and most of them were Air Force commandos. They were armed and wore bullet-proof vests with their Blue Helmets. They would escort me throughout my day in Port-au-Prince.

From the airport we went to visit the Helicopter Unit. Afterwards I visited the Army Engineers, a combined unit that included soldiers from the Ecuadoran Army, who were building and repairing roads in the capital, besides undertaking other projects in the north.

In both units I met soldiers who were excited about what they were doing. It was clear to me that their morale was high and their commitment strong.

To be blunt, I sweated far more than they did. The 35-degree temperature and the high humidity would accompany me throughout my time in Haiti, along with an ever-present bottle of water.

Colonel Ricardo Toro, MINUSTAH's Operations Officer, also attended these meetings. On the way to headquarters he took me to a supermarket in a residential area of the city so that I could see what was available and what I would need to bring with me from Chile. Even that soon, I understood that only a handful of Haitians (and of course foreigners) could afford supermarkets like this.

Prices were reasonable, and all I had to do was divide them by 6 to find out what items were worth in Chilean pesos. One thing I could never understand was why the country had more than one currency.

If you bought something or settled an account, the price was given in *gourdes*, a Haitian currency. But after that the price was given in Haitian dollars. And then, if you said you wanted to pay in U.S. dollars, they gave you that amount in *gourdes*.

The odd thing about all this is that Haitian dollars do not exist. So I never understood why every transaction always had to be converted into three different types of currency, of which only two were real: *gourdes* and U.S. dollars.

Later on, I would use this to illustrate that the state in this country was a virtual entity — just like its dollars.

From the supermarket our convoy made a tour of the city. We only went to certain areas, since part of the city was a danger zone, off limits except during operations. I learned that there were very beautiful areas in the capital, with many people walking around and street vendors selling all sorts of items. I saw a huge number of beauty parlours and barbershops. Later, people who knew the country well told me that it was a sign of Haiti's French cultural roots. Looking good is part of life in Haiti, never mind that most Haitian women (not the men) carry bundles on their heads.

During that brief drive, I noticed that most young Haitian women were slim and very attractive, with an elegant walk. The older women were mostly stocky. Also, most of the people I saw were black. There were some mulattoes, but no whites, except in the streets near the downtown hotels and in the sub-urb of Pétionville.

I saw street stalls selling fruit, vegetables, motor oil, even meat. The meat at these stalls was covered in flies and laid out on crude wooden tables of doubt-ful cleanliness. The same tables offered bags of water and various foods such as sugarcane and roast chicken. Garbage was piled up around the stalls. And since Haitian food is cooked over braziers, I saw many stalls selling charcoal.

When I flew over the country some time later, I saw that because of the reliance on charcoal, the country was severely deforested, especially in the northern and central zones — an ecological disaster. I was told that because of embargoes recently imposed on Haiti, even fruit trees were being cut down for firewood. The people had no alternative to charcoal — for them, cutting trees to produce it was a matter of survival.

The traffic was dreadful. The people were terrible drivers, and I wondered why there weren't more accidents in the city. I couldn't find a single vehicle that hadn't been dented, and most had no lights or mirrors.

Public transport was provided by tap-taps (single-cabin trucks; see Photo 1), though there were also some buses. The capacity of these was determined on the principle of "the more the merrier." People even rode on the roofs and running boards.

Passengers got on anywhere and paid the driver when they got off. You might think that in this chaos, there would be a lot of free riders. On the con-trary, in Haitian culture, this was frowned on — *everyone* paid up.

The tap-taps were brightly painted and covered with religious proverbs and portraits of soccer players. Pictures of Ronaldinho, the Brazilian soccer star, were common, and the Brazilian flag was flown on most vehicles.

Brazil's national team had come to play Haiti on August 18, 2004, as part of a program to encourage people to hand in their weapons. Lula, the Brazil-ian president, had attended the game, which his side won, 6–0.

Photo 1. A Haitian tap-tap

I learned later that truck and bus drivers were the biggest dangers on the road. They drove cast-off American school buses—the yellow ones—which were used in Haiti as intercity transport for goods and people. They drove very fast, with people on the roof, and sometimes even in the wrong lane no matter what was heading toward them. There were only three or four traffic lights in the entire capital, and policemen were nowhere to be seen.

Many roads lacked sidewalks. Someone who knew the country well told me later that it was because the streets had been designed for the bourgeoisie, not ordinary citizens. At dusk, I noticed that most of the street stalls used what are known as *chonchones* in Chile: tins with oil and candles. Electricity was scarce, and most of the city was in darkness.

After a brief tour of the city, we drove to the Hotel El Rancho, where the MINUSTAH officers were staying. That hotel was in the Musseau sector on the road to Pétionville. From there we set off for the Hotel Montana, which was nearby. I would be staying at the Montana, since that is where Generals Heleno and Lugani were lodged. The Montana was the most luxurious hotel in the city, a gorgeous building with all the amenities one could hope for: pool, tennis court, gym. The downside was that during the mission I would have little time to enjoy any of them. Perhaps in other circumstances, it would be an ideal place to rest. As it turned out, I would rarely use the hotel's pool or eat in its restaurant.

That day we had lunch at the Montana with Captain Zavala, Lieutenant Colonel Bermúdez (commander of the Army Helicopter Unit), Colonel Bisbal, and Major Díaz.

From the hotel, which was on a hill near the western sector of lower Port-au-Prince, we could see the whole city, including the neighbourhood of Cité Soleil, the site of many of the troubles and shootings I would be confronting during the mission.

We then drove to the MINUSTAH headquarters, the old Hotel Christopher, where Colonel Toro briefed me on the troops' operations. After that we met General Lugani. I was received by his assistant, Major Armando Peressí, an Argentine Army officer, and by General Heleno's two Brazilian assistants.

I entered Lugani's office with Colonels Toro and Bisbal and Major Díaz, and we started off discussing general topics. As Lugani explained it, the crisis in Haiti exceeded everyone's worst imaginings, and whatever solutions were found could not be strictly military in nature. That matched what my Chilean comrades who had been on the mission had told me.

He told me repeatedly that he could not be staying on the mission beyond his original term, since he was Director of Operations for the Argentine Army General Staff and he needed to return to his regular duties at home.

During our conversation he praised the Chilean troops, pointing to the example they had set for the other participating countries. He spoke excellent French and showed a good understanding of the mission.

After that, we met with General Heleno. We started out discussing soccer (Brazil had just beaten Argentina in a friendly game). We then talked about the mission. I soon realized that General Heleno was engaging, affable, and uncomplicated, besides being — as Ambassador Valdés would confirm — a very intelligent man.

As we began to discuss the mission in depth, he told me he did not want to return to his country with dead soldiers or injured civilians. He added that taking casualties would not solve Haiti's problems and that he was against using military force indiscriminately, though some members of Haiti's middle class were demanding he do just that. The Brazilian people would find such force unacceptable.

He told me how happy he was with the Chilean troops and that he was eager to return to his country. I added this to what General Lugani had told me, and deduced that the mission that lay ahead would be rather daunting.

I had given each general a bottle of Chilean wine. Before I left headquarters, General Lugani called, and we three generals sat down in an office to discuss matters.

Now the talk was more frank and relaxed. General Heleno told me that the possibility that Brazil might become a permanent member of the UN Security Council was affecting relations with some of the larger countries. That explained recent criticisms of MINUSTAH and the Brazilians' conduct of the mission.

Both generals insisted that the aid promised by the large donor countries had failed to arrive. That left military force as an option, but military force was not going to address the country's development needs.

We also discussed media criticisms of the mission. Some American commentators were arguing that the solution was to send in the U.S. Marines.

MINUSTAH was being accused of failing to provide security and of backing down from the criminal gangs. According to them, since Haiti was not complying with the UN resolution, U.S. forces would have to make them comply.

According to General Heleno, Ambassador Jean-Marie Guéhenno (Under-Secretary General in charge of the DPKO) had asked him whether U.S. military forces could also participate in the MINUSTAH operations.

Guéhenno was the UN's greatest authority on peacekeeping missions. He reported directly to the Secretary General — in other words, MINUSTAH worked directly for him (before being named the UN's Secretary General, Kofi Annan had been the DPKO's director).

General Heleno told me that he had written back that the Americans could provide intelligence, logistics support, cartography, medical aid, and indirect support for MINUSTAH, but in no event could it provide a parallel military force.

As for Haitian perceptions of Americans, Heleno told me that the arrival of the American forces with the Multinational Interim Force Haiti (MIFH) had been controversial. Some people did not like American soldiers very much; others welcomed them, because of the massive resources they brought with them (so they remembered from the 1990s). Elderly Haitians remembered that the Americans had run Haiti for almost thirty years in the early twentieth century.

More interesting was that if elections were held at that time, Aristide's Lavalas movement would win — something that was contrary to American and French interests. I was also told that a Lavalas victory would be a step backwards for the country and guarantee the return of violence.

General Heleno explained to me that though Aristide was wildly popular, he had failed to advance the country. Moreover, a number of Haitians suspected that Aristide had links with the street gangs.

Both generals thought that if the American military came to Haiti, MINUSTAH should end its mission and leave the country. American forces were famously reluctant to submit to international authority. The coexistence of two forces in Haiti was simply not feasible.

Clearly, the complex relationship between MINUSTAH and the Americans was far from being resolved at that time, and I suspected that I would have to deal with the issue.

I would often look back on this conversation and note how prescient my two fellow generals had been.

I said goodbye to both men. We had established that I would return around September 14. General Lugani's commission would be ending on September 22, and a week would be more than enough time to ensure a smooth transition.

After a short stop at the hotel where Colonel Toro was staying, we drove in convoy to the home of Ambassador Valdés. Valdés was a prominent politician and public figure who had served as Chilean Minister of Foreign Affairs and as Ambassador to Spain, the UN and (later) Argentina. At the UN in 2003, Valdés had criticized the American invasion of Iraq.

Along the road to his house were banners in Creole: "Ambassador Valdés, enforce MINUSTAH's mandate!" Other banners demanded fair elections.

His house in Musseau, off John Brown Avenue, was guarded by Philippine soldiers. There he often met Haitian political leaders. He would work there, and later so would I. It was his second office as much as his home.

The living quarters of the senior UN representative in Haiti were imposing. They included a large garden and an entrance road lined with tropical trees. Valdés was always accompanied by heavy security, provided by civilians contracted by the UN. Some were South African and others European; most of them were ex-paratroopers or Special Forces. They never left him alone and performed their duties with great professionalism.

Whenever the national units held a celebration, Valdés almost always attended. When he did, he was always accompanied by General Bacellar or myself. He was held in high esteem by the entire military contingent. He liked to mingle with our personnel. Ignoring the usual protocol, he would chat with them, pumping them for information about their duties.

He also attended the patriotic celebrations of the various contingents as well as change-of-command ceremonies, and he was there when UN decorations were bestowed on the mission's personnel.

After I had taken up my position, on a trip to Les Cayes, we were with Valdés at the airport (Photo 2). Before boarding the Puma helicopter that would take us back to the capital, we started talking about football. He told me he was a supporter of Colo Colo, Chile's most popular team. I took out a handkerchief I always carried in my pocket to mop my brow, which had the logo of Colo Colo. I spread it out and told him we should take a photograph to celebrate.

Finding two Colo Colo fans in this remote corner of the world is not something you would expect. It helped relax the tensions inherent in our respective jobs.

During the first week of the mission I would attend a weapons destruction ceremony as part of MINUSTAH's disarmament program. The ceremony took place in a stadium near Peace Square. Two young Chilean men approached

Photo 2. With Juan Gabriel Valdés at Les Cayes

me, perhaps because they had seen the national flag on my sleeve, and asked me if they could have their photo taken with me. I told them that there was something missing in the picture. Again I took my towel out.

They were also Colo Colo fans, though I suspect that if they had been fans of the University of Chile's soccer team, they would still have agreed to have their picture taken.

As time went by, my bond with the ambassador evolved from a formal relationship heavy with protocol — so characteristically Chilean — to a close personal friendship that we have maintained to this day. As you will read, this friendship would be born of crises, conflicts, and gunfire.

When General Bacellar died, in the room next to mine, the ambassador, seeing that I would be living alone in the hotel, invited me to live at his house. I thanked him for his offer. In many ways it would have been perfect, since we would have more time to continue our conversations. However, his departure was only a few months away, and the new SRSG would probably find my presence in the house a bit awkward, so I remained at the hotel. Even so, I will always remember that gesture.

Going back to that first visit to Ambassador Valdés's home: While we were talking, the other people invited to the meeting began to turn up. These included Juan Enrique Vega, a shrewd man who had been Chile's Ambassador to Cuba during the Allende administration. He later held a diplomatic position in Geneva. Now he was an adviser to Valdés.

Also attending were other Chilean military serving in Port-au-Prince. Among them were Frigate Captain Zavala and Colonels Bisbal and Toro.

Ambassador Valdés explained how the current situation in Haiti had begun and how this had affected the configuration of the UN forces, which in his opinion were not large enough to cope with the situation.

In his view, Haiti was facing a situation similar to the one in Rwanda, where the hatred between the Tutsis and the Hutus ran so deep that they were ready to hack each other to death with machetes.

He told us he had the highest opinion of General Heleno, whom he described as a thorough professional and a friend.

And he told us that at various times, when asked to do so, he had been reluctant to use force to impose order. Yet it was unacceptable that places like Cité Soleil were out of MINUSTAH's control and in the grip of criminal gangs. Later on, Valdés and I would agree that indiscriminate force was not the right solution.

Valdés then told us something that registered sharply with me: the governments of the region must not allow their troops to leave a trail of death in Haiti. No one on the mission wanted anything of the kind, yet escalating military and police action was a real possibility as long as the criminal gangs—who hid among the civilians—continued to attack the population and the UN soldiers.

During these conversations I came to understand that the mission was extremely complex and that several actors with conflicting agendas were involved. Besides the UN and the mission itself, there were the sponsor countries (the core group), the Organization of American States (OAS), the Haitian authorities, the provisional government, and newly emerging politicians and NGOs.

Over lunch, the issue of safety kept arising, and I remembered my discussion that day with Heleno regarding the use of force. I pointed out to Valdés that according to Chapter VII of the UN Charter, on a mission like MINUS-TAH the use of force was appropriate if it was in keeping with the rules of engagement and behaviour (ROEs), bearing in mind that the purpose of military action was to ensure compliance with the UN mandate.

At that time, an operation to enter Cité Soleil was being prepared. It had been planned by Colonel Toro in his capacity as Operations Officer. Toro had told the ambassador that the operation might well claim the lives of 10 Blue Helmets as well as many civilians.

Toro had also told the ambassador that a Haitian businessman who owned property in Cité Soleil had asked Heleno to postpone the operation while he built a wall around one of his buildings. The project would create jobs for local people, which would help reduce tensions in the area.

Valdés was rather upset, since the planning for this operation had involved a great deal of work and coordination. In his view, the businessman was being selfish and was only protecting his own interests. The request could not possibly be granted. Toro concurred — the operation should go ahead as planned.

After this meeting we moved to the dining room. I took this opportunity to give Valdés some books: one from a mutual friend, the other chosen for him by me.

During dinner, the ambassador made a little speech, in which he told us he looked forward to my early presence on the mission.

I kept asking myself why Heleno was so reluctant to use force. Perhaps he thought it would be ineffective unless accompanied by financial aid and political reform. And perhaps he felt it would worsen the already precarious situation in Haiti — which was Valdés's own view. On reflection, I am certain they were both right. Later, when I analyzed MINUSTAH's structure, I would find more arguments to support their position.

I thanked the ambassador for dinner, then had to leave before it ended. My flight back to Chile took off at 10 p.m. We landed in Santiago at 12:30 the next afternoon, four and a half hours late. Once again, of course, I did not catch much sleep.

My commission in Haiti would be far more complex than I had anticipated. I doubted whether the Chilean people were aware of the significance of the UN mission, even though the second-in-command would soon be a Chilean and 500 of our countrymen were already there. Our country's involvement was already heavy.

On February 28, 2005, three Brazilian soldiers were wounded in the capital during an attack by gangs. After that, an operation was launched to establish a checkpoint (CP) on Mariela Street. It would be the first effective CP established by MINUSTAH forces.

A few days after my return, I read in the international press that the operation mentioned during my first conversation with Ambassador Valdés had taken place. According to the reports, it had succeeded. Troops had entered Cité Soleil, and Dread Wilme — the infamous criminal who was the operation's target — had been killed. When I saw a picture of the man in the Haitian newspapers, I thought he looked more like a rapper than a gangster.

This operation, "Iron Fist," brought only momentary peace to Cité Soleil. MINUSTAH had taken no casualties, but its forces had taken fire from the gangs. The Chilean Helicopter Unit had been responsible for ensuring operational control for headquarters. I was told later that our aircraft had drawn heavy fire. Fortunately, our men escaped injury.

Our military engineers had deployed two dump trucks to fill in the ditches the gangs had prepared in order to trap the MINUSTAH vehicles so that they could be shot up point blank — a tactic that had been used on us more than once in the past.

The courageous actions of Sergeant Gerardo Montenegro were commended by the Mission Command, in a letter sent by General Heleno to the Engineering Unit Commander. Montenegro had bravely infiltrated the area early in the morning. From there he had supervised the work of the troops, during which four Blue Helmets were wounded. Though our vehicles had taken heavy fire, they had refused to stop until they had completed their task.

As a result of complaints related to this operation, the UN launched an inquiry into the soldiers' conduct. This inquiry reported back: "The MINUSTAH response to the commission's request for clarification about human rights violations by the MINUSTAH forces during the operation that took place in Cité Soleil on 6 July, 2005, was completely satisfactory."[1]

Despite this, certain groups would later accuse MINUSTAH's leaders of human rights violations — without mentioning, of course, that inquiries had already been made and that our troops had complied with the UN's own ROEs.

I did not expect Dread Wilme's death to improve security much in Haiti, especially in Cité Soleil. I was sure that soon after his death, others would replace him. Because a more comprehensive solution was unavailable, it was only a matter of time before violence returned to previous levels. Events would prove me right; gang violence receded for a short time, but no longer.

I remember talking to Colonel Toro during that dinner with Ambassador Valdés about whether the troops would be able to control Cité Soleil after the operation. He told me that only one security post — CP16 — manned by a platoon of Jordanian soldiers, would be maintained. That post would be in the heart of Cité Soleil, to establish a permanent presence. As it turned out, there would be a delay in establishing that post.

I replied that the only way to secure and exploit the operation's success would be to occupy the ground with troops. He told me this would require a senior-rank decision, since to be really effective, the soldiers would have to leave their vehicles and conduct foot patrols and searches — as had been done in Bel Air by Peruvian soldiers during the operation described earlier.

Besides that, he added, such an action would have to be authorized by the UN Police (UNPol) and by the Haitian police on the ground. And he suggested that in time I would realize what would actually be involved.

Toro also told me that combat intelligence was needed, but all they had came from informants whose real intentions were not fully understood.

While I was reading the news reports, I surmised that the Chilean forces would avoid casualties only if they stayed in an area where there was little action, such as Cap Haïtien.

I understand now that the statement that there would be zero UN casualties actually meant that the commanders would make every effort to avoid them, not that the mission would take no casualties. By then, there already *had* been casualties, and the situation was delicate, with constant violence in Port-au-Prince, though not in the northern zone, where most of the Chileans were deployed.

It seemed that in Chile, people's impressions of the mission were based on what our troops faced in Cap Haïtien, where things were relatively calm. But the real trouble was in the capital, where Chileans had also been deployed.

Moreover, most Chileans (including some of our military) had long assumed that their troops were in Haiti to engage in humanitarian assistance and that there would be no violence. The possibility of Chilean casualties simply did not occur to them. I wondered how our people would react to one of us being sent home in a body bag—a situation that many of the contingents deployed in the capital city had already faced.

On July 5, when I returned home from a military ceremony in Peldehue, María José, my 11-year-old daughter, told me she was worried about hurricanes, since they often struck Haiti. She had probably seen the news on TV. So as not to worry her before my departure, I told her that the TV news had been inaccurate. But I have to admit—I lied to her, since an average of five hurricanes struck the island every year, with significant losses of life and property.

The last severe hurricane to strike Haiti had been in 2004. It had struck Gonaïves, the country's third-largest city. The Argentine forces deployed there had had to be evacuated by helicopter. During that event, the Chilean crews of the Puma helicopters had helped rescue hundreds of people from towns cut off by flooding. They had also helped transport food, building supplies and medical staff from MINUSTAH and various NGOs, all in an attempt to control the chaos left in the hurricane's wake.

Hurricanes are not at all rare in Haiti. The one in Gonaïves claimed almost 3,000 lives. Of course, not many people in Chile or the rest of the world heard about it. It was seen as a minor news item because it happened in Haiti. I began to understand that though all of us are equally human, not all countries are equally important. Unfortunately, I was to see the truth of this in the coming year.

Note

1 Report by the Secretary General about the UN Stabilization Mission in Haiti, UN Security Council, July 28, 2006, 7.

CHAPTER THREE

At the Preparation Area

I RETURNED HOME from my flying visit to Haiti with about two months to go before I returned for a year. I crated my weapons (including a Galil assault rifle and an Uzi submachine gun) and other gear and took it all to FACH Group 10, which flew it to Haiti on July 5 in a Hercules C-130 transport.

Meanwhile, I kept working as director of the DGMN. On July 11, I attended a UN conference in New York on arms control. The following day, I visited Ambassador Heraldo Muñoz, our UN representative, whom I had met a year earlier during my nomination process. We had a friendly meeting, during which we discussed the situation in Haiti. He had up-to-date information on events in the country.

I also met with Colonel Marcos López and told him that since I was in New York, I wanted to talk to the DPKO authorities about my upcoming mission. The conference I was attending was in the same UN building.

On July 13, accompanied by Colonel López, I met with Vincent Ngooi, a Lieutenant Colonel of the Singaporean Army, who was serving in the Force Generation Department of the Military Division of the DPKO. He briefed me on how the MINUSTAH force had been designed. This was a highly informative meeting, during which he told me that I could name a Chilean officer to be my assistant at MINUSTAH Headquarters (just as General Lugani had named an Argentine assistant).

Later I met with Lieutenant Colonel Li Pen of the Chinese Army, Military Operations Services Officer of the Military Division of the DPKO, who told me about the structure and command relations of his department and its relationship with the mission.

Colonel López had also arranged for me to meet Lieutenant General Randhir Kumar Mehta, head of the Military Division of the DPKO, who was in charge of all UN military missions worldwide.

While waiting, I met his Chief of Staff, Colonel Doyle of the Irish Army, who was very kind and who tried to explain why his boss could not attend — apparently his presence had been required by a problem with an African mission. He suggested I meet with Wolfgang Weisbrod-Weber, who was in charge of the European and Caribbean Regions of the Operations Division of the DPKO. My meeting with him turned out to be the best of that day.

Regarding Haiti and the purpose of the mission there, Weisbrod-Weber believed that military, structural, and economic efforts should dovetail but that the priority must be to hold elections that would bring in a legitimate government. The elections needed to be as transparent, legitimate and independent as possible. This would enable development plans to advance. Nothing could be achieved in Haiti unless elections were held, so everything should be focused on that objective.

He told me that after Aristide's departure, and especially in light of Haiti's political history, it was vital to bring in a legitimate government — one that could begin adopting measures to build a more democratic, institutionalized society.

I finished my activities that day thinking about what Weber had said. I found myself agreeing with him, though time would make me change my position. A year later, I wondered whether the best way to help the country might be something completely different, perhaps impracticable from a political point of view, but in the light of the shortcomings I observed during my commission, perhaps not all that far-fetched. My conclusion — shared by many people at the UN who had spent several years in the country — was that the best thing for Haiti might be to spend several years building a solid state structure, since it was useless to talk about elections at a time when there were no state institutions and a democratic culture was lacking. Some even talked about twenty years of UN support.

On Friday morning, General Mehta of the Indian Army received us in his office on the thirty-sixth floor of the central UN building. He was waiting for me with Colonel Doyle. He began the meeting by insisting on explaining his absence the previous day. I replied to his explanation that I fully understood.

General Mehta was about 65 years old, and tall, thin, serious, warm, and intelligent. He had all the makings, so to speak, of a British officer — something that was only reinforced when he visited me in Haiti: his style (which included carrying a baton) and his approach to protocol were clear indications of Britain's influence on the Indian Army.

Officers in the Chilean Army retire around age 50, and most Chilean generals are under 55 when they retire. As a result, they take home a world of experience and have several years to remain useful to their country. General Bacellar himself was 58, and the Commander-in-Chief of the Brazilian Army was almost 68.

After the greetings, we began to discuss Haiti. General Mehta told me that Haiti was among the most peaceful missions of the 17 for which he was responsible: there were no dangerous neighbours, and no subversives or guerrilla forces—only criminal gangs. He added that the key to the mission was collaboration between the MINUSTAH Military Commander and the UN Police (UNPol).

Had I been sharper, I would have seen his insistence on this matter as a clue. In time I would understand that one of the main difficulties with the mission was conflict between the UN's military forces and UNPol.

To reassure him, I told him I had come up from Special Forces, where teamwork was essential, and that I had worked in military–civilian relations in my country, so I knew how to relate to civilians.

He expressed the UN's interest in having more Chileans—captains and military women—especially in Sudan and even in Haiti, and he asked me to tell our leaders in Chile about the advisability of increasing our presence at the UN.

He added that it would be useful if Chile sent an officer to serve as my assistant in Haiti; the UN had increased the number of MINUSTAH staff by one expressly for this purpose.

We discussed the dates when I would be in Haiti, and we agreed that a week— or even five days—of exchange would be more than enough to take over from General Lugani. We agreed that I would arrive in Port-au-Prince on September 15. That way I would have at least a week to assume my predecessor's functions. We parted company warmly. This ended my round of meetings at the UN.

Back in Chile, on July 18, the new Minister of National Defence, Jaime Ravinet, received me in his office to talk about Haiti. He pointed out that the situation in that country was complex and that until economic aid arrived, there was little the military forces could do, though security and stability should be provided by MINUSTAH.

He also told me that the idea was for Chilean troops to stay in Haiti until 2006. Meanwhile, the police presence would be increased gradually, the combat units would be withdrawn, and we would help other countries form a Haitian police force.

In keeping with the idea I had formed after the meetings at the UN, I told him it was vital for Haiti to hold clean, credible elections. Only then could a proper state emerge and national development begin.

I pointed out that we were under Chapter VII of the UN Charter, which added a significant level of risk for our soldiers. This could have strong political consequences. If our country were to receive back from Haiti a coffin holding a Chilean soldier, the impact might be tremendous, and I did not believe the country was prepared for it.

Before leaving, I told him how pleased I was with the commission and that I felt honoured to represent the army and my country. The meeting was a success, and I felt that he would be sympathetic to and supportive of my approaching mission.

After I left his office, I held a press conference with several journalists, with whom I shared some of my perspective on the mission.

On August 16 I met with General Heleno, who was visiting Chile with Ambassador Valdés, in the office of Army Commander-in-Chief General Cheyre. The two of them had come to participate in a seminar organized by Under-Secretary of War Gabriel Gaspar.

During that meeting with General Cheyre, we had a frank discussion with General Heleno, who insisted that despite the complaints being received, MINUSTAH was properly handling the situation in Haiti. He added that the violence being depicted by the media was not widespread. In his view, except for some parts of Port-au-Prince, things were under control and lives were being lived calmly.

General Heleno expressed his admiration for the work the Chilean troops were doing in Cap Haïtien, which had initially been a very difficult area but now, thanks to our soldiers' efforts, had been restored to calm. He hoped other MINUSTAH contingents would follow our example. He also praised our Helicopter Unit and our engineers. And he pointed out that our soldiers had earned the citizens' support.

Regarding his last comment, as I would confirm later, the Chilean habit of reaching out to people would be key to our mission's success, along with the professionalism of our soldiers.

General Heleno noted how difficult it had been to deploy certain contingents that had been poorly trained. He seemed worried about the cultural problems some of them were experiencing, problems that made it more difficult for them to gain the population's support.

I met up with Heleno again the next day, during the seminar at the Defence Ministry.

In his presentation, Ambassador Valdés began by pointing out that Haiti was not a failed state, but rather an "unthinkable" state where poverty levels were atrocious and life expectancy even worse. He dismissed criticisms of MINUSTAH's use of force, noted that the mission had prevented a civil war.

He emphasized that more time was required to achieve sustained progress, and he feared that the international community's will to help was weak. In particular, he worried that after the elections, some countries might consider withdrawing from the mission, as if the elections alone would solve everything.

According to Valdés, Haiti was a very fragile state, and even after transparent and fair elections were held, the country would require long-term international development aid.

General Heleno, in turn, explained what MINUSTAH was doing and the challenges it faced. These challenges could be summarized as follows: Haiti needed international aid, and that aid had to be two-pronged: a political and administrative system had to be nurtured, and in the meantime, military force was necessary. He pointed out that the country was facing what was at root a police problem — specifically, criminal gangs had sunk their roots deep into a society beset by extreme poverty.

José Miguel Insulza, Secretary General of the Organization of American States (OAS), also made a brief presentation. He concurred with Valdés and expressed his support for the electoral process, describing the OAS's on-the-ground efforts to register Haitian voters.

After these meetings I continued my preparations for Haiti. According to UN and Army regulations, all personnel on this mission were to be vaccinated against tropical diseases, so I had to have vaccines for hepatitis A and B, measles, yellow fever, typhoid fever, and tetanus. I also started taking chloroquine, since dengue fever and malaria are still serious health problems in Haiti.

Along with the medical exams required by the UN, I had to undergo a psychiatric exam. The psychiatrist asked whether this new mission might not be too much for me. Smiling, I answered that it was not, that I was sure everything would be all right. So he signed my medical pass.

I had very little time left before I was due to leave. I spent it with my family and friends.

CHAPTER FOUR

Green Light at the Gate

WHEN PARATROOPERS are about to jump, a green light above the aircraft gate lights up, indicating they are in the jump zone and need only wait for the bell and for the commander to give the order. Then they must jump!

Once the green light turns on, there is no turning back.

On the morning of September 12, 2005, I went to the Church of the Sacred Heart on avenida El Bosque to say goodbye to Father Fernando Karadima, my spiritual guide and friend. I would be leaving on the mission that afternoon, and he had invited me to celebrate mass with all the parish priests. Some of those young men had become my closest friends. It was 10 a.m. when I arrived at the church.

The aisle was full of priests, about forty of them, together with four bishops, all of them old friends. Among them were the military bishop, Monsignor Juan Barros, and Bishops Horacio Valenzuela, Tomislav Kolyatic, and Andrés Arteaga.

Father Fernando dedicated part of his sermon to me, asking the Virgin Mary to protect me. After mass, everyone greeted me affectionately. Then Father Fernando gave me an envelope in his office, asking me to open it when I arrived in Haiti. From then on, I would think of the mission as pastoral to a degree, because of the help I was giving a sister nation.

After lunch, I went with my wife Tere to say goodbye to my mother. As always, I tried to minimize the danger of my trip. I told her this separation

Photo 3. The airport at Santiago: goodbye to my family

would last only two or three months and that things in Haiti were calm, so there was no need to worry.

In the afternoon we left for the airport, where the family of Major Carlos Díaz — who was traveling with me — was waiting, together with the staff of the DGMN, my brothers and sisters, friends, and a few officers who were there to say goodbye (Photo 3).

After a nine-hour journey, Carlos and I arrived in Miami, where we spent four days.

We arrived at Toussaint L'Ouverture Airport in Port-au-Prince on September 17, after a flight of less than two hours from Miami. I was struck by the number of Haitians on board. All of them were traveling with large bags and several suitcases, which suggested to me that besides their personal belongings, they were bringing goods to sell.

I asked a flight attendant whether flights this full were normal. He told me that all of American Airlines' three or four daily flights between Miami / Fort Lauderdale and Port-au-Prince were full in both directions.

"That's strange," I thought, since I had imagined Haiti as a place of deep and widespread poverty. I would later realize that more than two million Haitians were living abroad, especially in Canada and the United States, and that many of them were sending remittances to their families.

There was no other explanation for the large number of travelers to and from such a terribly poor country, where most people earned less than US$2 a day.

A band playing *troubadou* — a Haitian style of music — had positioned itself at the terminal entrance. Oddly enough, all of the many times I passed through the airport, they would be playing the same tune.

I had arrived in the operations area — the "jump point" — and was set to embark on the mission I had dreamed about since February 2004.

I remember from that first day the intense heat and humidity. I do not like the heat much, preferring the rain and cold. But as soon as I was appointed to serve in Haiti I had decided I would "confront" the issue of heat and humidity — that I would face it with no complaints or accommodations. I started doing that my first day in Haiti, to everyone's dismay, since it meant little air conditioning.

I knew that if I didn't take that approach, I would soon find myself glued to that appliance, which would prevent me from being on the ground with the troops. I did not want that to happen, since I have always believed that a commander has to experience whatever the troops are facing. If I avoided dealing with the same conditions, my credibility with them would be zero.

GENERAL EDUARDO LUGANI was waiting for me at the airport in Port-au-Prince, along with a delegation of Chilean troop commanders. With them was Sub-Officer Alex Leiva — better known among the commandos as El Ratón ("The Rat"), who was serving with the Helicopter Unit. I had arranged for him to be in charge of my security in Haiti.

I went straight to the Montana, where Generals Bacellar and Lugani were staying, and where I would be as well. It had been Ambassador Valdés's idea to billet the commanders there, to ensure they lived as close as possible to MINUSTAH Headquarters. The best thing about the Montana was that it had guaranteed running water and electricity — no small consideration in a city where few places had these basic amenities on a regular basis.

When I got to my room, I found some of the crates I had sent ahead. The Rat had also deposited my weapons there. I changed into combat gear and immediately, as the heat sank in, started sweating as never before. I headed out to begin meetings to take over as Deputy Force Commander.

That afternoon I was invited to the home of Marcel Young, the Chilean Ambassador to Haiti, and his wife Isabel Araya, to celebrate our country's Independence Day. There I would also meet other Chileans and some Haitians as well.

Ambassador Young impressed me immediately as an excellent person and a distinguished representative of Chile. This impression would only strengthen as time went on.

That same afternoon I encountered General Urano Bacellar, who had replaced General Heleno as Force Commander (FC, in UN jargon) a month earlier. He, too, made an excellent first impression. He was a wonderful person, and the fact that he was an outstanding paratrooper in the Brazilian Army meant that we quickly struck up a friendship.

General Óscar Izurieta, Commander of the Military Institutes, had told me when we said our goodbyes that I didn't know how lucky I was that Bacellar would be my commander. He had been in Washington with him and they had become friends. General Heleno himself had spoken highly of him during his visit to Chile.

I later found out that they had graduated from the same class at the Brazilian Army Military College, as had General Elito, who would subsequently replace Bacellar.

I returned to the hotel and went to bed thinking that so far things had gone smoothly. During the night, the sound of gunfire made it clear to me that the situation in the capital was far from stable.

The next morning I took a Puma helicopter with Ambassador Young to Cap Haïtien to celebrate Independence Day with the Chilean battalion.

Cap Haïtien impressed me as very poor and very hot. The presence of several Haitians at the ceremony was a sign of the good relations our fellow countrymen had developed with the locals.

Two Chileans were with them: Andrea Loi, who was in charge of the Human Rights Division of MINUSTAH in Fort Liberté, and Mercedes Bustamante, who worked for the OAS in the Cap Haïtien office, also in human rights matters. Both women had an excellent working relationship with our soldiers and were of great help to us. Indeed, considering the precarious conditions in which they worked, their actions had been commendable and noteworthy.

After the ceremony I visited the military camp in the blazing heat and took a look at the battalion's tents, which housed about twenty men each. It was extremely hot, with hordes of mosquitoes. The air conditioning had collapsed from overuse, but even when working it had not been much use in these conditions. Yet our men seemed used to it.

I saw that new barracks were being built to replace the tents. The UN was in charge of that work, the idea being that the troops should have tolerable living conditions so that they could lead normal lives, which in turn would allow them to function properly.

During the several visits I made to that unit, I inspected the progress of the construction and realized how slow and bureaucratic the UN system was, especially when it came to troops' facilities. The opposite was true of the civilian facilities, and I urged the administrative authorities to be more diligent. It

Photo 4. DFC Handover Ceremony: Generals Bacellar and Lugani and I

would be several months before these quarters were finished. Even after I had completed my mission, some units were still sleeping in tents.

I returned to Port-au-Prince that afternoon with the impression that the Chileans in Cap Haïtien were accomplishing their mission and that our men's morale was excellent, but that their living conditions could certainly be improved.

I spent the next several days at headquarters meetings, which were conducted by various officers. I also paid my respects to the mission's representatives.

The ceremony at which General Lugani handed over to me took place on September 22 at the Chilean Engineers Unit, which was next to the Chilean Helicopter Unit, beside L'Ouverture Airport and about 40 minutes from headquarters. It was conducted by Ambassador Valdés, who was accompanied by the Ambassadors of Argentina, Brazil, Chile, and the United States and by several other MINUSTAH colleagues, civilians whom I had not yet met. I do not remember any Haitian authorities attending (Photo 4).

All the commanders of the military units attended the ceremony. A delegation with soldiers from each country was formed. Orders were issued in English so that everyone would understand.

The ceremony was short and simple. Lugani gave an emotional speech, thanking all of the mission's personnel. Afterwards, my curriculum vitae was read out. Then I signed a document with Bacellar in which the transfer of command was completed.

After the ceremony I noticed that several Peruvian officers from the Force Commander Reserve Unit would also be under my command, so to speak. They were Peruvian commandos, some of whom—so I would learn—had participated in the famous rescue operation at the Japanese Embassy in Lima after it had been taken over by guerrillas. .

I approached them and asked them to meet me to one side of the tent, where snacks were being served. There I told them something along these lines: "I'm a commando and Special Forces man like yourselves, and you're the Command Reserve, so from now on we're a team, a single patrol. I'm sure that will be the case.

"Next week I'll come and have lunch with you to have a taste of your *ají de gallina* [chicken with peppers], but no *pisco* [grape brandy], please, because we'll never be able to agree whether it's Chilean or Peruvian."

Their laughter and the way I talked to them created a friendly atmosphere, and I realized we'd soon build a good relationship. In time, things would exceed my expectations—we would forge an excellent friendship, based largely on coming under fire together. We would have lunch together at least once a month. I have very good memories of these men and to this day stay in touch with many of them by e-mail. Experiencing extreme situations creates special bonds that go beyond any other consideration.

Later that afternoon, after the ceremony, we went to the airport to see Lugani off, and he repeated what he had told me before: "I'm only going to give you one piece of advice, since at the professional level you have all the skills you need to do this properly. Take time out to rest when you need to, and go back to your country every two months."[1]

I would realize soon enough that this was excellent advice.

The following day I went to the office early—at about 6:50 a.m.—and took out some photos of my family and other things I had brought to make the place a little more human. The office was small and on the first floor of MINUSTAH Headquarters, with nothing but a metal desk and two chairs. The aides in the foyer also had metal desks.

The Military Command staff included General Bacellar and his two assistants, Lieutenant Colonel Hoover Sales and Major Marcelo Dutra, both from the Brazilian Army, along with Major Díaz, NCO Leiva, and me.

Since all of us except Major Dutra were paratroopers, paratroop jokes and codes of conduct flew thick and fast. For example, on the first day, I put a coffee mug on the office floor. Whoever wanted it, it was understood, would have to do several push-ups under the watchful eye of General Bacellar and amid much laughter.

Likewise, whenever someone made a mistake—including me—he had to pay with push-ups. This broke the ice and relaxed the atmosphere—with our commander's permission.

Before my arrival the team had lunched in their offices or in the mess on the first floor. After I arrived, we started lunching together in the Force Commander's conference room.

A headquarters meeting was held every morning at 8 a.m. During that meeting, items on the agenda were reviewed by the Chief of Staff. Every Friday there was a general HQ meeting chaired by General Bacellar and me, where issues concerning the top officers and the military and operative management of the mission were discussed.

At least three times every six months, the Battalion Commanders attended a meeting with the FC. At those meetings—which, by the way, were always in English—we evaluated our officers' performance. They always lived up to expectations, which boosted our troops' prestige.

Some of the commanders who did not speak English were assisted by interpreters. This drew negative comments from headquarters, since the mission required that commanders speak English. Put simply, these officers were failing to comply with a UN requirement.

Each and every day, including Saturdays and sometimes Sundays, I was in my office before 7 a.m. and worked there till 9 p.m. The pressure of my job was heavy from the start, so I preferred to spend my time working at the office. The Internet allowed me to stay in touch with my family and with events in Chile.

I soon realized there would be few opportunities for exercise, since there were no proper facilities. In the early days, with Major Díaz, I went jogging on the streets—toting my gun and running between the cars with him—but this was dangerous, so as time went by I exercised more sporadically.

On Saturday afternoons, mass was celebrated at the Argentine hospital and sometimes at the Brazilian unit. We usually attended mass with General Bacellar. We enjoyed attending with the Brazilians because of their cheerful enthusiasm, which was reflected even in their hymns. It surprised me that their military chaplains carried the cruets and other elements for mass in camouflage bags, which made me realize that they saw themselves as ordinary soldiers.

As I mentioned earlier, before leaving Chile, Father Fernando Karadima had given me an envelope. He told me it contained a picture of someone who had been to places where there was extreme poverty and that she would probably help and watch over me. I opened the envelope and found a picture of Mother Teresa of Calcutta.

I hung it on the wall by my chair, thinking how right Father Fernando had been, since this holy woman knew, like no one else, how to address poverty.

Photo 5. The Hotel Christopher, general headquarters of MINUSTAH

Later, I moved my office furniture around so that my desk faced the sea. Now, as it turned out, I had a view of the troubled place that would demand so much attention and cause so many worries: Cité Soleil.

Soon after starting my commission, I packed my rucksack with emergency items and placed it at my office door in case I had to fly somewhere immediately. I did not want to have to fumble for things I might need right away.

At about 8 a.m. on my first day as DFC, I was told of a meeting of the MINUSTAH sections that I needed to attend, since General Bacellar was visiting a military unit outside the capital.

I went to the ground floor and walked into a meeting with about twenty people. I waited for someone to introduce me to the others; instead, I was simply pointed to the empty chair at the head of the conference table, which was covered with telephones and monitors. I sat down and waited for someone to kick-start the meeting.

Since no one said anything, I asked the person next to me who was in charge of the meeting, to which he replied: "You."

I drew a breath and said, in English: "Well, I am General Eduardo Aldunate, new Deputy Force Commander of the mission, and I hereby declare this meeting open." I let them all speak, without really understanding how things were organized or whom they represented. They spoke in English or French, which made me realize that the little French I had learned would come in handy.

It dawned on me then that when Ambassador Valdés, his Deputy SRSG, and the FC were all away, I was next in line.

After the meeting I toured the building, visited the offices, and introduced myself in the different wings of this former hotel that had been turned into the MINUSTAH General Headquarters. Visiting all the departments took me several days. So began my official stay at MINUSTAH (Photo 5).

Colonel Toro's presence was extremely useful, since he had served as Operations Officer for about eight months and was fully conversant with the situation.

The Chief of Staff was Colonel Michel Duhamel of Canada. For some reason, that position had been reserved for his country. There were only three Canadians on the mission, all of them officers at General Headquarters. All three had had a lot of experience on peacekeeping and other missions, including in Afghanistan and Bosnia.

The lack of a military contingent from that country was rather odd, given that Canada has a large Haitian population and that Canada's ceremonial head of state, Governor General Michaëlle Jean, was born in Jacmel in the south of Haiti.

Colonel Duhamel was an outstanding officer. It was my good fortune that I was able to work alongside him until July 2006. During those months I came to appreciate his skill as a coordinator.

One of his duties was to assess the performance of about 100 officers at General Headquarters from 23 different countries. More than once I saw that he was very strict about minor disciplinary issues. This affected several officers, since in the final performance reports sent to the DPKO he mentioned certain points that he knew would affect these officers when they returned home. However, I always respected this sphere of his command and understood that he always tried to be fair.

Duhamel, who had a wealth of experience on international missions, sometimes observed mediocrity or dereliction of duty. In our region these things might not have warranted a misconduct report. He always said that if these officers had been selected because of their outstanding skills to serve on the mission in Haiti, this should be reflected in their actions.

One of my first steps, since I had a psychologist on staff at General Headquarters, was to order a study of the working conditions both at headquarters and in the various units. To this task I assigned Major Natalija Bockaj of the Croatian Army.

Her study found that on the whole, the situation was being properly handled by the Unit Commanders in the various regions and in the capital; also, that through sports and social activities and the appropriate use of day fur-loughs, the forces were able to cope with the tensions inherent in the opera-tions they conducted.

This was not the case among the Jordanian units deployed in the capital, since they were unable to play any sports and their living quarters were not up to scratch. To make matters worse, they were located in the most strife-torn districts of the city and their personnel tended not to use their furloughs.

The commanders and I thought that these troops should play sports and invite personnel from other contingents to visit them. Unfortunately, because of the tense atmosphere in the capital, that proved quite difficult.

As the days went by, I found myself caught up in a whirl of meetings and visits to the units. The meetings were attended by people from several coun-tries, most of them civilians. Some had served together on other missions and specialized in specific issues. Most would spend more than two years on a given mission before being redeployed. From the start, I built up a good work-ing relationship with all of them, especially the experts on politics, human rights, and the media.

The first thing I always did when I arrived at the office was go to the Joint Operations Centre (JOC) in the basement to pick up information on the pre-vious night's activities (this was also General Bacellar's routine). From there I went to my office, where I opened the MINUSTAH e-mail to check my mes-sages, of which I usually got more than I wanted. Around 8 a.m. the staff would hold a briefing meeting, chaired by General Bacellar or myself. We eventually handed this duty over to the Chief of Staff.

One of us had to attend the 8:30 a.m. meeting with the Senior Manage-ment Team (SMT), which was chaired by Valdés. Attending this would be the mission's five or six directors, including the directors of politics, the press, UNPol, and military issues.

After that meeting, which took about an hour, we would walk downstairs to attend another meeting with the chiefs of the MINUSTAH branches. Elec-toral, judicial, and political issues were always the main topic, and General Bacellar or I would invariably provide an update of the security situation.

On Tuesdays one of us would visit the Primature, the Prime Minister's res-idence, where we would meet with representatives of the provisional govern-ment.

On Friday mornings we attended a security meeting with all branches of MINUSTAH. This meeting usually opened with a presentation by Bertrand, the man in charge of the mission personnel's security. That was followed by an overview of security problems, during which the military commanders reported on the situation in the country.

On Friday afternoons at 3 p.m. we held the weekly staff meeting, which usually took about two hours. During it the military contingent's work was reviewed. We were required to attend all of these meetings, as well as other meetings that cropped up every day and at any time, of which there were never fewer than four a day. I joked with General Bacellar that until the gangs attacked us, our main threat was these endless meetings.

Over time I began to coordinate attendance at these meetings with General Bacellar. So that I could be with the troops, he attended all of them. When we began encountering new problems, the knowledge I had acquired about the situation on the ground would prove crucial. Even so, I know all these meetings placed enormous pressure on him.

Note

1 Brigade General Eduardo Lugani, Argentine Army, Deputy Force Commander, MINUSTAH, September 2005–September 2006.

CHAPTER FIVE

First Steps on the Ground

IN SEPTEMBER 2005, when I arrived in the country, the situation was complex. There was an interim government, and elections were still regarded as a distant prospect — indeed, many believed they would never take place. Violence was steadily increasing in the capital, though the rest of the country was stable and safe, since it was controlled by MINUSTAH.

In Gonaïvҽs, north of Port-au-Prince, minor issues were being handled by the Argentine contingent. The main cause of conflict was the lack of coordination between the Haitian National Police (PNH) and the UN Police (UNPol). As in other parts of the country, this problem was compounded by the actions of political representatives or "caciques," who had close links with some of the gangs and whose credentials as upstanding citizens were questionable at best.

In the northern region, Cap Haïtien, where the Chileans were posted, things were satisfactory. During their first few days in that zone, our forces had experienced some very tense moments, especially with ex-officers of the former army — the ex-FAd'H, as they were called. This situation was skillfully handled by the commanders and never posed a real threat to the security of the area under their command.

In the northwest, at Fort Liberté, where the Spaniards and Moroccans were deployed, some minor problems had arisen in Ouanaminthe, relating to the border control, but in general the situation was in hand.

I will return to this situation of "virtual" border control. By "virtual," I mean that the frontier posts were in constant conflict with the Dominican authorities, mainly because an enormous number of Haitians were being deported from the Dominican Republic every day. There were also problems involving customs: goods were constantly being smuggled from one country to the other.

There were no major problems in the central area. As in the southern part of the country, the main problems were policing ones—robberies, kidnappings and other crimes. But there were no paramilitary groups. Nine-tenths of our security issues related to conditions in Port-au-Prince.

The recent history of security was disturbing.

On February 19, a group of armed men stormed the National Penitentiary and freed 493 prisoners. It was later discovered that this had taken place with the complicity of agents of the Haitian state.

On March 20, MINUSTAH launched an operation to recover the Petit Goâve police station, during which several armed criminals and a journalist were killed.

In 2004 the Sri Lanka Battalion launched an operation to recover a police station that had been taken over by a local gang. This resulted in the death of one Sri Lankan soldier and more than 30 injured, though the troops regained control of the premises.

A similarly violent situation arose on March 21 in Terrier Rouge, where the police station—which had been used as a base to attack a military patrol—was recovered.

On March 31, a military operation was launched in Cité Soleil to restrict the movements of criminals and at the same time to allow the free movement of people along Route #1, the main road. On April 14, a MINUSTAH soldier was shot and killed by gangs in Cité Soleil.

On June 1, a group of armed men had set fire to Port-au-Prince's central market, Tête Boeuf, claiming 17 lives.

On July 6, MINUSTAH launched an operation in the capital to neutralize the leader of one of the Cité Soleil gangs. I discussed that operation earlier.

Besides all this, many bodies were being left in the streets. Many of these showed signs of torture—an indication that lynchings were taking place in Haiti, most probably as a result of the dysfunctional judicial system.

This sort of violence—at a level barely imaginable in Chile—indicates the level of insecurity the mission had to deal with, especially in the capital.

To summarize, the situation in most of the country was under control, but there were also specific parts of the capital where insecurity levels were high.

I thought it best to confront the toughest issues right away. So, early in my assignment, I told General Bacellar I wanted to visit Cité Soleil. He liked the idea and said he wanted to go with me.

Photo 6. With General Bacellar in Cité Soleil

Donning bulletproof vests and helmets and carrying rifles, we set off one morning to visit the area. For this we had arranged the support of Jordanian armoured personnel carriers (APCs), since it was the Jordanians who were responsible for the area (Photos 6 and 7).

MINUSTAH regarded Cité Soleil as a danger zone and forbade its civilian personnel to enter it. The night before, Jordanian troops had come under heavy fire from the gangs.

Since my vehicle was not armoured (unlike General Bacellar's), we drove to Checkpoint 2, where we clambered into a Jordanian APC to enter Cité Soleil. We sat on top of the vehicle and felt the tension rise as we entered the area.

The gangs usually shot at UN vehicles, but I knew that if I wanted to understand this place, I could not hide inside the carrier and look out through the hatches. I also realized that our behaviour was being observed by the soldiers, so we had to be brave and experience the same insecurity they faced every day. So I sat on top of the vehicle, well aware of the risk this entailed. General Bacellar did the same.

General Bacellar, Major Díaz, NCO Leiva, and I sat on top of the APC with our rifles off safety. With us up there were some Jordanian soldiers, all heavily armed. We set off down a dirt road. Most of the houses we passed had been sprayed with bullets.

Photo 7. With General Bacellar entering Cité Soleil

Shortly after starting out, we heard gunfire in the distance and coming closer. A Jordanian soldier beside us began firing his M-16 until General Bacellar ordered him to stop.

At that point, we were all keeping our field of fire, but we could see no one shooting at us.

We passed several Jordanian vehicles that were controlling the route, and I noticed that all the soldiers were inside their APCs, which seemed strange since it is difficult to control the population from there.

We finally got to CP16, an old market occupied by around 30 men, who were sandbagged to fend off any attack (Photo 8). A platoon of Jordanian soldiers was posted there on a six-hour rotation. They were under constant fire, especially from the west.

Living conditions were abysmal. The floor was covered with weeds, the walls peppered with holes caused by the constant gunfire from the gangs.

Through interpreters, we spoke to these men. I thought that having a platoon shut inside a building under constant gunfire was not the best solution. From my perspective these men were ducks in a barrel, target practice for the gangs. Clearly, there was an urgent need to take physical control of the streets here.

The Jordanians' morale was surprisingly good, considering that their unit had borne the brunt of the casualties.

Photo 8. Reviewing CP16

This visit proved extremely useful during later meetings with the provisional government authorities, where I would respond to demands for more action from the MINUSTAH military force by asking them to show me the presence of their own government, their own police, and their own development projects, since the UN could do nothing without those. This did not go down well, but there was no denying the complete absence of the PNH in those places.

I always believed that the Cité Soleil issue could not be solved by force. The situation was more complex than that. Improving the people's living conditions would have a significant impact on the violence. During that first reconnaissance trip, the people's extreme poverty caught my attention, and I was sure that not all of them were criminals. The lack of effort to help those people — indeed, the government's glaring absence — did much to explain the insecurity and violence.

After visiting Cité Soleil we inspected National Route #1, another of the city's danger zones. From there we returned to headquarters. That day we did not see a single PNH officer on the streets — or a single member of UNPol, which was even more worrying.

It was time to meet the rest of the units. I began with the contingents deployed outside the capital, starting in Cap Haïtien, the most remote region in the country, where the Chileans were stationed. Lieutenant Colonel Hernán Castellón was their commander. They seemed to be faring well and were excited about what they were doing. They had the situation in their zone under control.

I toured the Chilean unit more thoroughly than during my first brief visit. In fact, I went to all the barracks and met with some acquaintances who had served with me in various units in Chile. I left feeling certain that all was running smoothly in the north.

Next I visited the Peruvian unit, which was deployed in the capital in the Shodecosa sector, adjoining Cité Soleil. That unit was commanded by Lieutenant Colonel Flores, whom I had met during the command transfer ceremony.

Next I visited the northeastern zone — Fort Liberté and Ouanaminthe — where the Spanish soldiers were stationed under the command of Colonel Luis Flores, an officer of the Spanish Marine Corps and an extremely pleasant fellow.

This area was under the shared watch of the Spanish and Moroccan contingents. From there we headed for Terrier Rouge, where the Moroccan forces were waiting for me offering dates and almonds. They had scheduled a meeting at their camp, where there was a large tent. Inside we sat on enormous couches, and I was served very hot tea and briefed about their situation. Afterwards we played football.

At the Spanish camp I uncovered two fascinating facts. The first involved logistics — a private Spanish company was providing support for this unit. The second was that some of the Spanish soldiers were women — good-looking women at that. Operational issues aside, I asked what it was like living with women in these circumstances. Colonel Flores told me that the Spanish Navy had adopted a policy of full integration, to the degree that some of the accommodations were mixed, with men and women sharing rooms.

When we visited Ouanaminthe on the Dominican border, my personal security was provided by a very attractive female Spanish soldier, armed with a rifle and wearing a bulletproof vest, who carried the same heavy equipment as the rest of the soldiers. Women on the front lines had to be a rather delicate issue, especially during times of stress but also because of crowded facilities.

One of the female soldiers in that contingent had gotten pregnant by her boyfriend, another Spanish soldier, by the end of their mission.

Next we visited the Nepalese at Hinche, Saint-Marc and Mirebalais, in the north-central zone. They were a well-trained and highly effective force. After visiting their three camps, we had lunch at Hinche, where they served traditional Nepalese food, which was very spicy.

By now I had learned several things. First, I should take into account the different customs of each country, which varied greatly. Second, I should eat whatever they ate. Third, they expected me to accompany them to the most difficult areas under their responsibility—which I never failed to do.

I was especially struck by the Nepalese toilets. These were just a hole in the ground with a place on either side for each foot. They seemed inadequate to me, but their commander explained that that was their custom, so I did not insist. I encountered them again in the Jordanian soldiers' camps.

From there we visited the Argentine contingent, which was stationed to the north of the capital in Gonaïves. Theirs was a mixed army/marine battalion. Their barracks were on the side of a hill they called The Rock. They also had a platoon billeted in Port-de-Paix in the northwestern zone.

This was a complex area. There had been trouble in Gonaïves before Aristide's ousting, and this was also the area that had been struck by Hurricane Jeanne 18 months earlier. Jeanne had claimed about 3,000 lives and forced some of the Argentine personnel onto the roofs of their facilities.

The commander told me that local political leaders were in cahoots with the criminals—a situation repeated throughout the country. And while at Gonaïves I noted another recurrent fact about most of Haiti: the PNH was not working properly, since its members served the interests of the local elite.

A few days before my visit, a patrol of Argentine soldiers in Saint-Michel de L'Attalaye had been attacked by gangs, which the soldiers had driven back.

Later on, during the elections, a mob in the Grande Saline area would attack and set fire to a polling booth. That incident—perhaps the most serious during the elections—would be contained by the Argentine troops' swift intervention.

I visited Raboteau, a district of Gonaïves, with the Argentine commander. Despite all the problems and the lack of security, the Argentines there were doing an excellent job.

At each of the contingents I visited, I was briefed on the difficulties involved in coordinating security missions with UNPol, especially the police units, the FPUs, which had been deployed in their areas yet acted independently of the military units. This would be a chronic problem during most of my time in Haiti.

Our next stop was the Sri Lankan contingent, stationed in the south near the capital, in Jacmel, Petit Goâve, Grand Goâve and Killick. This troop's military protocols, like those of the Nepalese, showed strong British influence. They were highly efficient soldiers and had gained full control of their area.

From there we flew to the southern region, where a Uruguayan battalion was deployed, covering Les Cayes, Jérémie and Port Salut. This area—like Cap Haïtien, where the Chileans were—faced hardly any security issues, and the Uruguayans were doing a fine job under the command of Lieutenant Colonel Pim.

In fact, during my twelve months in Haiti, not a single problem arose in the south, which spoke well of the Uruguayan troops, most of whom had long experience as peacekeepers.

On all of these trips I made use of the fact that our helicopters flew low to observe the landscape. This confirmed for me that the country almost entirely lacked roads and was severely deforested and that large numbers of people were living a difficult and isolated existence without water and electricity.

Later on, as the elections approached, this helped me understand why our patrols were taking more than eight hours to travel from one place to the next and why we had to arrange nearly 200 donkeys to transport polling boxes and other necessary materials.

It took me a week to visit the units in Port-au-Prince itself. I began with the Argentine hospital.

The mission's health system included primary medical care for the soldiers at their own units, all of which had doctors and infirmaries. Secondary-level care was provided by the Argentine hospital, which had dentists as well as specialist physicians.

The facility included portables. The doctors and personnel, most of them from the Argentine Air Force, had a large capacity to care for our troops, the mission's civilian and police personnel and even the civilian population in the event of an emergency.

My visit to the hospital allowed me to verify the staff's professionalism. I took the opportunity to visit the sick — something I would continue to do during my command.

When necessary, the injured or ill from the contingents were flown to hospital, which kept our helicopters and the two Argentine Bell helicopters on the go. Our Pumas could fly by night, which made them more efficient than the Bells.

After that I visited the Brazilian Engineers Unit, the Philippine Administrative Unit, and the Military Police Unit — a Guatemalan contingent that supported any necessary investigations involving military personnel.

Later on I visited the Brazilian battalion stationed at Camp Bravo, in a building on the University of Haiti campus. It was responsible for Bel Air, a downtown neighbourhood. When the Brazilians arrived in 2004, Bel Air was so dangerous and full of trash that it was impossible to walk through the streets. That changed when the garbage collectors arrived; the streets were now clean and people could move freely thanks to these soldiers.

The same battalion covered the presidential palace. The Brazilian troops that patrolled this critical district were billeted inside that beautiful, imposing white building.

The Brazilians had smaller units spread throughout the capital, including at Fort National, an old building on a hill inside the city and overlooking most of it. The PNH had been using the fort as a prison since August 2005. The soldiers used the prison cells for sleeping quarters.

The Brazilians had succeeded in restoring calm to the area. Besides cleaning the streets—which had been no mean feat—they had plastered pictures of football stars on the tap-taps, which (as I mentioned earlier) had improved community relations to no end.

The Brazilians and the Jordanian unit deployed in Cité Soleil were constantly at risk, as were the Peruvians in Shodecosa, who were shot at by criminals every day.

I had yet to visit the unit provided by Jordan. There were two battalions from that country on the mission, Jorbat 1 and Jorbat 2, both billeted in the capital with 750 soldiers each. The first had been tasked with Cité Soleil and Route #1; the second with the northern district of the city, from Croix de Bouquet to Cabaret.

A few days before my arrival in Haiti, an intermediate command for the mission had been established. This is how the DPKO (in New York) had decided to coordinate the units in the capital. Colonel Toro expressed to me concerns about that decision. From the start, arguments had been made against it. An intermediate command might have worked in other situations, but the decision had not taken into account the view from the ground in the capital.

To learn about these units I went to the Plaza Hotel, where that section's staff officers were billeted. There I was given a detailed briefing of the situation of the units in the capital by the general in command. I then visited Jorbat 1, which was headquartered in a place called Tony Warehouse on Route #1.

The contingents in Haiti were quartered mainly in civilian buildings, most of them renovated warehouses. These facilities had to be equipped with offices, bathrooms, kitchens and parking places for about 750 men.

As I had seen regarding the Chilean unit in Cap Haïtien, work was under way to adapt the facilities to their new functions. Some of the work was being contracted out to Haitian companies, and some was being undertaken by MINUSTAH, but a great deal was being carried out by the military units themselves.

The Jordanians were living in harsh conditions in all respects. Their quarters were basically sheds, which had to accommodate 750 men, with all that entailed, besides providing storage space for materials, vehicles, weapons and so on.

The Jordanians gave me a very warm welcome. I met with the officers, who briefed me on the situation and then served me a cup of scalding tea. I burned my fingers trying to drink it, which caused a great deal of laughter.

During this visit they kept asking me why other contingents did not have to face the same risks they were. Without question, the Jordanians were confronting the hardest task on the mission, and they were doing so on a daily basis. I realized they were speaking the truth. And I knew they also faced the worst living conditions.

So far the Jordanians had suffered the most casualties of any unit in the mission. Every day, at least 80 percent of the attacks on MINUSTAH forces were in the sector they were holding and against their personnel.

I told them their assignment had been determined in New York by the DPKO long before they arrived and that the locations for the various national contingents had been decided by the countries involved prior to their arrival in Haiti. I added that this was not something under my control. Any changes would have to be made by their superiors, and meanwhile, we would bring in other contingents to support them as necessary.

I noticed that the soldiers' helmets and bulletproof vests were of rather poor quality. I mentioned this to General Bacellar. He considered the heat they were taking in their zone and found better ones for them.

During that first visit to the Jordanians I did not have the opportunity to visit the personnel's bedrooms — something I had done on my visits to all the other units. The Jordanians had been reluctant to show them to me — perhaps their dignity prevented them. On my next visit I started with the sleeping quarters, which confirmed that their living conditions were poor — indeed, the worst of any MINUSTAH contingent. I lit a fire under the civil engineers whose task it was to remodel the Jordanians' quarters.

Each contingent received the food it had requested according to its soldiers' customs. The Jordanians' food was very different from that of other units.

Jorbat 2 was billeted to one side of the Route #1 and in better quarters than Jorbat 1. Its task was to provide security for the MINUSTAH columns operating inside Port-au-Prince — that is, for the humanitarian, electoral and development agencies as they moved around the city. It also patrolled the northern area, where it maintained a post on the highway near Cabaret, an hour from the capital.

As I had done with the other contingents, I visited Jorbat 2's area of responsibility as well as the troublesome local neighbourhoods, which gave me a good idea of the situation these soldiers faced. I had the impression that this contingent had been assigned the mission's most difficult task and that sooner or later it would have to be supported by other forces.

In general, these first visits were extremely enlightening for me as DFC, for they enabled me to meet all the personnel and tell them how important they were to the mission. I stressed the importance of following the rules of engagement (ROEs) and remembering the UN mandate, which was why we were here. And I pointed out that this was not a war mission or an occupation force.

Above all, these visits gave me a first-hand view of the actual situation each contingent was experiencing.

After these visits, I held a meeting with General Bacellar to share my impressions. He already had an accurate view of the situation. My fresh one only underscored that Cité Soleil was the main issue and that we had to do something to assist the Jordanians.

IN DECEMBER, Colonel Ricardo Toro said goodbye to the mission. His commission had been extended for two months owing to the security planning for the elections, which had been delayed. By that time he had been promoted to brigadier general and had to return to his country to take up his new post.

Ricardo had performed extremely well on the mission and had shown himself to be a man of strong character as well as a dedicated, hard-working officer. His actions had only raised our army's prestige. When he left, he received many awards for his work, evidence that all of MINUSTAH's personnel, civilian and military, held him in high esteem.

Colonel Horacio Sánchez Mariño, a distinguished officer in the Argentine Army and a veteran of the Malvinas/Falklands War, succeeded him as Operations Officer.

Horacio quickly demonstrated his skills, and I will always be grateful for his professionalism and personal qualities. When we were off duty, we talked about our countries. I would tell him about our experience in Chile, where we had built up a mature civilian–military relationship, and he would tell me about his experiences during the Falklands war.

He also showed a great appreciation for Chile and a desire to strengthen our relations as armies and countries — something on which we agreed. He made an enormous contribution to the mission, besides being a great source of support for me.

Horacio had a solid academic background, which was apparent in his advice as well as during his presentations at meetings with civilians. That was in addition to his knowledge as a professional soldier, which set an example for the rest of the headquarters officers. He also had an ideal temperament for addressing critical, high-pressure situations. That meant I could always trust his advice to be clear-headed and useful.

The days flew by between meetings and visits to the units. So ended my first two months on the mission.

THE MAIN PROBLEM was Cité Soleil, especially the difficulties of coordinating with headquarters. This required several meetings with General Bacellar and constant visits to the places where the military forces were billeted.

I met with Ambassador Valdés at least once a week. Some afternoons he would invite me to his house to exchange perspectives on the mission and the country. During those visits he was constantly receiving calls on his cellphone from various authorities, which suggests the enormous pressure he was under. He dealt with this calmly and was always optimistic about the mission. At a time when so many were not, this was extremely helpful.

I was careful not to let my relationship with Ambassador Valdés and the fact that we were both Chilean affect the chain of command, since my commander was General Bacellar. In any case, Valdés and Bacellar had an excellent relationship.

Something else worth noting is the sponsoring of a small school called "The Good Samaritan" in Croix de Bouquets, in the capital. The school takes in small children who have been abandoned or are otherwise at risk. This sponsorship was provided by the personal resources of the mission staff, who donated part of their salaries.

To raise funds, items were sometimes raffled at social gatherings to collect money for the school. Sometimes a number of Chileans in Haiti who were working on specific efforts — including ones sponsored by the Helicopter Unit, such as "América Solidaria" — joined us at these events.

These young doctors, dentists and architects, among other professions, did yeoman service. Chile ought to increase its presence in Haiti through initiatives such as this one.

At times like this, modern societies need more agencies that offer dignity to human beings. I find it distressing that the valuable efforts of these young people have gone almost unnoticed.

Throughout my time in Haiti, I kept reminding myself how little was known in Chile about what our people, both civilian and military, were achieving on this mission.

A mission like the one in Haiti takes its toll. The UN grants contingents three days' rest each month and a fortnight off every six months. These furloughs, however, must be preapproved by an immediate superior — be it a corporal or a general — and then reviewed and approved by the mission's Personnel Department.

Each member of the mission could use his leave to travel or rest. Most of our personnel went on leave at least once during their six months to the Dominican Republic — some to Punta Cana and others to places near the border with Cap Haïtien. Many used this unique opportunity to bring over their spouses and even their children, since it was perhaps their only possibility of taking their families abroad.

During one of these administrative leaves, two months after taking up my position, I went off to Punta Cana for three days with Major Díaz and NCO Leiva.

Ambassador Young had organized several meetings at his home with people he thought I should meet, including both Haitians and foreign diplomats. I found these crucial for learning more about the country.

The day before my vacation I met with the Dominican Ambassador to Haiti, José Serulle, at the home of Chilean Ambassador Marcel Young. After dinner our ambassador told his colleague that the following day I would be going on vacation to the Dominican.

"Aldunate," he replied, "we will look after you once you arrive." I did not take him seriously.

The next day we took a 50-minute Air Caribbean flight to Santo Domingo, the capital of the Dominican. On our arrival, Colonel Danilo Charles, the Dominican Military Attaché to Haiti, was waiting for us. He took us to a VIP room, noting that the Dominican Defence Minister was expecting us.

I thanked him for his offer but said I was on vacation, not in an official capacity. Besides, I was not suitably dressed to meet a senior minister. As you can imagine, I was wearing shorts and carrying a camera and a backpack — hardly appropriate for a top-level meeting. They just waved their hands at my excuses.

We were driven in two vehicles to the Defence Ministry, where Admiral Sigfrido Paredes Pérez, the minister himself, was waiting for us. He was very hospitable, and I was at a loss for words over my casual attire.

After discussing the situation in Haiti, the minister provided us with an official vehicle to take us to Punta Cana. After thanking him, we left. Three hours later we arrived at our hotel.

We had a wonderful time in that beach paradise. I ate and swam and ate some more, which is what one usually does at resorts like this. But I also took time to think about the mission.

I wondered why the Haitians weren't exploiting their natural beauty the way the Dominicans had, since they shared the same island and had equally spectacular geography. Of course, in the Dominican Republic there was a functioning state, and in Haiti the situation was very different.

I RETURNED TO HAITI, where the mission stayed on a relatively even keel until December.

Kidnappings in the capital had increased exponentially, and we had almost all our troops distributed through its various districts.

The elections were a principal focus of our work, but we were also trying to keep order in the country and succeeding quite well. Even so, we were concerned about Cité Soleil. It was clear even then this would be a difficult issue to resolve.

I attended various meetings with transitional government officials, foreign ambassadors, and visiting delegates. None of them acknowledged the actual situation in the country as a whole. In their view, Cité Soleil and the kidnappings in the capital were the only significant issues.

The situation in Haiti was far different from how it was being portrayed. The violence was ongoing, but it was not widespread. Unfortunately, there was little we could do to change people's impressions.

CHAPTER SIX

Same Old Story: International Interventions in Haiti

EXPLAINING THE ROOTS of the successive crises that Haiti has gone through would require extensive analyses of history and sociological, economic and political issues. That, of course, is beyond the scope of this book.

Whatever conclusion we reach after analyzing its history, the collective perception abroad—at least, the most widespread one—is that Haiti is a place with nearly all the world's problems: poverty, deforestation, lack of drinking water, violence, corruption and more recently AIDS.

Yet it would be unfair to cast Haiti in only a negative light. The country I came to know had strong and proud people, rich cultural expressions and a landscape full of development possibilities. Regrettably, it was not these things that had brought Blue Helmets to the country.

The problems Haiti is facing today are not new, and aid and intervention efforts to that country have never given Haiti a stable and orderly state. That the UN has been present in Haiti since 2004 reflects that truth.

It would seem—and I have heard this several times—that there are already people who think that MINUSTAH will suffer the same fate as past missions and that chaos will return to the country, which in turn will bring about another mission. I am reluctant to believe this, though of course it *may* happen.

I am optimistic, since the country I arrived in had changed for the better by the time I left. But the history of past interventions in Haiti reminds us how hard progress comes to that country.

In 1697, Spain recognized France's sovereignty over the western part of the island of Hispaniola. That colony quickly became one of the world's leading producers of coffee and sugar — through the toil of African slaves.

A popular uprising against the French, led by Toussaint L'Ouverture, Jean-Jacques Dessalines and Henri Christophe, began in 1791. The struggle ended with the defeat of Napoleon's forces, and Haiti achieved its independence in 1804.

The independence leaders organized a republic based on what they knew. As a result, the new state was a sort of continuation of the old colony. Christophe proclaimed himself emperor and built a fortress in Cap Haïtien named La Citadelle (a site well worth visiting). He also built a magnificent palace, Sans Souci, of which only ruins remain.

Yet the freedom his people had so long coveted failed to provide them with stability. Evidence of this: the 1789 census counted 700,000 blacks in the country, yet by 1824 there were only 351,000. This suggests how violent those times must have been and how deeply that violence marked Haiti's society.

Various conflicts followed independence, between the blacks and the mulattoes and also between the inhabitants of northern Haiti and those of Port-au-Prince. Before long, the country had descended into permanent crisis.

It is interesting that Miranda and Bolívar, the fathers of South American independence, visited Haiti and were given muskets and coffee to support their dreams of liberation. Dessalines, one of Haiti's founding fathers, suggested to Miranda during his visit that there was only one way to achieve independence, and it was reflected in his battle cry: "Koupé tèt, boulé kay" (cut off their heads, raze their homes).

Various military governments succeeded each other until 1986, when a new constitution was drafted, mainly in order to prevent the Duvalier family from taking power again.[1] Since then, Aristide, Cédras, and others had struggled to confront the country's perennial crisis.

In September 1993 the UN Security Council, through Resolution 1940, established the first UN peacekeeping operation in Haiti, UNMIH. Its mandate was to restore democracy, build a safe and stable environment and restructure the Haitian security forces. That mission did not fully succeed, because the Haitian military would not cooperate.

In July 1994 the Security Council authorized the deployment of a multinational force of 20,000 to help the legitimate authorities return, bring about a safe and stable environment and promote law enforcement. This multinational force was followed by other UN missions between 1994 and 2001: the

UN Support Mission in Haiti (UNSMIH), the UN Transition Mission in Haiti (UNTMIH), the International Civilian Support Mission in Haiti (MICAH) in 2001 and the UN Civilian Police Mission in Haiti (MIPONUH). Mention should also be made of the UN/OAS International Civilian Mission (MICIVIH) — a civilian human-rights mission — between 1993 and 2000.

Throughout this period there were several positive events. A degree of democracy was restored, which included the first peaceful transfer of power between two democratically elected Haitian presidents. A multifaceted civilian society took root and began to participate in a developing political culture based on democratic values. But there were also a number of setbacks. Owing to the permanent political crisis and the ensuing instability, the existing system was never thoroughly reformed.

The past century of Haitian politics can be summarized as follows. Political upheaval and social conflict led to coups d'état and assassinations. In 1915, American troops landed in Port-au-Prince. They occupied the country until 1934 but failed during those decades to sow the seeds of democracy.

In 1957 the Duvaliers came to power. "Papa Doc" and his son, "Baby Doc," maintained a violent dictatorship until 1986. During those years the country made little economic progress. Its economy was based largely on tourism and the export of textiles.

With the end of the Duvalier era arrived a new leader, a young and progressive priest named Jean-Bertrand Aristide. He was an excellent public speaker with a charismatic personality. He founded the Lavalas Party ("Avalanche") and gained the support of the poor. He was elected president in 1990, but was deposed two years later in a coup d'état led by General Raoul Cédras.

Living in exile in the United States, he received support for his call that the OAS impose a trade embargo on Haiti. The country's already weakened economy immediately collapsed.

Aristide returned to power in 1994, backed by a multinational force of 20,000 soldiers led by the United States. He seized this opportunity to disband the Haitian Armed Forces, which he accused of fomenting instability. He claimed that the Constitution gave him the power to do this by presidential decree. Actually, it was an illegal and poorly judged decision that left former soldiers jobless and without prospects. It only encouraged them to engage in illegal activities.

Aristide then founded the Haitian National Police (PNH) with the help of yet another UN mission, this one led by Canada. Nowadays this police force is more a problem than a solution.

In 1996 Aristide chose his successor, René Préval, who as it turned out would be the first and only Haitian president ever to complete his term.

In 2000 Aristide was re-elected president in an election some considered fraudulent and unrepresentative (only 10 percent of the eligible population turned out to vote). In this his second term, he engaged in populist actions, such as arming marginalized groups in the shantytowns (the *chimères*) to neutralize opposition. Irresponsibly, he politicized the PNH.

The first popular demonstrations against Aristide and Lavalas took place in mid-2002.[2] By early 2004 the situation was rapidly deteriorating. The Caribbean Community (CARICOM) offered to serve as mediator, and on January 31 it submitted a Proposed Action Plan. This was followed in February by an Application Plan drafted by the Group of Six. The participants included the Bahamas (representing CARICOM), Canada, the United States, France, the OAS and the European Union. Aristide accepted both plans.

The Proposed Action Plan called for major reforms, including a new Council of Ministers. Aristide would be allowed to complete his term. However, the opposition refused to back the plan. Soon after, CARICOM and the OAS led several diplomatic initiatives to break the political impasse and prevent the crisis from deepening.

In early February 2004, armed revolt broke out in Gonaïves. The crisis spread to other cities over the next few days, and rebels gradually took control of most of the north. Despite diplomatic efforts, the armed opposition threatened to march on the capital.

On February 26 the OAS in Resolution 862 urged the UN Security Council to "take the necessary and appropriate measures to address the crisis in Haiti and coordinate the action of both organizations" (OAS-UN).

In the early hours of February 29, Aristide left the country. Prime Minister Yvon Neptune read his letter of resignation. A few hours later, Chief Justice Boniface Alexandre was sworn in as interim president, in accordance with the constitutional provisions relating to succession. On the afternoon of the same day, the Permanent Representative of Haiti to the UN submitted a request for assistance from the interim president, authorizing the entry of troops into Haiti.

The UN Secretary General sent Hocine Medili as Special Envoy to Haiti. Subsequently he would serve as deputy head of the peacekeeping mission until January 2006, while I was on the mission.

In response to the Haitian request, the UNSC approved Resolution 1529 (2004) authorizing the deployment of MIFH and declared its willingness to establish a UN stabilization and follow-up force to support non-violent and constitutional political processes and maintain a safe, stable environment.

It was thought that MIFH would require three months to accomplish its mission — that is, until May 29, 2004. The UN resolution authorized its deployment in order to:

- contribute to a safe, stable environment in the country;
- facilitate the provision of humanitarian assistance;
- facilitate the provision of international aid to the Haitian Police (PNH);
- support the establishment of conditions for international and regional organizations, including the UN and the OAS, to assist the Haitian people; *and*
- coordinate, as needed, with the OAS Special Mission and the UN Special Adviser for Haiti, to prevent further deterioration of the humanitarian situation.

This resolution authorized MIFH to take the necessary actions to fulfill its mandate. This wording was interpreted as authorizing force if necessary.

On April 16, 2004, UN Secretary General Kofi Annan briefed the Security Council on the situation as follows:

After President Aristide's return to power, having been overthrown in a military coup in 1991, he passed a decree in 1995 to disband the Haitian armed forces.

This decision was not followed by an amendment to the Constitution reflecting the army's dissolution.

Moreover, former members of the military were demobilized without adequate provision being made for securing their weapons or for establishing reintegration programs or compensation packages, including pensions.

This resulted in serious discontent among former members of the military and sowed the seeds for future civil unrest.

As requested in the 4 April Pact, a commission will explore the issue of pensions for former military and make recommendations to the incoming Government on the advisability of reorganizing the army.

Over time, security in Haiti was undermined by the politicization and disintegration of the HNP and the concomitant rise of armed groups, known as *chimères*, on which the former President increasingly relied to remain in power.

In return for their support, these armed groups received financial assistance and were given free hand to intimidate political opponents as well as segments of the local population and to engage in organized crime, including drug trafficking.

Given these circumstances, many Haitians armed themselves for self-protection and unregulated private security companies further contributed to the unprecedented nationwide proliferation and trafficking of small arms.

It should be recalled that the Constitution grants every citizen the right to self-defense within the bounds of his domicile, but not to carry weapons without a permit.

Following the outbreak of armed conflict in the city of Gonaïves in early February 2004, which soon spread to other cities, insurgents gradually took over much of the north of the country.

Some members of the former military also returned to Haiti and took control of cities in the Central Plateau.

Other armed groups, such as community-organized groups, paramilitary and militia groups, armed street gangs and prison escapees joined the ranks of the insurgents.

Some of them have been embraced by the local population and senior politicians as "liberators."

The community-organized armed groups and gangs are highly fragmented, located primarily in impoverished urban areas and pose the greatest threat to security.

Moreover, many of these groups also turned to banditry and other criminal activities in order to sustain themselves.

The absence of the rule of law has reinforced a climate of impunity and other crimes, such as kidnapping, robberies and rape, are on the rise.

In addition, politically motivated intimidation now mainly targets Fanmi Lavalas supporters.

Moreover, Haiti has become a significant trans-shipment place for cocaine due to a lack of law enforcement, porous borders and corruption of some of the law enforcement agencies and their political sponsors.

This has resulted not only in increased violence and crime, but also in a higher consumption of drugs, as local intermediaries have increasingly been paid in kind, prompting them to resell it on the local market.

This problem would need to be addressed more aggressively by the international community and by the Haitian leadership and law enforcement agencies, both at the local and regional levels.

At the time of the deployment of the MIF on 29 February, the Haitian authorities were in control only of the territory around Port-au-Prince.

The MIF, which is drawn from Canada, Chile, France and the United States, has already deployed over 3,000 troops.

The MIF headquarters and the majority of its troops are deployed in the capital.

Since mid-March, the MIF has also established a presence in the northern cities of Gonaïves, Cap Haïtien and Fort Liberté.

The MIF conducts occasional air and ground patrols in other areas. The MIF's number of troops does not allow it to guard large numbers of static sites.

The HNP has joined the MIF in some patrols.

While the security situation has calmed down with the deployment of the MIF, the latter's restricted resources and geographic areas of operation, as well as limited disarmament activities has constrained its ability to address aspects of the insecurity.

The situation on the ground remains complex; in some areas, the MIF and the HNP coexist with the insurgents.

Armed groups still control parts of some regions. In addition, a variety of local security arrangements exist, involving civil action groups, former military, local gangs, escaped prisoners and some HNP officers who returned to their posts.

These groups coexist in some cities, dividing the area among them.

The security environment remains uncertain and will be influenced by the political process, the pace and effectiveness of the restoration of government authority and state institutions, particularly the HNP, throughout the country, the durability of the measures undertaken by the MIF, particularly with regard to disarmament, and the willingness of armed groups to cooperate with disarmament and reintegration plans.

To date, weapons handovers have been largely symbolic and pledges by rebels to lay down arms upon the establishment of a transitional Government have not yet been followed through.

In the light of these uncertainties and the institutional obstacles faced by the HNP in performing law and order functions, an international presence would need to provide a security umbrella under which the Haitian Government could re-establish public security and promote a feeling of safety among the population.

That would require that the international security presence, in conjunction with the gradually emerging HNP, confiscate visible illicit arms and seize arms caches.

It would also require deployment throughout the country and close coordination with international civilian police as well as the HNP.[3]

There were arguments against sending a mission to Haiti. Many people contended that, out of eagerness to provide help there, the Latin American nations were embarking on an ill-conceived and poorly executed diplomatic and military intervention. Put simply, we would not know how to get out of Haiti if we did not know why we were going in.[4] These arguments were valid, but the reality still was that unless other countries did something, a bloodbath would result.

My own view is that the international community had no time for careful analysis: the situation was too urgent, and immediate action was needed. There would be time for armchair analyses later on — the immediate objective was to prevent a tragedy.

MIFH began its deployment in Haiti as authorized by the UN Resolution. Within a short time, 2,000 American, 910 French, 329 Chilean, and 525 Canadian soldiers — 2,600 in all — arrived there under General Ron Coleman of the United States.

The U.S. contingent was stationed to the north of Port-au-Prince, at Hinche, Jacmel and Les Cayes. The Canadians were billeted in the southwestern sector of the capital and at Miragoâne, with a smaller contingent at Petit

Goâve. Most of the French forces were stationed in the north of the country, at Cap Haïtien, Port-de-Paix and Fort Liberté, with smaller contingents at Saint Marc and Gonaïves. The Chileans were mainly to the southeast of the capital, guarding the airport, with some troops at Hinche in the centre of the country.

It was a difficult mission. On March 12 a U.S. patrol was fired on, leaving one marine wounded and six Haitians reported dead. Even so, the heavy military deployment brought relative calm to the country.

On March 17, Gérard Latortue, Prime Minister of Haiti, with the support of the Conseil des Sages (a group of seven distinguished persons), formed a transitional government of 13 members. Its task was to establish a broad political consensus with representatives from various political groups and civil society organizations, which had signed a document titled "Consensus Pact on Political Transition."

The signatories reached a general agreement on the transition period. Municipal, parliamentary and presidential elections would be held in 2005, after which a new elected president would assume power. Later this schedule would be extended for various reasons. The same document included measures to be taken during the transition period regarding security, development, decentralization, elections, corruption and judicial reform, as well as an initiative to hold a national conference for establishing a new social contract, strengthening political parties and civil society groups, reincorporating former armed forces personnel and professionalizing the PNH.

The document called for various commissions to handle issues such as financial crime and recent violations of human rights. And it emphasized the need to assist victims of the previous government and to open a dialogue between the signatories and the UN regarding MIFH and the continuation of peacekeeping operations.

Lavalas denounced the pact, claiming that Aristide had been deposed in an illegitimate manner.

In his report to the Security Council dated April 16, the UN Secretary General hailed the Consensus Pact for uniting Haitian leaders from different parts of society. However, he added: "Not all the important political movements had participated in it, as they could have done, and every Haitian should have taken the opportunity to significantly participate in a widespread national dialogue."

In accordance with Resolution 1529, and based on the findings of the multidisciplinary team that had visited the country in March 2004, the Secretary General recommended the deployment of an operation to be called the UN Stabilization Mission in Haiti (MINUSTAH).

In response to that recommendation, on 30 April the UNSC approved Resolution 1542, which established MINUSTAH for an initial period of six months. It also called for MIFH to transfer its authority to that mission on 1 June.[5]

Juan Gabriel Valdés of Chile was appointed UNSG Representative. In other words, he was placed in charge of the entire mission. He would continue at that post until the day President Préval took office. On May 7, 2006, he would be replaced by Edmond Mulet of Guatemala.

MINUSTAH's immediate objective (as had been MIFH's) was to prevent a massacre of the Haitian population. After July 2004, during the second stage, other mandates would be added, such as to support the transitional government and the country's electoral process. It is noteworthy that Chile is the only country that has had a presence on the mission from the beginning, with MIFH and now with MINUSTAH.

In hindsight, I have to admit that MINUSTAH has not succeeded fully. Yet I still have hope. I believe there is an opportunity to achieve something more lasting in Haiti provided that certain conditions are established.

First, the participating countries and organizations need to understand that this must be a long-term effort. They should draw lessons from East Timor, where the UN withdrew too early, before all underlying problems had been solved.

Second, economic and humanitarian aid should be provided when required. That said, I have my doubts whether Haiti's needs in this regard are clearly understood. The problem is not strictly speaking a shortage of aid. Too often, projects are delayed or cancelled because they have been poorly designed or because the Haitian authorities refuse to cooperate unless they themselves handle the funds—a situation not many donors are willing to accept.

Third, it is vital for the Haitians to participate in their own development—that is, to determine for themselves what kind of society and institutions they want. Otherwise, efforts by donor countries will be futile. In this regard, I seriously doubt whether it will be enough to 'patch up' old Haitian institutions.

The problem, perhaps, is that Haitians have never demanded enough of their own institutions. Unless they learn to do so, the task of rebuilding the country may be insurmountable.

The test for Haitians will be whether they can administer their own institutions. For them to do so, they will require international aid to design organizations according to their own realities, and Haitians will have to take part in these aid programs with the goal of taking increasing charge of them.

The international community's lack of perseverance and the lack of support from Haitians themselves partly explains the failure of the missions that preceded MINUSTAH.

Notes

1 Félix Ulloa, *Haiti: 200 Years of Elections and Constitutions* (Port-au-Prince: Editions PFA, 2004).

2 Augusto Heleno, "El Componente Militar de la Misión de las Naciones Unidas para la Estabilización de Haití," *Military Review*, January–February 2007: 2–3.

3 UN Security Council, "Report of the Secretary General on Hati," April 16, 2004.

4 Juan Gabriel Tokatlian, "Haití, una intervención equivocada," Análisis de coyuntura, *Observatório Politico Sul-Americano* 8 (July).

5 UN website, MINUSTAH, accessed August 29, 2005.

CHAPTER SEVEN

MINUSTAH

ACCORDING TO UN Security Council Resolution 1542 (April 30, 2004), MINUSTAH had been established to support the transitional government, aid the political process, protect the Haitian people's human rights and support the elections.

In the words of Ambassador Valdés: "This resolution was one of UN's largest, most ambitious missions, and at bottom, it seemed that rather than solving an emergency situation, the challenge of the mission was to recreate a country."

MINUSTAH was expected to ensure minimum security for Haiti, besides coordinating a multitude of programs. This would involve synchronizing its actions with the transitional government, the NGOs, Haitian society, the Core Group (i.e., countries participating in the process), the UN and other international actors. Clearly, this was a highly complex mission.

To accomplish all this, MINUSTAH had an annual budget of US$500 million and a force of 7,500 soldiers, 1,897 police, 449 international advisers and 526 local civilians. Do not assume that all of these resources arrived immediately; in fact, it took eight months for most of them to arrive in Haiti.

This mission had a curious structure: there were two parallel forces, each depending on the Special Representative of the Secretary General (SRSG) of the UN. The first was a military force led by the Force Commander; the second was a police force, UNPol, led by the Police Commissioner. These two components should have coordinated their actions closely, since they shared responsibility for security.

Various documents of the UN DPKO regulated how the military and police components were to carry out their tasks. In theory, this should have been clear enough; in my experience, it was anything but. In accordance with the initial UN resolution, the military force had 6,400 men, which increased to 7,500 during the election period and totaled 7,200 as of August 2006.

The UN Police (UNPol) had about 1,897 men from 34 countries. Of this force, 1,000 were in the assault units — that is, in Formed Police Units (FPUs) — whose main function was to handle riots. The officers from these units were drawn from China, Nepal, Jordan and Pakistan, among other countries. They had powerful weapons and armoured vehicles — indeed, they had even more of them than some military contingents and were organized rather much like army companies (100 soldiers).

UNPol also had police whom the UN had contracted on an individual basis. Many of them were retired in their own countries and had been recruited by MINUSTAH to advise and assist the PNH, not specifically for operations. They included officers from France, Canada, Spain, Argentina, Ghana, Guinea and other African countries. Some, including some Chilean *carabineros*, were helping organize the PNH.

Our *carabineros*, who have solid training that is recognized worldwide, barely participated in the development of the new police force. Instead, Canadian, American and French police had been tasked with the most important issues facing the PNH. In my view, this was a mistake — Chileans would have been more familiar with Latin and Caribbean cultural ways.

The Chilean Investigative Police was represented by four professionals led by Deputy Prefect Segundo Castro, who worked with the *carabineros* in UNPol and did an excellent job.

The various military contingents shared a similar structure and discipline, and their working methods were much the same. Whether soldiers came from Sri Lanka, Chile, Peru or Jordan, soldiers have many things in common that enable them to understand one another at work.

At the military force's headquarters were 100 officers from 22 countries, who carried out the usual advisory functions of any military entity: Personnel, Intelligence, Operations and Logistics. Additional functions included Disarmament (DDR), Civil Affairs and Planning. And there were other sections that supported the work of the contingents through the Force Commander.

The soldiers had little problem understanding one another during ground operations. They found it more difficult to work with the UNPol officers and the African and European police. This was not because of language barriers or diversity; mainly, the issue here related to divergent doctrines and procedures.

We solved this problem over time; that said, we would have done so more quickly had there been a single command from the outset with the authority to compel the military and UNPol to cooperate more closely.

The biggest stumbling blocks related to how the mission had been organized, which affected how security operations were carried out. Specifically, the dual command—UNPol and the military—had resulted in dual responsibility for security.

UNPol's commissioner let me know from the start that he was a "parallel" commander with authority equal to mine as the FC and that he was only answerable to Valdés, who was chief of the entire mission.

This meant we had to coordinate operations with him. With his agreement, we would operate together within an area, though he always commanded his own personnel. This dual command meant that operations were always extremely difficult to plan and implement.

In an operative situation, there should logically always be a single commander who plans how all the actors on the scene are to be used, who leads and controls operations and who can be held accountable.

General Heleno, the first FC, described the situation this way: "UNPol had some very unusual features. First of all, UNPol was not under the authority of the Force Commander, which contradicts the principle of unity of command and sometimes even prevents unity of effort".[1]

The problem escalated to the point that some UNPol units thought they were participating in the mission under Chapter VI rather than Chapter VII, which involves very different behaviour—namely, the use of force as opposed to a merely advisory or passive presence.

We drew up a number of plans and issued various orders that, when carried out, resulted in only military force being present, instead of what had been planned, which was for UNPol to act in unison with our troops. It was impossible to get this police force to accomplish its mission.

In Port-au-Prince—especially at the checkpoints, where joint action was a necessity—our troops would arrive at dawn as planned, but UNPol officers would simply fail to show up.

UNPol was extremely reluctant to accept any type of command over its staff. That was fine when it came to administrative or advisory issues with the PNH, but a disaster when it was vital to have a single person commanding personnel, coordinating their activities and ensuring they carried out their duties.

These problems were compounded by the fact that the PNH—perhaps as part of their national ethos—do not like being given orders by foreigners. So we had to be extremely careful when assigning any mission to them. Such assignments had to be channeled through UNPol.

The presence of the PNH as a third actor in security issues made matters even worse. Because of its doubtful competence and structural weaknesses, we could not rely on that force for ground operations. Had we done so, our own efficiency would have been compromised.

The first time I set eyes on Mario Andressol, the PNH Director General, I saw proof of what I had long suspected: he could not trust his own people to ensure security.

PNH officers were supposed to provide the one thing our troops lacked: knowledge of the locals, the criminals and the culture of the various zones. Yet in Cité Soleil, not a single Haitian police officer was present, let alone a police station. There had once been two stations, but both had been torched by gangs, and there were no plans to rebuild them, despite my pleas to the prime minister and, later, to President Préval.

Another problem was that the PNH was poorly outfitted. Yet another was that we did not know which PNH officers had ties to criminal gangs — we only knew that many of them did. According to Andressol himself, over 30 percent of corruption in Haiti could be linked to PNH officers.

Coordination with UNPol was extremely difficult because of the dual command and the use of the PNH, which resulted a highly complex operational environment. The coordination issues were only partly resolved by the time I left Haiti.

General Bacellar and I ran into this problem time and time again. We learned from it that in situations as complicated as the one in Haiti, where the lives of personnel are at stake, there needs to be a single command. Only then can decisions be made quickly and efficiently.

There are no two ways about it: there should always be a single commander. Regrettably, UNPol regarded itself as a parallel force to the military, even though its people knew full well they had neither the force nor the presence throughout the country to act as one, much less the capacity to operate on their own.

Our operations were developed by about 100 officers at headquarters. UNPol did not take part in this planning. Its own operations were organized by four people with limited command, advisory, and control capacity. The PNH's planning capacity was minimal.

Because the situation was so serious, I set up weekly meetings in my office with the UNPol commissioner and the PNH director to coordinate operations. The latter's frequent absences meant that these meetings did not always proceed as planned.

This situation was not resolved until August 31, 2006, during a videoconference with the DPKO, when it was finally agreed that there should be a single command for operations.

The situation throughout the country was roughly the same as in Port-au-Prince. In some places, UNPol was subordinate to the military force; in others—in Gonaïves, for example—there were permanent misunderstandings among the senior officers. The undisputed winners in this situation were the criminal gangs.

Only near the end of my time in Haiti did we succeed in acting jointly. This was largely thanks to a good personal relationship between the UNPol commissioner, Richard Graham Muir, and myself. Also, the circumstances were so grave that we had no choice but to coordinate ourselves. Albeit a little too late.

Another serious problem was the lack of an intelligence organization to gather and analyze information and deliver two things: strategic intelligence for running the mission; and—no less important—useful information for our soldiers regarding the threats they faced every day.

Our soldiers were serving in a foreign country, yet only a few people in MINUSTAH spoke the local language—which is not, as many people think, French but rather Creole. In addition, Haiti has different cultural mores, a police force that in practice does not exist, and no reliable databases. So it was a dreadful oversight not to establish an intelligence office. Valdés himself would state that "without this vital instrument, it was very difficult to participate in these missions."[2]

This issue was partly resolved around eighteen months after the mission began when the Joint Mission Analysis Cell (JMAC) was established under Resolution 1608 of the UNSC. Unfortunately, the people first assigned to that group lacked the necessary training. Despite their best efforts, they found it difficult to provide useful, timely information. The strategic information eventually delivered to the commander-in-chief proved to be of little use to the contingents.

In practice, operative intelligence was obtained through our contingents' own "street savvy." This material was useful, but it could have been improved through a structured military intelligence organization.

I found it hard to decide how to use our forces, considering that we did not know the language, had no knowledge of looming threats, and could not provide even the minimal intelligence, especially since contingents were rotated every six months.

A Chilean commander on the mission told me that when he requested intelligence on the gangs in his AOR, he was told it did not exist. PNH intelligence, it should be noted, was not useful to us. Its officers could not be relied on.

The UN had judged that units assigned to an area of responsibility (AOR) should be able to operate there after two weeks. Apart from administrative and acclimatization issues, it takes time to get to know a zone of operations, including all the threats it poses. We succeeded at this *despite* the minimal intelligence available to us.

In JMAC there were 15 personnel, along with UNPol and PNH officers and various civilians. But these people did not understand the basic requirements, which were to provide our troops with gang-related information and our SRSG with useful advice, so the results of this office were negligible. General Heleno would later state: "The UN failed to provide intelligence services for its peacekeeping missions. The mission is therefore heavily reliant on rumors. I was forced, on several occasions to use troops with information that had not been confirmed. This situation, particularly at times of crisis, creates unnecessarily high levels of stress."[3]

As is so often the case with intelligence units, JMAC was very good at recounting past events, with well-designed spreadsheets and plenty of Power-Point presentations. It had powerful computers and an air-conditioned office. But in the end, its people were unable to predict the enemy's actions for the troops on point. They could not join up the dots and deliver what we needed from them the most: possible scenarios based on gathered and analyzed facts, that would be useful to the commander-in-chief and other end users. For that, it was necessary to have eyes and ears on the street as well as specialists in information analysis. We didn't have those things.

One of the mission's mistakes was that it failed to confront the intelligence situation at the headquarters level. This error would be corrected in July 2006 by General Elito Siqueira, who replaced General Bacellar as FC. We assembled a group of officers to analyze the information received from the units and to provide useful intelligence for the troops. This decision raised problems, since the DPKO was insisting that the mission rely solely on JMAC. But General Elito was emphatic: there would also be a intelligence group specifically for the troops.

This was not the end of the mission's intelligence problems. Within MINUSTAH there was an organization in charge of UN personnel security, responsible for procedures, vehicle security, document safekeeping and so on. During my stay this was led by Bertrand Bourgain, a former French colonel who had served most of his career in the Foreign Legion. He was also a para-trooper, a man of action and a friendly, amusing person. The problem was that he often misunderstood his role. As a result he would cross the line, assuming that he was responsible for obtaining information and briefing the mission commander.

I often attended meetings with Ambassador Valdés at which Bertrand would start talking about the gangs, security around the country and other issues that had little or nothing to do with his role.

This was a problem, and to make it worse, the person in charge of JMAC was someone who though he tried hard lacked basic technical knowledge. Bertrand exploited this weakness.

Since Bertrand was very good at his job, Valdés unfortunately put great stock in his views, even though I kept insisting to him that he follow the appropriate channels when he wanted to be briefed on the mission.

At meetings, Bertrand would keep harping about security issues that were outside his purview. We would patiently hear him out, though my patience started to wear thin as the days went by. I felt that he was not helping the mission, so at several meetings I tore a strip off him in front of everyone and told him to keep his nose out of things that were none of his business.

Looking back, I do not blame Valdés for listening to Bertrand. JMAC had just been formed and had very little credibility, which meant he had nowhere else to turn for information.

Bertrand was regularly turning up at meetings with information on security issues — information I had never heard before. So Graham Muir and I took matters into our own hands. We had the support of an excellent French police officer, Bernard Foucre, who besides being highly efficient was ready to deal with tricky situations.

Things came to a head in January, when two election officials from the OAS were kidnapped on Toussaint L'Ouverture Avenue. This created a huge problem for the mission. At about 3 p.m. that day, Ambassador Valdés called and asked me to rescue them, since Bertrand had said he knew where they were being held.

I replied that I had requested information from Bertrand about this at 8 a.m. and that I was still awaiting an answer. Though I had the Peruvian commandos ready for the rescue operation, Bertrand had not provided any information, which for me was proof that his intelligence was based on hearsay, which he then used as leverage.

As it turned out, all the "detailed information" he had given our Mission Commander had been based on rumour.

I got along well with Bertrand, and I considered him a solid professional. But on this mission — as in any situation where the pressure is constant and people's lives are at stake — procedures needed to be clear, and they had to be adhered to. Organizations can be destroyed by back channels and parallel authorities. If a proper working structure doesn't exist, you have to develop one.

This information chaos was compounded by the fact that in the early days — at least while I was present — UNPol and the PNH sometimes provided unclear and poorly processed information. We had placed several PNH officers within JMAC, yet their information usually wasn't accurate.

At MINUSTAH meetings, civilian groups sometimes provided information, but it was extremely difficult to analyze it systematically. Also, some of the larger embassies in Haiti shared information with us, which partly made up for our lack of in-house intelligence.

It struck me as odd that some of these reports emphasized that ex-FAd'H officers were a significant threat to security in Haiti—indeed, perhaps the biggest threat. These insinuations ebbed over time after no basis was provided for them.

Actually, these former military men were mainly trying to recover their salaries and pensions. As soon as we saw their meeting places and examined their weapons, we realized they were not a security threat, at least not for now.

It seemed that one of our problems regarding information was Bertrand. I already mentioned, he normally worked outside the channels we were trying to implement. It was our own fault—we lacked an orderly intelligence system. In this regard, my idea was to channel all information through JMAC, which should be the sole conduit for useful intelligence.

Also affecting the mission was the presence of an intermediate command in Port-au-Prince—the Sector Command, which had its own headquarters. MINUSTAH's FC had about 10 units reporting to him from around the country, and this had affected the chain of command—specifically, his control over those units. So the DPKO had created an intermediate command in the capital. Without consulting the FC in Haiti, the UN had issued Resolution 1608, dated 22 June, 2005, whose Section 2, subparagraph (b), read as follows:

> There will be an increase of 50 military personnel in order to create a sector headquarters in Port-au-Prince, on the understanding that MINUSTAH will optimize coordination between military and police components at all levels to ensure efficient, better-integrated operations, including the designation of UNPol officers in these headquarters.

The mission of this intermediate command can be summarized as follows:

a. Ensuring freedom of movement in Port-au-Prince.
b. Protecting MINUSTAH personnel and equipment involved in humanitarian tasks.
c. Neutralizing armed groups.
d. Protecting the lives of civilians from the gangs.
e. Planning and coordinating the Disarmament, Demobilization and Reintegration Program (DDR).
f. Controlling, coordinating and supervising military actions in Port-au-Prince.
g. Ensuring compliance with the ROEs by military staff.

An outstanding officer, Brigadier General Mahmoud Ajaj Al Husban of the Jordanian Army, was appointed Sector Commander. In September the staff for the new command began to arrive. They were billeted downtown at the Plaza and were provided with PCs and other equipment.

With the elections approaching, the same UN resolution increased the MINUSTAH forces to 7,500 men, with the arrival of a second Jordanian battalion.

All of this meant that we now had a military commander, the FC, who was directly in charge of all units outside Port-au-Prince. At the same time, the following contingents were under the command of the Sector Commander:

- Two Jordanian battalions responsible for security in Cité Soleil, Cité Militaire and the northern area as far as Cabaret.
- One Brazilian battalion in charge of Bel Air and the eastern zone of the city.
- One Peruvian company as a reserve force in charge of the industrial complex of Shodecosa.
- One company from Sri Lanka in the Killick–Martissant area.

All of this sounded promising, and General Bacellar, together with everyone at HQ, threw his heart into this new structure.

Once I arrived at the mission, only days after the unit had been established, I realized it was not going to work. General Bacellar had already noticed this too, but there was nothing we could do.

General Bacellar and I were not focusing on what was going on outside Port-au-Prince — that is, in the rest of the country. Generally speaking, there *were* no security issues in those places where the AOR Sector Commanders had freedom of action (as well as the appropriate equipment). Except perhaps in Gonaïves, threats of violence were rarely followed through with and petty crime was the only real problem. So our military activities in the rest of the country were more operational and administrative than tactical.

I do not recall any situation from that time outside Port-au-Prince where headquarters was compelled to provide support or a solution.

The situation was very different in the capital. Threats from gangs normally required a quick response, because of their influence on the mission and their impact through the media. Yet to respond to those threats, Bacellar as Commander-in-Chief, or myself as DFC, now had to follow a bureaucratic chain of command that involved relaying orders through Sector Command. Reaction times were extremely slow as a result. The political and strategic repercussions were far swifter.

Ambassador Valdés, the transitional government and even the authorities in New York were focused on events in Port-au-Prince, mainly in Cité Soleil and along Route #1, where the crimes and kidnappings were taking place. Every conversation with New York and with the transitional government began and ended with events in these places. I cannot remember making a single reference to any other area in the country regarding security issues. Our headquarters was spending at least 90 percent of its time analyzing the events in Port-au-Prince—a good indication of where our problems lay.

A key task for any commander is to determine what the strategic site is, to focus on it and, where necessary, to participate in it personally. This was not possible in the situation at hand.

I do not blame the senior officers. I am only stressing how important it is to have a structure in place that allows those with military and political responsibility to perform their duties properly.

I mentioned earlier that I could see Cité Soleil both from my office and from my hotel room. Yet neither General Bacellar nor I could operate directly or quickly in this area, since an intermediate command had been created for the purpose.

Given the situation, we had to proceed with caution. There was a commander in charge of that area, and we could not go directly to the units to gather information or issue orders from the mission's commander-in-chief, even though General Bacellar was often prepared to do so. So, for that matter, was I. We knew that doing so would create problems for the Sector Command and be especially damaging to the Jordanian contingents' morale.

By February 2006 the Sector Command had been terminated and the senior officer could again operate at the heart of the problems: Port-au-Prince.

This was not the only problem with the mission's structure. Once he took command, General Elito quickly realized that military helicopters were not under his jurisdiction; instead they were under the command of a civilian authority, the same as the military engineers. The civilians in charge of air operations sometimes refused to let us use the helicopters, and every time we needed them, we had to explain why.

The civilian authorities did not seem to realize that the senior officer was accountable for the lives of our contingent and that a detailed analysis had been carried out for every last mission. Nor did they seem to realize that in the mission's chain of command, senior officers ranked far higher than administrators.

It was common sense that administrative, maintenance, logistics and specific regulatory offices should have a civilian technical commander. But when it came to military equipment, no civilian had the authority to prevent its use for properly planned military operations.

General Elito solved this problem, but it was no easy task. I myself got dragged into many arguments over this issue with the mission's administrative staff.

There were various other structural problems with the mission, many of which were resolved while I was there. But until they were, they caused a great deal of concern and affected the mission's success.

Good personal relations can mitigate certain structural problems — at least, that has been my experience. I will always be grateful to many of the civilian professionals from around the world with whom I worked who helped us solve many of these problems. Bureaucratic obstacles can be overcome provided one finds reliable allies, has sound arguments and achieves positive results on the ground.

From the many meetings I attended, I learned that some efforts were poorly coordinated, mainly because of the multitude of stakeholders both within and outside the mission.

Despite Ambassador Valdés's efforts, it was not easy to develop a general strategy, especially since the country had a weak and inefficient provisional government. This made it extremely difficult to deal with the challenges at hand. Compounding this, many people believed — mistakenly — that the elections and the arrival of a new government would solve everything. At the same time, others were demanding that we take more decisive action against the gangs.

As senior officers, we felt that we could be improving our methods but also that it was beyond our power to solve the country's problems. As time passed, though, the operational and security situation gradually improved, which freed us to deal with many of the bureaucratic problems noted earlier.

I also felt we should be more efficient regarding our soldiers on the ground. After all, they were the ones risking their lives.

We learned along the way, and we could have done more. We might have spared the lives of some soldiers and achieved the UN objectives more fully if we had paid more attention to what the ground was telling us. A lesson for all commanders is that it is sometimes good to heed the privates and corporals when making proposals or issuing commands.

All who participate in these missions realize that they are placing lives at risk and that some soldiers will fall in the line of duty. I had to order missions on which our soldiers' lives were lost. A better structure might have prevented those deaths. I believe that an efficient organization should be the main objective of every commander. I have no regrets about the battles I had to fight to accomplish this; I only regret that I did not win them all.

I hope things will improve regarding the issues facing MINUSTAH and that the people who lead future UN missions will use the lessons learned to make these international efforts more effective.

Notes

1 Augusto Heleno, "El Componente Militar de la Misión de las Naciones Unidas para la Estabilización de Haití," *Military Review*, January–February 2007: 6.

2 Juan Gabriel Valdés, presentation to the War Academy of the Chilean Army, March 30, 2007.

3 Heleno, "El Componente Militar de la Misión," 8.

CHAPTER EIGHT

Chilean Blue Helmets in Haiti

CHILEAN POLICY on participation in peace operations is determined by Supreme Decree no. 94 (November 6, 1996), published in the *Official Gazette* no. 36,358 on May 8, 1999, which modified and adapted previous regulations.

A brief summary reveals Chile's clear commitment to taking part in peace operations within the UN framework. The president's instructions attached to the decree include a number of suggestions regarding how these activities should be conducted.

For some time, Chile has had personnel from the army and other institutions acting as observers or participants in international conflicts. According to a fascinating study recently published by Colonel Antonio Varas,[1] the army's contribution dates back to the time of the Chaco War and continues today, with the numerous peace operations in which the country is involved. This participation is also described in a leaflet published by the EMDN.[2]

Five Chilean army generals have been involved in UN and other missions. In particular, General Luis Tassara spent several years on a mission in India and Pakistan. Later, General Sergio Espinoza served in a similar post for several months.

The above-mentioned Supreme Decree authorizes Chilean troops to expand their traditional functions as UN observers. They have done so on missions such as the one in Haiti, which could require the use of force within the framework of Chapter VII of the UN Charter, which refers to peacekeeping missions "which permit the use of force in legitimate defense and include the possibility of the use of force for the protection of civilian, humanitarian agencies and vulnerable ethnic groups."

Our objectives and working methods in Haiti have been delineated by authorities at various levels. They were perhaps expressed best by General Cheyre: "We will not fight Haiti, we will not take sides, we will not serve the interests of a nation, a power or a sector. Instead we will contribute to peace, that peace which the media have shown to have been disturbed and that peace which is the aim of our force."[3]

Among the various documents regulating a country's participation with these missions are the UN's mandate for Haiti, the Memorandum of Understanding (MOU), and the LOAs. The UN has determined that personnel on these missions will adhere strictly to the UN Rules of Engagement (ROEs).

Chile's Defence Ministry organized the Haiti mission through the Joint Centre for Peace Operation Training (CECOPAC). That centre's work has made our country a model among its peers. Chile's military are well equipped to train personnel for these missions and have achieved internationally recognized standards.

Once our soldiers have been assigned to a peace mission, on the basis of specific personnel requirements they are incorporated into units that are trained by Cecopac and then on the ground in the Peldehue area. Clearly, our Armed Forces place great importance on targeted training. Indeed, the results show that our soldiers have lived up to expectations in terms of both discipline and efficiency.

Since 2000 the Chilean Army has deployed about 4,000 peacekeepers to missions in Haiti, Cyprus, Bosnia, and the Congo, among other places. Since 2004 the Chilean Navy has deployed a company of 150 marines to Cap Haïtien, as well as a number of officers to MINUSTAH Headquarters. The Chilean Air Force has about 70 men in Haiti in the Helicopter Unit, besides a number of officers in air support operations. Chile's *carabineros* have sent around 20 riflemen to Haiti, while the Investigative Police have sent four officers, most of whom support UNPol in MINUSTAH.

In Haiti alone we have posted as many as 600 men at a time to our military contingent. While I was there, I received two Chilean contingents (who are replaced every six months). Overall, then, about 3,500 Chilean military men have served in Haiti over the past three years.

The military are deeply honoured by the armed forces' contribution to Chilean foreign policy. Some people have used the term "military diplomacy" to describe military participation.

The armed forces have benefited greatly from these missions, through contact with other armies and by the chance to test training, equipment and systems under real-life conditions. These missions have undoubtedly boosted our combat readiness; they have also provided feedback for our teaching, instruction and training systems.

No less important is our contribution to deterrence. On the ground, acting in concert with other armies, we have been able to show the strong capacity of our troops and equipment. Participation has also boosted Chile's prestige, in that our country has now joined an international "club."

At one point the media began to discuss the advisability of participating in the Haiti mission. Some felt there was nothing to be gained — that the conflict did not justify the loss of Chilean lives. Others said that we should support a sister nation, that we could not hope to matter on the international stage unless we took part in such missions and that free trade agreements were not everything. Still others thought it advisable to debate the costs of participation. All sides made valid arguments.

In this respect, I feel that the financial costs were not presented clearly enough by the military. The Armed Forces were novices when it came to such issues and had no clear idea how to respond. What *was* quite clear was that the costs of joining peacekeeping missions were usually returned to the participating states by the UN and that there was a complex formula for determining that amount.

I believe that over time we have made progress. But I also think that Chilean society could have been kept better informed.

As far as funding is concerned, once it has been established which countries will send which types of units, a contract is established with the UN, which employs several methods to decide how the countries involved will be compensated financially. By way of example, a helicopter has a value to the mission that depends on the type of machine and the number of hours it is used. The UN takes a measure of these things and then reimburses the country that provided the helicopter. The same for all other equipment.

After a talk I gave at a university in Santiago, one of the professors asked how much it was costing Chile to participate in the Haiti mission. His concern was that we ought to be using those funds for our own social programs.

I replied that most of the money we were spending on the mission would be paid back by the UN. That aside, our country was gaining international prestige as a result of our soldiers' contributions to the mission, and that was valuable to Chile though also difficult to quantify. And I added that it was crucial for our country to show how effective its military could be, and that the "military diplomacy" was worth something, in the sense that our soldiers were learning — and teaching — a great deal by serving with those of other nations.

I thought it rather short-sighted to evaluate the mission on the basis of how much it was costing. Unfortunately, by this time the salaries of our personnel were becoming an issue. By contract, the UN was paying all soldiers on the Haiti mission a fixed salary of US$1,028 per month, paid directly to the country of origin. In Chile's case, according to existing law, the salaries for Defence Ministry staff in Haiti were tied directly to those of the Foreign Office employees there. Some people argued that this was rather expensive. Some people even thought that our soldiers' pay should be cut to reduce the cost of sending them on international missions.

It was suggested that when our soldiers went abroad, they should be paid an allowance for food and lodging—which wasn't necessary on these missions, by the way, for they were provided with food and stayed in military camps.

To some, salary reductions sounded like a good approach to cutting the costs of peacekeeping missions. But it did not sound that way to the soldiers who went on them, given that those missions—besides benefiting them professionally and culturally—enabled them to improve their finances, which partly made up for their separation from home and for the risks they faced.

To send our soldiers on peacekeeping missions, even though they are volunteers, without a financial incentive is asking too much of their professionalism and their vocation for service, especially when one considers the dangers involved and the living conditions they encounter. In any case, I believe that focusing on this issue lowers the level of discussion.

Very few critics discussed the risks our men faced or the fact that the UN salaries were intended to reflect the dangers faced by our soldiers, who wore our national flag on their sleeve and who were trying to help a sister country.

We were driven by other things—mainly, by the desire to fulfill our duty to Chile and by the pride we took in our training. In all the conversations I had with soldiers who had survived dangerous situations, never once did I hear them raise the issue of salaries. When I raised the issue myself, almost all of them said they would be using the extra pay to fund their children's education or to pay down a mortgage.

It is unfair to reduce a major incentive for those who are risking their lives in difficult circumstances. A country that decides to send its soldiers on peacekeeping missions, where they will be risking their lives to strengthen the nation's international prestige, needs to find better ways to economize. A soldier deserves decent wages.

It is worth noting how other MINUSTAH countries dealt with this issue. In some cases, soldiers of all ranks continued to be paid their salaries in their countries' national currencies and, in addition, received the US$1,028 paid by the UN, regardless of rank. The country's government was compensated for the material it contributed.

In other cases, soldiers' salaries were kept in the national currency. Some of the money obtained from personnel salaries and the compensation for material was divided up by rank. In this way everyone from lieutenant to general was given a sum according to his seniority, with something left over to pay for equipment repairs. The international press later reported that certain countries were abusing this formula.

I would make one observation. Because of the almost certain destruction of material during a mission, after several years the armies using this latter formula have to pay higher replacement costs if they wish to maintain their operational status.

From what I saw, all of the Haiti mission's trucks had to be written off after being driven on the local roads, or they required major repairs. I think a serious mistake is being made if these funds are not used to purchase replacements or pay for maintenance.

Now that Chilean soldiers are being sent overseas as peacekeepers, it is important to teach senior officers international humanitarian law as well as the English language. I had been trying to improve our personnel's English for some time. To that end I had established the Army School of Languages and toughened the officers' training curriculum. An analysis of the language skills of Chilean soldiers today shows how far we have progressed toward fielding a truly bilingual army.

A soldier with a good command of English makes an enormous difference, since other countries judge us in large part according to our communication skills. In this regard, our personnel in Haiti were also taught a few words of Creole at the Language School and were given a card listing common Haitian phrases.

Taking part in peacekeeping missions gives our soldiers direct access to the practices of more advanced armies, which undoubtedly benefits them as well as the Armed Forces as a whole. Besides that, these missions show other countries the quality of our personnel, who are our main capital as an institution as well as a tangible asset to our nation.

Before discussing Chile's presence on MINUSTAH, I want to say a little about MIFH, in which Chile also participated. Of all the countries presently in Haiti, the only one that also served on MIFH is Chile. The Haitians have noticed that, and so have the other countries now there.

I remember clearly the role played by General Juan Carlos Salgado Brocal, who at the time of MIFH was Chief of the National Defence General Staff. He was an outstanding general: highly intelligent, exceptionally well trained, and possessed well-honed political skills. Under the system he developed, responsibility for our participation with MIFH was assumed by EMDN, which in turn created an organization to handle all the legal, financial and administrative issues involving the DPKO. This was not easy, but General Salgado's personal supervision ensured that our participation matched our interests on these missions. We learned as we went along and have drawn several lessons from this complex process.

Beginning in February 2004, Chile contributed 329 men to MIFH. They included General Staff officers deployed in Miami in the South Command of the U.S. Army, others in the force's headquarters in Haiti, medical personnel in the field hospital in Port-au-Prince, and a Chilean battalion, also stationed in Port-au-Prince. That battalion included a company of Special Forces, a company of riflemen, and a reserve company that also undertook missions and patrol work in Hinche and other parts of the central zone. The members of this force began arriving in Haiti on the night of March 3 on a Boeing 707 and a Hercules C-130.

It was MIFH's assignment to establish the bases for MINUSTAH. Transferring this unit such a long distance was a challenge we met successfully, and one that earned us enormous international prestige as a military force. But it was undoubtedly a risky endeavour.

Among other things, the Army Directive stipulated that the Chilean battalion should "pacify and create the conditions of governance and functioning of the institutions, in a critical zone of Haiti, affected by the severe crisis that had led to the International Organizations' decision at the request of former President Aristide. It should assume control of the jurisdictional zone that will be assigned by the commander of the Multinational Force, restore safety on the streets there and establish peace."

Great importance was placed on strict compliance with the objectives of this mission, on following the rules of engagement (ROEs), and on preserving Chile's prestige.

One paragraph described the mission of Unit Commander Colonel Mario Messen: "You will consider at all times that the unit you command is part of the Chilean Army, meaning that its behavior, actions and professional performance must be worthy of the institution's historic prestige and loyal to the doctrine of the army and the rules of International Law."

The Chileans arrived in Port-au-Prince on March 7. Now they had to rapidly achieve operational efficiency while acclimatizing to conditions very different from those at home.

After four months in Haiti this "expeditionary force" returned to Chile. It had completed its mission successfully while suffering no casualties. It had helped establish peace and prevent the massacre of civilians that had seemed so imminent when it arrived.

The unit had been assembled just before departure as an emergency force and was 8000 kilometres from its base, on far different terrain than it would ever have encountered in Chile, facing a complicated operation. That it succeeded at its task speaks highly of us.

The possibility that Chilean forces might take casualties, and that the Chilean people might have to be told about them, made the risks of this mission even higher. Fortunately, our troops suffered no casualties.

As soldiers we had been ready to take casualties. In fact, Chilean soldiers' training—particularly in Special Units—involves a high degree of danger, which we deal with professionally and which instills excellent combat skills.

Chilean participation on MIFH had been a success, both for our foreign policy and for our defence policy. The troops displayed a level of efficiency that surprised many armies, to our country's benefit.

But in light of the UN resolution that had sent this mission, and the circumstances in the country, something more than MIFH was needed. Haiti needed far more help than this.

So the UN decided to send a second mission, one with broader objectives. On June 1, 2004, the UN transferred MIFH's responsibilities to this new mission, named MINUSTAH. Then on May 11, through Official Letter 542, the President of Chile requested the Senate's authorization for troops to leave the country, pursuant to Article 4 of Law no. 19067.

I arrived in Haiti 16 months after MINUSTAH began operations. For the information on MIFH I am extremely grateful to Lieutenant Colonel Rodrigo Carrasco, who served as second commander of the first Chilean battalion in Cap Haïtien, and whose experiences proved vital to me.

Chilean forces were distributed as follows:

At headquarters we had eight Chilean officers in advisory posts relating to intelligence, disarmament, operations, logistics and training. Some of these officers worked at Central Headquarters, others near the airport, which was the site of the mission's logistics and administrative offices. Like me, they were all in Haiti for twelve months. The contingents were there for six months.

The Joint Helicopter Unit's principal mission was to transport MINUSTAH equipment and personnel, carry out aerial reconnaissance, train and set up patrols, and transport the authorities. They had clocked about 2,500 hours' flying time in the two years since the start of the mission (around 550 hours' flying time per shift). They had carried out medical airlifts within the country and had transferred the sick to the Level III hospital in the Dominican Republic.

The equipment for the Helicopter Unit and the Mechanized Infantry Battalion units was transported in June and July 2004. This meant packing aircraft, spare parts, vehicles and general freight and shipping all of it to Haiti on the Navy barge *Valdivia* and in a Russian Antonov aircraft.

The Joint Helicopter Unit comprised about 90 soldiers, including pilots, administrative personnel and mechanics and logistics experts from the Army and Air Force. They were stationed next to the Port-au-Prince airport along-side the Argentine Helicopter Unit. They were adjacent to the combined Chilean and Ecuadoran Engineers' Unit, the first joint unit composed of two institutions engaged in a UN mission. The Army and the Air Force took turns commanding them.

Noteworthy is the night flying capability of our pilots and crews. They had developed it in Chile; then while in Haiti they raised it even higher, by which point few countries in the region could equal our level of training. During their six months in Haiti, our pilots got to fly more than they would have in two years in Chile.

The accommodations for our pilots and crews were good, but this requires some explanation. Our personnel were lodged in containers that accommo-dated three or four persons each. For recreation there was a gym under a tent awning with some basic equipment and an area behind the camp that had been cleared for volleyball or jogging. Whenever possible, trips were organized to the beaches north of the capital, with all the necessary security arrange-ments since we had to cross the city to get there.

The FACH personnel had a modern, fully air-conditioned marquee with a capacity of about 70. Known as the "dome," it had been used by FACH under extreme conditions, including ice camps, but it was still in good condition. This was where the personnel took their meals and watched TV and movies. There were also facilities for instant messaging back home.

The helicopter facility had a joint infirmary for crews and backup person-nel, run by a FACH doctor, who also joined the medical teams on aircraft when patients had to be transferred from various parts of the country. The army's male nurses also worked at the infirmary.

The army personnel had a marquee provided by the UN that was very long and narrow, with the same personnel capacity as the dome but without good insulation or air conditioning, which meant it was usually hotter inside than outside. A TV screen had been set up inside that received the signal from the national television channel when conditions permitted.

The FACH mess and recreation facilities were far better than what the army had been provided. Also, the FACH personnel could videoconference with their families every week. A telephone line had been put in for the army.

The food, which was provided by the UN, was excellent. It was prepared by our own cooks, who designed the menus on the basis of our own culture and culinary traditions.

The army personnel adopted a mongrel they christened "Velo." It became the unit's mascot. They refused to tell me where the name came from, though our mechanics and pilots certainly knew. I hope that noble beast is in good hands today.

Let me share a disloyalty that seriously compromises my credibility as the most senior Chilean military officer. When I arrived at Port-au-Prince, the two units in the capital, using the Chilean Army as a model for their food, used to put casserole and *empanadas* (meat pies) on the menu. I am a real *empanada* fan and one day I cornered the two commanders, Engineering Lieutenant Colonel Marcelo Iturriaga and Colonel Javier Cancino from the Helicopter Unit, and asked them to put them on the menu on Tuesdays and Thursdays so that I could have the luxury of eating empanadas twice a week. Fortunately they gave me their wholehearted support.

Some of the helicopters were equipped with FLYR, a system for sending signals. It meant that from headquarters — or wherever the system was set up — we could see on a crystal-clear monitor what the helicopter was recording. This was very useful, especially given the restrictions we faced when it came to entering certain zones where the gangs were unfriendly to say the least.

I felt proud to see our pilots and crews carrying the national flag through Haitian airspace. Unfortunately, for technical reasons involving complex maintenance owing to the number of flying hours, our aging Pumas had to be returned to Chile in August 2006. This left the mission with low transport capacity and deprived our crews of an exceptional flying school. In Chile we faced a restricted budget; in Haiti we had an abundance of fuel.

Because of the risk of being shot by the gangs, our aircraft were outfitted with Kevlar, a material designed to withstand small-arms fire. Since we were in one of the capital's danger zones, the pilots always had to fly above 2,500 feet to avoid being hit by snipers. Even so, they were hit twice, which fortunately did not create a serious problem. On one occasion an aircraft was shot near the tail, which could have proved disastrous.

Our aircraft were used to transport U.S. Secretary of State Colin Powell to the Parliament in 2004. This was a critical time, since demonstrators launched a small-arms attack, which was put down at great risk to our personnel.

Later on, our aircraft would also be used to transport the presidential candidate René Préval to meetings with the transitional government at perhaps the most critical moment of the election campaign (more on this later). In fact, a crucial meeting would be held at the offices of our pilots, one that led to a solution at a difficult time for the mission.

The Helicopter Unit was in a dangerous neighbourhood, which meant that the personnel could not leave their facilities and were restricted to the marquees I mentioned earlier. At the end of my mission, a plastic swimming pool with a capacity for ten people arrived, and the two units got together to coordinate its use.

One day I went out for a jog on the airport track — though it was 45 degrees out — with Major Jorge Castro, whose combat name was "Coyote." That day I

Photo 10. The Helicopter Unit's lounge plane

noticed two old planes sitting at the end of the track about 1000 metres from our unit.

Afterwards I met with Lieutenant Colonel Bermúdez, who was in charge of the Army Helicopter Unit, and suggested — though I'm sure it sounded like an order — that we copy the Argentines' idea of doing up an old airplane as a lounge, since our personnel had no entertainment facilities.

One night, after the pilots and technicians had studied the matter, I was invited to watch the plane being towed into "national territory" (our base). Bermúdez and his men had examined the structure of the old plane. With the Chilean engineers' help, they found a truck to tow it to the base.

That night I climbed into the cockpit of the plane, which was hooked up to the truck. The operation was swift and effective, and once the plane had been installed in the right place, they proceeded to put everything back to how it had been before, with no trace of movement.

The plane was done up as a lounge by the entire unit, with the enthusiastic participation of the FACH and army personnel, and officially opened by Ambassador Valdés on March 11, my birthday (Photo 10).

The South American contingents worked together so well in Haiti largely because since the 1990s there has been a marked increase in exchanges and mutual cooperation among the South American armies. They have exchanged professionals, undertaken joint training and simulation activities, and held congresses and seminars in order to share experiences and lessons learned. All of this greatly benefited our joint work in Haiti. So I agree with Colonel Sánchez's statement:

> The joint deployment in Cyprus by Chile, Argentina, Brazil, Peru, Bolivia and Paraguay, as well as of the exercises that began in the 1990s, constituted the basis of our success in Haiti.
>
> This training increased our capacity to operate together, encouraged mutual knowledge and enabled us to put our doctrines into practice. When the contingents arrived on the island, the South Americans knew each other well, and the General Staff officers soon created a tight community, based on a common culture and values.[4]

One of the main lessons I took from my work with the various contingents — especially at General Headquarters — was the importance of rapport and mutual professional recognition of the sort that exists among South American military officers. It is what enabled us to carry out our work in an atmosphere of camaraderie and friendship. The joint operations we conducted in Haiti were good experiences that only strengthened our unity.

Civilians have sometimes raised questions about the links that have been forged between our country's Armed Forces and those of our neighbours. Actually, we ought to integrate our forces even more in order to increase our capacity to operate combined forces.

Institutional cultures are sometimes difficult to change. Serving on missions like MINUSTAH speeds up the process — which is another advantage to contributing to them.

When I compare what we were like at the beginning of the mission with what we are like now in terms of interoperational aspects, I have to conclude that MINUSTAH has been of great benefit to Chile's soldiers.

Next to the Helicopter Unit was a construction engineers' company, with equipment and personnel from the Chilean and Ecuadoran Armies. Our engineers spent most of their time building roads in the northern zone, in Limbé near Port-de-Paix and toward Ennery. They also repaired the airport road in Cap Haïtien and carried out several projects to support the force and assist the local people.

When times were difficult in the capital, we called on the engineers to reinforce the checkpoints (CPs). This involved them in risky operations on Route #1 and Cité Militaire — an area controlled by criminals, where they were shot at by snipers. For the Iron Fist Operation in July, they added steel plates to one of their machines, which were shot at by the gangs.

When one talks about military participation in these operations, examples such as this show that our soldiers in the Engineering Corps are an extremely useful instrument for post-conflict missions. Our engineers showed great professionalism in Haiti, and their joint work reinforced their friendship with our Ecuadoran colleagues, who were delighted to work with our personnel.

The only complaint I heard from our engineers — so I told Ecuador's President Alfredo Palacio when he visited our Engineers' Unit in July 2006 — was that the Ecuadorans liked rice far too much when it was their turn to cook mess.

AT THE TIME of writing, Chile had a mixed battalion comprising Chilean Army personnel (a Mechanized Infantry company) and Navy personnel (a company of Marines) distributed among the Carrera, Prat, O'Higgins and Morín barracks in Cap Haïtien. Besides these the battalion had men stationed at several points in the north zone, such as Plaisance and Pignon, where there was normally a riflemen's platoon commanded by a lieutenant.

In keeping with UN regulations, this battalion had a Level I medical care centre. It was staffed by two physicians — one an emergency specialist, the other a surgeon. It had first-rate equipment and auxiliary staff capable of handling emergencies and even minor operations. These two doctors also provided medical care for Haitians at various sites throughout the city. In a country with such poor health care, the people benefited greatly from this.

There was also a chaplain, normally attached to the army, who stayed for the same length of time as the contingent — that is, six months.

Besides ministering to our personnel, the chaplain provided religious services for the neighbourhood's mainly Catholic community. This was in addition to his many humanitarian activities. All of these were much appreciated by the community, yet they have barely been reported. According to Colonel Horacio Sánchez,

> the Chileans occupied Cap Haïtien and swiftly took control of its jurisdiction. It was their first mission with troops, but they proved that they were extremely well prepared. The Chileans' work in their sphere of action, whose center of operations, Cap Haïtien, is one of the most populous cities in the country, required an enormous effort. They wisely reached out to the Haitians, giving the population courses at their camp, where they taught them various trades. This yielded excellent results and very soon, requests flooded in from all over the island for MINUSTAH to use the Chilean contingent's formula.[5]

The engineers in the north were with the Morín barracks near Cap Haïtien and also in Limbé, where they lived in containers while constructing a road to Port-de-Paix (Photo 11).

Photo 11. Mechanized Infantry Unit Stacks at the Carrera Barracks, Cap Haïtien

The Chileans spent most of their off-duty hours in barracks. Through a national TV signal, they were able to keep daily track of Chilean events. Other national contingents were similarly equipped. Playing sports, watching TV, surfing the Internet, and keeping equipment in good repair took up a large part of their off-duty time.

As in all contingents, about 15 percent were on leave at any one time. Most of them used these furloughs to visit resorts in the nearby Dominican Republic.

Whenever possible, Sunday outings were organized to Cormier and Labadie—two gorgeous beaches with warm, crystal-clear water to the northeast of Cap Haïtien (Photo 12). They traveled there in military caravans with guards included. For a few dollars our men could eat fresh-caught lobster or the local snails. Very few Haitians visited these places, which could only be reached by a sturdy vehicle because of the poor condition of the roads.

Labadie is a beautiful beach, which was visited every week by large cruise ships from Miami. The passengers would come ashore in small boats. Suddenly the view would change: the water would fill with motorboats, jet skis, parachutes, and dinghies—everything tourists need for a good time. In the afternoon the visitors would return to their ship, often without realizing they had just been in Haiti.

Photo 12. Labadie Beach, north of Cap Haïtien

In Cap Haïtien the Chileans established their operations centre next to La Citadelle, a fortress built by Henri Christophe in the 1810s. It is set on a hill with a view to the north down a valley to the city. A visit completely changes your perspective on this unusual country and its history.

Four members of the unit were injured during this time. The most critical moments came in November 2005, when a Marine patrol commanded by Second Lieutenant Francisco Recassens was ambushed near Plaissance. The lieutenant was wounded in the hand and later had to be repatriated to Chile. Three NCOs were also wounded, but less seriously. When I saw what remained of the jeep, I was amazed they had survived.

I went to see Lieutenant Recassens with Ambassador Valdés while he was at the Argentine hospital in Port-au-Prince (Photo 13). He told us how quickly the ambush had flared and how they had escaped certain death by returning fire immediately. I told the young officer this proved how well trained he and his men were and that he should feel proud about this.

That ambush had been an anomaly: Cap Haïtien was generally peaceful and had not seen serious security problems during the nearly three months I had spent on the mission to that point.

Another incident occurred in Cap Haïtien, during the presidential elections in February 2006. While supervising a polling booth, Marine officer Luis

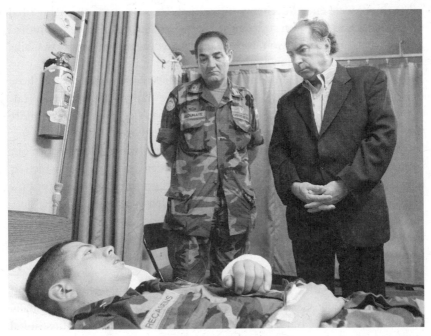

Photo 13. Ambassador Valdés visiting Second Lieutenant Recassens at the Argentine Hospital

Huenul was attacked with a knife. He suffered a wound to his hand while struggling with a group of assailants.

And in July 2006, Army Corporal Mauro Rojas Fierro contracted malaria, which created quite a stir in Chile, though it had apparently happened because he had stopped taking his chloroquine tablets. As a result, senior officers tightened their surveillance of what had been an individual responsibility.

Otherwise, the situation in this zone — which had been one of the most problematic in the country when the first contingent arrived in 2004 — was usually fairly calm, thanks to the preventive work carried out by the Chileans.

Times when our personnel were threatened were heavily publicized in Chile, alerting the population to the risks our people were facing. This worried me. I detected among Chileans a limited ability to accept that there might be deaths or injuries on the mission. This in turn suggested that they were unaware of the environment in which our troops were working.

They knew we were in a very hot place with beautiful beaches, that we were helping impoverished people, and that there were a few criminals who were a long way from where the Chileans were posted.

I called Santiago and spoke to various authorities, to remind them that what had happened to our personnel in the incidents was regrettable but insignificant compared to what the Jordanians, Brazilians, Peruvians and other troops were encountering in the capital. Those groups were being fired on every day and had been suffering casualties as a result. If those troops had known what a fuss these two minor events were causing back home in Chile, they would have looked down on us.

I was also worried because our pilots — and even our engineers and those of us at General Headquarters — were more likely than our troops in Cap Haïtien to be shot at by gangs. By that point there had been 9 deaths and more than 70 wounded on the mission. None of them had been Chilean.

I told the various authorities that it would be advisable to improve our communications, since we were on a mission under Chapter VII, in which by definition danger was present. I suggested that they devise a strategy for how to respond if one of our men happened to be killed by criminals.

Regarding Lieutenant Recassens and Corporal Rojas, the Defence Ministry responded by providing strong support to the families. This was laudable, because when you are in this situation, that type of institutional response is a big morale boost for everybody.

Our personnel's morale was very high at all times, even during the difficult days of January 2006. Several of our Marines — "Cossacks," as they are usually known — and some of our Army troops asked to be transferred to the capital so that they could contribute to the mission in the most dangerous zone. Whenever I visited our men in Cap Haïtien, the only thing they ever asked was to be transferred to Port-au-Prince, where they knew there was more action and thus more to contribute to the mission. Our personnel's esprit de corps and desire to be in the thick of the mission contrasted with what I read in the papers, which focused excessively on the impact that the danger they faced might have on Chilean society.

The Chileans in Cap Haïtien were bracketed by Spanish and Moroccan units in the east, Argentine units in the southwest, and Nepalese units in the south. In keeping with our planning, all these contingents maintained close operating links and often undertook joint activities. In fact, several combined operations were carried out with soldiers from these countries. The purpose of these was to "show the flag" in the zone and to locate possible criminals.

Most of these missions involved small units led by an officer or NCO, traveling over bad roads and unable to contact base. From these missions I learned a key lesson: lieutenants and sergeants play a crucial role in peacekeeping. *They* are the ones who actually carry out the UN's mandate.

During actions, besides being present in key places at crucial times, senior officers focus mainly on reminding people what the mission's goal is — what we call the "commander's intention." This requires effective management and control.

On a day-to-day basis, in the streets, it is the patrols and the young officers who command them that have to confront the reality — the gangs — and then develop tactics to address that reality — tactics that often have a strategic impact on the mission as a whole. Based on what our soldiers accomplished, and the Haitian people's admiration for them, I can say that the mission results reflected well on how our country trains its soldiers, for they accomplished their mission in Haiti.

Our men in the north gained the local people's support as a result of effective leadership. Our officers repeatedly reminded their men how important it was to win the hearts of the local people, which they did through actions that benefited the community they served.

The battalion command was rotated every six months between an Army and a Navy officer. On the whole, the sailors and soldiers worked well together. When a Navy commander was in charge, the meeting places were known as chambers; when it was the military's turn, they were known as casinos.

I want to highlight the work of the female Chilean soldiers on these missions during my time in Haiti. The Army would later commend the female personnel at Cap Haïtien for their work in supporting the unit, and in logistics and other activities outside the base. Our female soldiers performed superbly, meeting the mission's demands and earning their male colleagues' respect. When people talk about women in the Armed Forces, Haiti is a good example of how much they can contribute. By the time I finished this book, 14 women from the Army had joined the Chilean contingents.

I have already said something about our personnel's living conditions. Now I will say more. On top of each soldier's camp bed was a mosquito net, next to which lay that soldiers' combat equipment, ready to be taken out on patrol.

Everyone slept in shorts, since the air conditioning was inadequate. It was even hotter under the mosquito nets, and there were swarms of mosquitoes in the barracks. By the time I arrived, the soldiers had already got used to them. In that typical Chilean way of looking on the bright side and giving things nicknames, our men had christened their insect repellent "Bug Appeal" since the more they put on, the more mosquitoes they attracted.

Later on, more solid "stacks" were completed, containing the same camp beds with mosquito nets. But these, at least, were a little cooler. They took longer to build than they should have.

The soldiers built their own sports fields, where they used to play five-a-side and jog around the units.

Most of the equipment was good, but the wear and tear on the trucks, owing to heavy use on poor roads, required a huge logistic effort to overcome. Simply to maintain the tires and suspension systems was torture for the logistics officers and their mechanics, not to mention those who supported the mission from Santiago or Valparaíso. Minor spare parts were obtained in the Dominican Republic and were flown in when necessary.

Service stoves were purchased from the French contingent, which had served on MIFH in the past. As time went by, we bought better equipment.

Traditional Chilean dishes made with ingredients requested from MINUSTAH were served in the barracks. (All contingents were on the same footing in this regard.) The soldiers were very well fed, right down to *empanadas* — in the Navy style, which the Army officers had maintained.

On weekends, conditions permitting, the units engaged in sports and social activities. There was even a karaoke machine, which everyone tried, including me during my visits.

All our personnel were properly uniformed, except that their boots were black. I insisted that these be replaced by sand-coloured boots, which absorb less heat and do not need polishing. The change was made the year I returned to Chile.

Every soldier wore a Kevlar helmet and a flak jacket, both of which were to be worn at all times outside the base. Similarly, it was compulsory to carry a weapon whenever off base. In addition, each soldier wore a CamelPak — a bag holding two litres of water.

The individual equipment included five to seven ammunition clips. Those clips increased each soldier's carry weight by at least 18 kilos — something I remembered every time I visited Cité Soleil. In that damp heat you felt as if you were in a walking sauna the whole day, but all the equipment was absolutely necessary.

Most of the personnel lost several kilos at the beginning and used to drink about five litres of water a day. As time went by and they got used to the climate, a couple of litres a day got to be enough, unless they were out on a mission, where the weight of the equipment and the adrenaline caused them to drink more water. In this respect, one of the lessons of the mission was that dehydration reduced efficiency in combat. To function well, we had to drink water constantly.

There was no safe drinking water in Haiti. We had to purify all of it at the unit in our own machines and store it in plastic containers.

The area for which the battalion was responsible was generally well controlled, and the personnel's morale high, so I expected no problems from this contingent. No problems is in fact what I got. This reflected well on the officers. Another cause was effective selection and training.

Official visits from Santiago were quite common and invariably ended with a hike to the Citadelle or to the ruins of Sans Souci, a palace built by Henri Christophe around the same time as the fortress. On these walks we would be accompanied by a crowd of young Haitians, who would yell, "Chile!

Chile!" since they recognized the flag patch each of us wore on his sleeve. They expected food or money in return, mind you.

In Cap Haïtien and also in Ouanaminthe on the Dominican border there were *carabineros,* who supported the Haitian National Police (PNH). Neighboring national contingents had mutual-support agreements in the event of emergency; our "partner" in this was the Spanish unit posted at Fort Liberté and Ouanaminthe.

Besides carrying out their operational duties, our units in Haiti gave classes in cooking, electricity, and mechanics; they also provided tutoring and health care. In short, they engaged with the population in ways that encouraged the local people to be glad of our soldiers' presence.

During ceremonies in Port-au-Prince and visits to Cap Haïtien, I always ran into Haitians and various authorities. I found that they felt very close to the Chilean unit—a clear indicator of good relations between our countries.

All Chileans in Haiti were ordered to win the people's hearts and minds— to make them feel that we were not an occupation force but rather were there so that together we could do something to improve their lives. I think that the Chilean contingent—and the rest of MINUSTAH—achieved this. Except for a few reporters' questions and isolated articles in the press, no one ever made me feel, nor did I ever hear, that they perceived us as an occupying force.

Someone once coined the phrase WHAM (winning hearts and minds). I think we accomplished this.

The Chilean personnel at General Headquarters and at "Logbase" (the mission's logistics base) at first lived in the El Rancho, in Musseau near Pétionville. In November 2005 they were transferred to the Plaza, opposite the city hall in downtown Port-au-Prince. This was far from ideal, since the previous hotel had been more convenient and was in better condition.

Some Fridays we all met with the HQ staff for a barbecue lunch provided by the hotel, to celebrate any recent birthdays. This was usually a moment of rest and relaxation for all of us, though we did not forget that while we were sitting around the barbecue, our colleagues were out on the streets controlling the gangs and providing security for Haitian society.

The food, provided by the UN, was shared by more than 100 officers from different countries. Argentine and Uruguayan yerba mate was served around Arab prayer mats.

Those on the mission for a year would usually return to Chile at least once, which was not easy because of the costs involved. Most of those who were in Haiti for six months did not return to Chile to see their families.

All national holidays and celebrations and various social activities were attended by Ambassador Valdés and the Chilean Ambassador to Haiti, Marcel Young. Ambassador Young was so fond of Haiti and so aware of Chile's commitment to that nation that he would enthusiastically propose new activities for the benefit of the people and was always showing our soldiers his appreciation.

He did a great deal for Haiti and was always looking for ways to tighten the bonds between our countries. He recommended cultural activities, and to our engineers he suggested road- and bridge-building projects. He welcomed all the Chilean military and made every effort to be with us. His house was always open to us. We would gather there to coordinate our activities, or simply to chat.

He was subsequently joined by Jorge Vidal, who was just starting his career as a diplomat. Jorge quickly won us over, and we included him in all our activities.

We military personnel spent most of our time with our combat equipment and the radio. There were times when we could have rested, though I for one definitely did not spend most of my time enjoying the beaches.

While in Haiti I tried a number of very good restaurants, all of which served French cuisine at affordable prices. I would usually dine with UN personnel and Haitian civilians. A dinner out was one of the few entertainments available that did not add to our stress.

Videoconferences were held every week in Cap Haïtien in conjunction with EMDN, though not with the rest of our units in Haiti. Some units had a telephone line for Chile with a system for charging individual calls. Our soldiers often used the Internet to stay in touch with family. After I returned from the mission, this videoconference contact was extended to the other units.

All the authorities, both the Haitian ones and those of MINUSTAH, always appreciated the Chileans' work. This filled us with pride but also placed a burden of responsibility on us, which we gracefully accepted.

Chilean pilots used to train Brazilian and Argentine soldiers and Peruvian commandos. They would also carry personnel from the other contingents on reconnaissance missions and patrols.

Our engineers used to help the other contingents. Our battalion interacted with Argentine, Spanish, Moroccan and Uruguayan soldiers. Our officers on the General Staff displayed great professionalism in all their missions.

Our personnel did an excellent job of portraying the Chilean military as highly professional. But I also I heard some comments — especially from officers of the units that had suffered the highest casualties — that the Chilean, Uruguayan, Spanish, Moroccan and Nepalese troops were stationed in the less dangerous areas and that it would be a good idea to rotate the contingents to even things out a little.

I always pointed out that when Chile joined the mission in 2004, it had been deployed to Cap Haïtien, where at the time there had been a great deal of violence (though never as much as in Cité Soleil). So I tended to shrug off these concerns. Even so, they were being expressed for clear reasons, and sooner or later changes would have to be made.

I also often heard criticisms that certain officers were favouring their home countries in minor situations, by praising their units' achievements over those of other contingents. Some officers even told me bluntly that the Chileans were in a conflict-free zone, as opposed to their own men, who were being shot at every day by the gangs.

On this type of mission a commander is evaluated largely in terms of his impartiality, especially when there is a contingent from his home country. I would note that I never received a request from Santiago to favour our contingent, nor would it have occurred to me to give the Chileans preferential treatment over the other contingents. I never strayed from what was expected of a commander of a multinational force such as this: that he treat everyone equally.

But a few situations did arise which showed me that these missions are never as clear as one thinks or hopes. During my term as Acting Force Commander (AFC), the violence reached its height in January 2006. The forces in the capital were conducting extremely dangerous missions, and there weren't enough soldiers to neutralize the threat. It was clear to me at the time that the "mother of all battles" was taking place in Port-au-Prince and that unless military force was focused on this situation, there would be no point maintaining calm in the rest of the country.

I felt like a boat in the middle of a storm, and the entire boat, except for one cabin, was filling with water. The people in the one cabin were safe at the moment, but they would sink with all the others unless everyone on board pitched in.

In view of the gravity of the situation, I gathered together all those at headquarters and asked them to suggest courses of action. The Operations Officer said he had contacted a commander who said he was ready to send a company to the capital immediately. Another contingent commander from outside the capital got in touch with me and said he was willing to send in his troops immediately as reinforcements. I remembered that our soldiers in Cap Haïtien had said, whenever I went to visit them, that if there were problems in the capital, they were ready to go there.

I preferred to work methodically, so I issued an order for each unit to prepare a platoon (30 soldiers) to be sent to the capital as soon as ordered and to be ready to send a company (100 soldiers) if the situation worsened.

As the days went by, I received information directly from the senior officers of one country, telling me that to move a unit from their zone to the capital, I should have requested permission from their country. Also, that I should not forget that according to the MOU and the protocols signed with the UN, each state had operational *command* through its own command system and that the mission's FC was responsible for operational *control*. On the basis of this argument, any transfer would have to be authorized by the country itself.

I asked this authority to explain whether, in an emergency, this applied to all contingents. In other words, in the midst of a crisis, with troops being deployed and under attack, should I call each of the authorities of the 13 contingents? That wouldn't be very practical, to say the least.

I told him that through their contingents, MINUSTAH member countries were not only in charge of a particular zone but also contributing to the mission as a whole and that because of the dynamics of events in the capital, the rules as they understood them were unworkable, especially when we were talking about small squads.

I told him in no uncertain terms that the situation was serious, that I would make the decision to transfer troops to the capital, regardless of the country they were from, that I would assume the consequences of my decision, that his country should do the same, and that I would inform New York of this matter.

In all of this, I was fully in line with what the UN had stated in documents issued by the DPKO in 2004. Apparently not everyone had been informed of this.

I experienced a similar problem with another contingent commander, who told me that his men had not come to Haiti to take part in combat in the countryside. In other words, there were missions they could not accomplish.

I explained the obvious — that there were threats in all the cities in the country, and that the UN mandate had made it quite clear we were acting under Chapter VII, so his attitude was unacceptable. In any case, I told him I would inform the DPKO in New York in order for it to repatriate the unit to its country, since it was no use to us here, and that if he stuck to his position I would immediately remove the unit from the mission.

Nowadays I realize how difficult it would have been to send a contingent home from this mission, but I was determined to do so. Fortunately, the officer quickly realized his mistake, and his unit was deployed as planned.

Notes

1 Antonio Varas Clavel, *Visión histórica de la participación en Operaciones de Paz del Ejército de Chile* (Santiago: Biblioteca del Oficial, 2006). [Historical perspective of the participation of the Chilean Army in peacekeeping operations].

2 EMDN (National Defence Chiefs of Staff of Chile), "Misiones de Paz, devolviendo la esperanza," Santiago, 2004. [Peacekeeping missions, giving hope back].

3 CiC Conference, Juan Emilio Cheyre, at the War Academy, July 14, 2004.

4 Horacio S. Sánchez Mariño (Colonel of the Argentine Army), *La Campaña en Haití: Una experiencia sudamericana* (Argentina: n.p., 2007).

5 Ibid.

CHAPTER NINE

Violence in Haiti

VIOLENCE HAS long existed in Haiti, and many of the root causes of that violence persist to this day. So it is unreasonable to ask a military force to do something that is not its responsibility: provide a long-term solution to an existing problem. This may partly explain why so many missions preceded MINUSTAH.

When MIFH was launched, the situation and past experience predicted the worst. Fortunately, the worst did not happen, which is why, I think, its successor, MINUSTAH, has succeeded in fulfilling its mandate: to provide security and stability.

Today I can safely say that MINUSTAH has achieved concrete results. For example, it has prevented a civil war and the massacre of civilians. Since 2006, Haiti has had an elected government, after the most transparent and participative electoral process in its history. Under the new authorities the scenario is far better than it was in 2004.

Yet international aid must be continued; otherwise, Haitians will be back to square one until the next time the UN or some other organization intervenes. The country still faces profound and complex challenges, and a two-year mission will not solve them all, though it will make solutions more possible.

The violence in Haiti has political, social, and economic roots and has long been exacerbated by the absence of a functioning state. In hindsight, I can see that Haiti is a good example of a post-conflict scenario, one that suggests a need for non-traditional strategies.

In Ambassador Valdés's address to the Army War Academy in March 2007 he said: "Perhaps the best definition for the situation of the country is that of a state whose institutions have collapsed rather than a failed state."

During the period covered in this book we experienced severe episodes of violence. Things came to a head in December 2005 and January 2006, when the situation escalated to about 260 kidnappings, mostly in Port-au-Prince, and we had to deploy almost all our personnel just to ensure minimum stability.

Future studies might try to explain why, in a country so poor and so structurally backward, there have not been more serious outbreaks of violence. I cannot answer that question. But I would say that in our region there are more violent places than Haiti.

Though we tried to show we were fulfilling our mission, people were only concerned about Cité Soleil. Rather unfairly, the situation in that neighbourhood reflected strongly on the mission as a whole.

Haiti's 2005 census[1] indicates the situation in the country at the time. Also revealing is that the UNDP Human Development Index[2] ranked Haiti 154th among the world's countries that same year. In Haiti it is difficult to find reliable statistics, though the Internet does provide some data.[3]

Charcoal is the country's main cooking fuel. It is used by 68 percent of households in urban areas, rising to 90.9 percent in rural areas. That explains why deforestation is such a severe problem. Only 28 percent of Haitians have access to potable water, and according to some, the country's aquifers are drying up. The literacy rate is 61 percent, and only 45.9 percent of Haitians between 6 and 24 receive any formal education. The figure is only 25 percent in rural areas. Some suggest even those figures are too generous. Twenty-eight percent of Haitian children are malnourished. The child mortality is 71 deaths per 1,000 live births. During my stay in Haiti, the doctors in charge of the country's AIDS control program told me that 3.4 percent of Haitians were infected. For pregnant women the figure was 2.4 percent. AIDS is the main cause of death in Haiti, with thousands dying from it every year. Fifty-four percent of Haitians are economically active. The main occupation is agriculture. The unemployment rate is over 60 percent. Per capita income is US$1,800 per year. Some economists suggest this figure is far too high and that the actual amount is less than US$600 per year — one of the lowest in the world. According to a 2006 IMF report, the country's growth rate is barely 1.2 percent.

Clearly, Haiti has a subsistence economy rather than a productive one, in that 66 percent of the people engage in farming, 25 percent in services, and only 9 percent in industry. Yet during the nineteenth century, Haiti was one of the wealthiest countries on earth.

According to some experts, the Haitian economy was declining owing to inefficient governments as early as the 1970s — a situation made worse by the sanctions and economic blockade of the 1990s. That blockade had been declared by the OAS in the wake of Aristide's departure. In Ambassador Valdés's view, that blockade had verged on criminal, since the country's elites had been able to keep exporting their products through other countries. It was the poorest Haitians who suffered all the consequences.

Just a glance at the swarms of people on the streets of the main cities barely eking out a living by selling every imaginable thing from makeshift stalls makes it clear that the country suffers from underdevelopment and little industrial activity.

During my strategy classes at the War Academy, I had always drummed into my students that a commander must *study* a situation, not just look at it. In other words, one must somehow grasp the central issue. In Haiti you did not need to be an economist or a political scientist to realize that the problems there ran far deeper than the violence on the streets. Violence and insecurity were only symptoms. The real threats to the country were to be gleaned from the statistics I mentioned earlier.

Every time I received visitors from abroad — which happened quite often — they would spend no more than three days in Haiti before starting to give their opinion on how to improve the situation. Yet we had many talented people on the mission, and more than 100 officers at headquarters, who were well aware of what could and indeed must be done.

"Specialists" often told us that after fair elections, Haiti would rapidly set off down the road to development, since it had comparative advantages to exploit. They talked about the country's tourism potential, and about setting up assembly plants to exploit the country's proximity to wealthy markets.

Indeed, Haiti has enormous possibilities. Its culture is rich in traditions and values, and the land itself has plenty of development potential. Also, it is only a 90-minute flight from Florida, yet Haitian labour is far cheaper than in Canada and the United States.

But who is going to invest there until the country can offer a secure environment to do business? And that will only happen after Haiti has built a functioning police force and court system. And who will want to visit the country's beaches until minimal services, such as roads and sanitation, have been provided? Especially when safe and attractive resorts are available on the other side of the island, in the Dominican Republic. Until structural issues are addressed, tourists are unlikely to swap Punta Cana for Labadie, and investors are not going to pull out of China or Indonesia and relocate to Haiti to manufacture the products sold under American brand names.

Perhaps now is the time to ask what kind of aid Haiti actually needs. Remembering, of course, that any aid will be futile without the commitment and cooperation of the Haitians themselves.

A false premise, on which many visitors insisted, haunted me throughout the mission: "Once the military provide security, development and investment will follow." Yet at the time, the security level was more than acceptable everywhere in the country except in Port-au-Prince.

How many development schemes were launched in Cap Haïtien or Les Cayes, where all was calm and secure? None of any importance while I was there.

I would suggest that all the missions to Haiti so far—including MINUS-TAH—have made this same error: they have tried to break the country's fever and neglected to treat the disease that has caused it. That disease, in my view, is political immaturity. Haiti had never in its history established rule of law. In a civilized society, no one can be above the law.

Within a few months of my arrival, I fully agreed with Generals Heleno and Bacellar that the country's problems called for deeper reforms and ongoing, well-considered international aid. On these same lines, Ambassador Valdés often told me that Haiti more than anything else needed long-term international aid.

I realized that many of the country's problems had been exacerbated by poor decisions by the international community. The effects of those decisions were being felt by those on the mission and, worse still, by the Haitian people themselves, who had suffered the most casualties during this long crisis. A large part of the problem was that the police and the army had both been politicized. Haitians were continuing to suffer from that legacy.

At MINUSTAH meetings, past UN missions would be discussed. But it was always understood that Haiti's unique culture would have to be taken into account if solutions were ever to be found to the problems it faced. Other countries' experiences can never be perfect templates. Lessons can be transferred to some degree, but a given country's problems are always largely original.

Haitians lack consensus on how to address their challenges and establish the rule of law. I only hope they find that consensus one day and develop laws that reflect it. Meanwhile, that lack of consensus was indicated by how they handled the coming elections and confronted the problem of gang violence.

The most immediate threat to Haiti's security was the criminal gangs. Young men armed with automatic weapons were making money through robbery, kidnapping and murder. Some well-informed people were certain they were financed by politicians.

There was plenty of speculation about the links between gangs and drugs. This was mainly because of the high-powered weapons these groups displayed and the large stocks of ammunition they had. We could not help but suspect that drugs were involved.

Unfortunately, some pro-Aristide supporters and other political stake-holders at the very least sympathized with violent groups. And some sectors of the society were benefiting from the resulting anarchy.

The Haitian state was dysfunctional, and the society allowed certain people to be above the law. Those things, and the country's poverty and high unemployment, bred criminal gangs. The violence could not of course be justified, but it was almost inevitable.

The only positive thing one could say—I don't know how much longer this will last—was that so far the country had not had to confront politically motivated guerrilla or terrorist groups. This should have made the gang problem less difficult to solve, since a political solution would not be required. In the event, the problem was plenty difficult enough without the political factors.

Making the situation worse were the media, and an international community with a poor grasp of Haiti's problems. A particular problem was outsiders' obsession with the problems in Cité Soleil.

Some people actually viewed the *criminals* as victims. Yet no society can allow armed gangs to attack with impunity the police, whose task it is to enforce security and prevent crime. The Haitian police were constantly being attacked in this way. To join the force at times verged on suicide. Crimes need to be punished if a society is to have any chance of working.

Nothing good can come of a society whose judiciary cannot enforce the law. I saw this again and again while I was on the mission. The Haitian police, besides being highly ineffective, were neither respected nor valued by other Haitians, and the courts basically did not exist. Even worse, Haitians knew all this and barely complained about it.

All of the country's ten provinces had criminal gangs, yet during the twelve months I spent there, I never received any intelligence about their activities. Those gangs were deadly, and they would dump the bodies of their victims on the streets. Regrettably, this was nothing new in Haiti. The mission focused entirely on the gangs in Port-au-Prince, and all our casualties and problems occurred there.

A few months after it arrived, MINUSTAH faced its first large-scale problem, which some people called "Operation Baghdad." Put simply, this was a show of force by Aristide's followers, and it ended with ten people dead and three police officers decapitated. The criminals meant this display of force to intimidate both the mission and the transitional government. They failed on both counts.

During my posting, I would receive several warnings of a new "Operation Baghdad." It never happened.

The commanders of our contingents, who faced security threats on a daily basis in their areas of responsibility, used to tell me that the police were unbelievably inefficient when faced with these crimes and that they usually kept off the gangs' turf.

Cité Soleil borders an industrial area, which leads me to suspect that some business people were paying the gangs protection money.

In December 2005 a criminal gang attacked and seized a police station. The few police on the premises fled. Our military unit was alerted and came out to take back the station. On arrival, they saw that the gang had already left. Unfortunately, before the military force arrived, the criminals had beheaded a man in his sleep. Several hours would elapse before the police returned to the premises.

This suggests the PNH's level of professionalism. And though it was an isolated act outside the capital, it showed the level of violence in the country.

There were about 50 gangs in Port-au-Prince, which exerted territorial control over specific areas.

According to a report by the International Crisis Group,[4] 1999 marked the emergence of the "chimères" — a pejorative term for criminal gangs. Some said that the term referred to those who had been excluded from the establishment, "the dispossessed."

Most gang members had been Aristide supporters operating in the marginalized neighbourhoods of the capital, mainly in Cité Soleil, Bel Air and Les Salines. They had started out focusing their attacks on those who opposed the regime. Most members were unemployed men between 14 and 30 who lived in poor neighbourhoods where police presence was virtually non-existent and who fought for control of certain territories. Kidnapping was their main source of funds. They used violence openly, gruesomely murdering those who opposed them, both men and women, with no regard.

A MINUSTAH specialist told me that by the time they were 18, gang members were hardened criminals who had survived much combat.

According to reliable sources, the gangs also made money from drugs, which further complicated the situation.

The press did its part, interviewing gang leaders, who said they were not criminals and were being persecuted by MINUSTAH. Others insisted that abject poverty justified their violence. All of this fostered a myth about Cité Soleil that would cause us many problems and make it difficult for us to explain our actions against these criminals.

The notion that these poor boys were being forced into violence was a half-truth at best. To suggest that murder and kidnapping were justified by poverty was stretching things. Yet it is also true that there *was* plenty of injustice in

Haiti that these gang members had *not* caused. Better for all if we remembered that and dealt with the situation accordingly.

The gangs had an efficient information system based on cellphones. We often requested cellphone blocking systems but never received them.

The criminals had links within the justice system and the PNH, which partly explained the complete lack of arrest warrants against those whom law-abiding Haitians had identified to us as gang members. They had shown a great ability to corrupt the police, and according to some of the country's police authorities, many PNH officers were colluding with the criminals.

The gangs had plenty of weapons and ammunition. This was partly explained by the Haitian government's inability to control its borders, be they land, sea or air.

The gangs had a strong impact on politics. They had been working with politicians for many years, forging unlikely alliances, as the coming elections would show.

The gangs were well organized, especially in Cité Soleil and Cité Militaire. Each had its own turf under the control of the gang leader. On that turf, there was no rule of law. Kidnapped people would be hidden on the turf of the gang that had grabbed them. That was according to the people who were later rescued.

When the criminals shot at our troops they hid behind women and children, which made it more difficult for our soldiers to respond. Indeed, many gang members *were* women and children. The women would hide the criminals' weapons under their skirts for them.

This limited our use of weapons, since no mission could possibly countenance the killing of women and children. The senior officers always remembered this, however hard civilians pressed us to apply a "firm hand."

The criminals' cruelty was boundless. In June 2006, two PNH agents were captured by the gang of Evans Ti Couteau (little penknife) and taken to Cité Soleil. Once they were in the hands of this band, they were tortured and chopped into pieces and their remains were thrown to the dogs. The gang members burned what was left of them.

That was the violence and sadism we were up against.

Cité Soleil fronts the sea, which allowed the criminals to use small boats to move their hostages from place to place. We did not have the resources to monitor or control these seaborne movements. The PNH had two boats, but neither had any fuel. MINUSTAH eventually provided some with the aid of another country, but when the police approached the coast of Cité Soleil, they came under heavy fire, even from smaller vessels.

That, then, is the situation we faced. The PNH was entirely absent from the zones where our Blue Helmets were posted. Our troops were under almost constant fire from criminals. How different all of this was from the rest of the country, where I rarely received reports of gunfire! Yet on a single night in January, our troops in the danger zones fired 10,000 rounds to fend off gang attacks.

We already knew where the gangs were, but the UN mandate and Resolution 1542 made it very difficult to go after them. The UN might be helping the political process, but it was failing to provide a solution to the violence.

It was very difficult for Generals Bacellar and Elito and me to persuade the contingents that for the mission's sake, they should stay calm despite the relentless gunfire—that there was a higher objective, which was to fulfill the UN mandate, which required us to support the political process, including the coming elections.

In October 2005 it was decided that the population of Cité Soleil would take part in the elections. If the people there were unable to vote, the elections would be invalid. This decision was the result of media pressure more than anything else, since the possibility of citizens actually participating in the electoral process was minimal.

Two voter registration centres were established in Cité Soleil. This involved mission personnel contacting community leaders known to have links with gangs. These people said they would help open the centres, which would be run jointly by MINUSTAH, the OAS, and the Provisional Electoral Council (CEP). These "leaders" assured us that the gangs would not attack as long as no soldiers or Haitian police were posted nearby.

I realize now that the Haitian people's rejection of the PNH and the authorities in general was justified by their past experiences with both. It was going to take time to build a good relationship between the people and their police and other authorities. In the absence of a functioning state, many Haitians supported the gangs, since they were the only ones offering any semblance of authority.

At this point in the electoral process, the neighbourhood leaders and some gang leaders went out onto the streets of Cité Soleil to dissuade criminals from shooting at our troops. It was part of the deal that had been struck that MINUSTAH would not have to tolerate Blue Helmets being shot at.

Oddly enough, most of the gang leaders registered to vote, and there were no security problems, even though we were required to keep our soldiers out of the danger zones. Clearly, the gangs were conniving with the police.

Once the enrollment period was over, insecurity and violence returned to previous levels. There were shootings and other confrontations in Cité Soleil every day, especially along Route #1. The Jordanian troops continued to take heavy fire each night. They heard thousands of rounds, especially around CP16. Much of this gunfire involved gangs engaged in turf wars, but a fair amount of it involved the gangs firing at MINUSTAH forces.

Presidential candidate René Préval was known to have influence over many local leaders. As a result, the situation stabilized somewhat in November. It was expected he would negotiate some kind of agreement with the gangs once he gained the presidency. Indeed, that is what happened.

But that truce ended on July 7, 2006, several months after Préval took office. One gang attacked another in an attempt to take control of Martissant. Twenty-two people died in the street battle, including three children murdered by the Ti Machet gang.

In the international press, the gangs were portraying themselves as defenceless victims of social injustice who were being indiscriminately attacked by the military. Nothing could have been further from the truth. Unfortunately, the press was giving more coverage to the criminals than to the people they abused and kidnapped. When a society is more concerned about criminals than their victims, it is in trouble. That was precisely the situation in Cité Soleil.

To make things worse, every week, dozens of criminals deported from the United States were entering Haiti and either joining the gangs or forming their own. In the latter case, they would start turf wars with existing gangs.

We knew that many of the gang leaders were seeking a political solution to their situation. They hoped that Préval, whom they assumed was close to Aristide, would extend them amnesty or at least deport them to a country where they would be safe.

I never expected that either of these things would help. My view was that if the gang leaders left the country, their gangs wouldn't disappear — new leaders would take their place, that's all. There would be no surrendering and no changes of ways — there was too much money to be made from drug running, kidnapping, and other organized crimes for either to happen.

To solve the gang problem would require the rule of law, but that day was obviously a long way off. I am not sure how quickly this will be achieved, since it is widely believed in Haiti that many of the country's political and social leaders have links with the gangs and that they are benefiting from the disorder on the streets.

It was difficult to provide security for the elections, because the gangs played dirty. But we were committed to the UN mandate and did not fall into the trap of applying force indiscriminately, as some wished. The problem was that security in Haiti had been "citesoleilized." In other words, the whole country was being treated as if it was as dysfunctional as Cité Soleil. That was a mistake, in my view.

To understand the security problems we faced, you need some accurate information on Cité Soleil. We suffered the vast majority of our losses there, and over 90 percent of MINUSTAH's efforts focused on that neighbourhood.

During my time as AFC, four of the five deaths of MINUSTAH soldiers occurred there. I bade farewell to all five as their commander, sending their coffins back to their homeland. They had only come to help the country.

Cité Soleil is bounded by Route #1 on the east, the sea on the west, and the Bois Neuf and Drouillard neighbourhoods in the north and south respectively. It is ironic that this area has the highest levels of violence in Haiti, even though it is right next to Shodecosa, the country's leading industrial park.

Cité Soleil is no more than 5 km long from north to south; it is 4 km at its widest point. It is home to about 300,000 Haitians. The land is marshy, and there is neither electricity or potable water.

During my posting, the absence of the state there was complete. The strongest criminal gangs fought constantly among themselves for turf. They had carved Cité Soleil into zones, which were controlled by leaders such as Amaral (in Bellecou), Evans Ti Couteau (in Boston), Ti Blanc (in Simon), Alain Cadet ("Pinochet") (in Drouillard), and Belony (in Bois Neuf).

Besides an utter lack of any state presence, this area suffers from severe unemployment. There is nothing to help people improve their lives. Poverty and lawlessness have coexisted there for many years.

No one thinks that the *favelas* in Rio de Janeiro are an accurate indication of security in Brazil as a whole. Yet Cité Soleil is assumed to represent the security level of Haiti as a whole.

The gangs there had light weapons of various calibres, ranging from .38 and 9 mm guns to AK47s, Galils, M4s, and FALs. They also had plenty of ammunition. This could be explained largely by the lack of border controls.

The gangs' main activity was kidnapping. Their targets lived mainly in Bel Air and Pétionville, the capital's middle- and upper-class neighbourhoods. The criminals would kidnap people while they were moving on the roads and transport them to Cité Soleil for hiding. Over 90 percent of the victims were Haitian, which is why ransoms were demanded in cash. These crimes typically took place between 8 a.m. and 10 a.m., while our forces and presumably the PNH officers were being deployed.

Some kidnapping victims were poor. This may seem strange, but remember that more than one million Haitians are living in the United States and Canada and send money back to their families. It was they who would pay the ransom.

Most of Cité Soleil's buildings are of one or two storeys and are typical shanty dwellings, in this case made from bricks made by hand by the local people from a concrete-like material. The walls are bullet riddled, mainly as a result of gang wars. Most of the streets are dead ends and are too narrow for vehicles. Some streets are broad enough for tap-taps to operate.

Photo 14. Houses with bullet holes in Cité Soleil

When fighting our troops, the gangs would block the streets with containers and abandoned vehicles. Or they would flood a street with water so that when a military vehicle came along, it would bog down and become an easy target. More than once when this happened, we had to come to the rescue.

The streets were nearly always covered in garbage, in vast amounts that prevented the passage of vehicles. What vehicles were moving were always full of people traveling from place to place or going to market to sell their wares.

On many roofs the gangs posted permanent sentries, armed with mobile phones and long-range guns, ready to inform their leaders of our presence and to fire at our patrols (Photo 14).

Within Cité Soleil, besides several NGOs, there were a number of religious organizations running schools and clinics. It was no coincidence that the houses where we had detected the presence of gang leaders were next to an NGO or a clinic.

In Port-au-Prince, streets are named in a peculiar way. The main street is given a name; the ones running perpendicular to it are called that name, plus a number. So if Soleil is the main street in the locality, then the streets are called Soleil 1, 2, and so on.

Soleil 9 is one of the principal streets of Cité Soleil. There is a building on it adjoining a derelict church on the main plaza. That is where we set up CP16, about 1000 m from Route #1. It was manned by a section of Jordanian soldiers. Farther north on that same street, about 1500 m away, we set up CP21 and CP23 with two armoured vehicles, also manned by Jordanian personnel. After June 2006 we began rotating the Jordanians with Brazilian and Chilean soldiers, among others.

On the perimeter of this zone, Route #1 crossed the city from north to south. Along it we had placed CP15 (beside a water tower) and CP2, both with Jordanian personnel. With two or three APC vehicles, they carried out patrols and monitored the local traffic.

CP13 was established in the south beside the industrial zone of Shodecosa. It was manned by Peruvians, who kept a close eye on the southern exit from this route. Inside Cité Soleil, CP12 was set up for the same purpose. It was controlled by the Peruvians as well. That is where I would be given a warm reception by Amaral's gang.

The most dangerous zones were undoubtedly CP15, CP16 and CP2. Those were the checkpoints where we suffered the most casualties. To protect our soldiers, we deployed defences and containers.

As of August 2006, there had been no Haitian police presence or any action on the part of the Haitian state for the benefit of these people, despite the fact that within Cité Soleil a police station had been razed, like the one outside the zone on Route #1.

While I was on the mission, we were unable to convince the Haitian authorities to reopen at least one police station in Cité Soleil, even though several times I had personally asked Préval to do so.

There were a number of schools in Cité Soleil, the main one being opposite CP16. Though it was in good condition, we did not succeed in having it reopened. That is regrettable — it would have restored some peace and normalcy to the local people. By the time I left Haiti, the Haitian authorities still had not reopened it.

The gangs held a huge cache of weapons and munitions. Someone was financing their weaponry, and I sensed that drugs were at the centre. Several investigations had found that Haiti was a transshipment point for American-bound drugs. The volume of cocaine in transit had been rising sharply in recent years, with about 10 percent of what came in staying in place for local consumption.

In July 2006 I invited the DEA's Haiti office chief to a meeting at my office. He told me that 8 percent of the drugs entering his country[5] were arriving from Haiti, and he was emphatic that the gangs were involved in the trade, which paid each gang rifleman US$100 for his efforts on a given run.

When I asked him whether 8 percent of his department's interest was in Haiti, he answered with silence.

I think that most of the residents of Cité Soleil are poor but decent people. Some of them may have relatives in the gangs, which use women and children as human shields when firing on our soldiers, which drastically reduces our soldiers' scope for manoeuvre.

Whenever the authorities asked me to take action against the gangs, I would ask them how many dead women and children would be acceptable to them. Eventually they stopped asking.

As AFC, I never hesitated to use force, since it was part of our UN mandate. I used it in various operations, some of which even led to casualties among our personnel. But I always remembered that acting rashly (as some wanted us to) would not further the election process. And if that process failed, it would mean we had failed in our mandate.

So Generals Bacellar and Elito never resorted to the rash use of force, however strong the temptation, and neither did I.

During our Tuesday meetings, people in the transitional government used to urge MINUSTAH — especially Ambassador Valdés, General Bacellar, and on several occasions me — to use more force against the gangs. I would keep telling them that it wasn't our presence that was required — it was theirs. This would be met with polite replies but no action.

I was aware of the dangers and difficulties the transitional government would face when re-establishing a presence in Cité Soleil. I was willing to share that risk. But I also believed that initiatives such as reopening schools would improve the atmosphere, and the government wasn't taking them.

The absence of courts and a functioning police service worked against us. Criminals were walking the streets with impunity, with no worries about being arrested.

The city's business community continued to call for harsh action from us. At several meetings with MINUSTAH, they made it clear just how dissatisfied they were with our military force's behaviour, which they blamed for the lack of safety. Obviously, they kept quiet about the government's role.

I began to sense something fishy going on between them and the politicians. I began to wonder whether they even *wanted* a political process that would put the country back on track.

One day, one of the mission's senior people rang me and asked me to call one of Haiti's top businessmen, who wanted to talk to me.

I rang him out of curiosity, and he told me he wanted to meet me to discuss security in Cité Soleil. He then asked me to write down his office address and to wait there. I politely asked him whether he had a paper and pencil. When he said he did, I gave him my address and said, "Whenever you wish to speak to me, come and see me at my office." That ended the conversation.

Right after that I went to see the person who had asked me to call the businessman. I told him in no uncertain terms that I would not accept another situation like this: I was commander of the military force, and his suggestion had shown a lack of respect for my position.

In the 1990s, Aristide had dissolved the Haitian Army (FAd'H) and handed some of its weapons over to civilians. But the Cité Soleil gangs and those in other parts of the country had nothing to do with FAd'H's former soldiers, and the weapons they used were much more modern than the army ever had.

Some experts told me that in Haiti there were more than 200,000 weapons in civilian hands. Prior to my MINUSTAH posting, I had been Chile's national authority on weapons control. From that experience I had learned there is no foolproof way to determine how many illegal weapons there are in a country. So I was somewhat skeptical of that figure. That said, I was well aware that weapons and ammunition were readily available to the gangs.

There is no question that the easy availability of guns was a problem in Haiti, one that was worsened by the country's loose borders as well as by drugs. This created a complex situation as far as controlling violence was concerned. MINUSTAH's disarmament programs had little effect. The Disarmament, Demobilization and Reintegration Program (DDR, as it is known in UN jargon) carried out its tasks through the Haitian National Disarmament Commission.

The number of weapons gathered up by DDR was insignificant, though such programs had worked on other UN missions and in other circumstances. Such programs worked when two or more irregular armies were laying down their weapons in exchange for political concessions, educational and social supports, and so on. This was the model most often used in El Salvador, Guatemala, Africa, and other parts of the world.

In Haiti, the problem was that armed gangs were profiting from violence. In that situation, implementing a disarmament program was going to be more complex. In two years, fewer than 150 weapons were handed over to us voluntarily, and many of those were in extremely poor condition.

The underlying issue was that given the lack of safety on the streets and the absence of a police force, criminals who handed over their weapons were likely to be attacked by other criminals. They had no incentives to give up their weapons and plenty of incentives to keep them.

According to the authorities, PNH officers were themselves involved in criminal activities. This, too, made it highly unlikely that Haitians who were not linked to any crimes but who had weapons would surrender guns that ensured their safety. I surmised from all this that the DDR program was doomed to failure as presently designed.

As an example of how hard it was to implement this program, the PNH itself sometimes arrested those who took part in it. The participants had been given identification, but the police were ignoring this and were treating them like criminals.

In fact, the gangs often murdered those who took part in this program, in order to sow terror among the population. And of course, the judicial system's inefficiency did not help disarmament efforts. Those enrolled in the program were sometimes locked up with common criminals. Other times, the police did not know what to do with those alleged to have taken part in crimes, because their criminal records could not be confirmed. We encountered one problem after another.

Add to all this, that DDR programs are effective only when the person surrendering his weapons receives something in return, such as a job or training. So, while these programs were implemented, because the country was so poor, they proved inefficient. General Heleno put it this way:

> In the case of Haiti, there are no formal groups in conflict or peace agreements.
>
> Most weapons are owned by members of various groups, living in shanty towns, and in other inaccessible, densely inhabited, extremely poor areas. Unemployment continues to prevent marginalized sectors from being reincorporated into society.
>
> Under these circumstances, compulsory disarmament requires an effective intelligence system, without which we run the risk of causing severe damage to innocent civilians.[6]

A few months after I returned to Chile, a new initiative was launched to gather up weapons and reintegrate criminals into society. I think it will be a long time before this new program achieves its goals.

My experience has been that DDR programs are well intentioned but ineffective. Criminals never lay down their arms. I think it would be more effective to try other solutions, such as tougher penalties for gun crimes.

In Cité Soleil, in view of the total absence of the state during the time I was there, non-governmental organizations (NGOs) such as the International Red Cross, Doctors Without Borders and Doctors of the World worked on behalf of the neediest people. As soon as I took up my post, I met with some of them to offer my cooperation.

During the twelve months I was on the mission, I never had a problem with the NGOs, though a couple of difficult situations did arise. I was sure they were really trying to help people, the same as our soldiers were, and that all we had to do was to understand everyone's role so that we could coexist in that difficult environment. I'm sure that if nothing else, we learned to communicate well.

I realized from the outset that it would sometimes be difficult to work with NGOs. They tend to prize their independence, whereas in the military we tend to prize coordination among all players. That coordination is difficult to achieve with these groups, though in the end, I believe we succeeded.

My goal was to establish trust and good communication with them. I invited them to my office to establish points of mutual cooperation so that I could instruct our senior officers on how to handle them.

In Cité Soleil the NGOs undertook 62 projects between 2005 and August 2006. They involved themselves in preventative medicine, road resurfacing, environmental management, the revamping of public infrastructure, and other activities. And they trained Haitian men and women in these things.

MINUSTAH for its part had, since 2004, launched 228 quick action projects (QIPs) at a cost of almost US$2,500,000. Some of these had been in Cité Soleil.

I realized soon enough that many offers of financial aid from certain countries never materialized. The press would report that this help was coming, and then it did not. Bureaucratic red tape was certainly one reason, but reasons were of little use to the Haitian people, who needed all the help they could get.

Looking back, I can see that the battalions themselves would have been much more effective if they had had resources to undertake their own development projects.

For those of us who were constantly visiting Cité Soleil, it was difficult to see the impact of the NGOs' projects. I often discussed this with our MINUSTAH soldiers. They felt, the same as I did, that the only effective force there was our troops, who besides providing security undertook several initiatives to support the community. Unfortunately, these were barely publicized.

We made an effort to win over the people by helping them in their daily lives. When the Brazilian battalion moved into Cité Soleil, replacing the Jordanians, they quickly developed a number of initiatives to benefit that community. Among other things, they paved a section of Soleil 9, fixed up the main square, and removed the rubbish. They did this with their own resources and, more important, with the people of Cité Soleil.

The Brazilian unit also submitted a project to install an electricity generator in the centre of the district, but this initiative got lost in the mission's bureaucracy.

While carrying out these public works, we deployed on the streets, since we knew that by engaging with the people, we would be weakening the gangs, who might start shooting at any time.

One of these projects involved securing a school in the middle of that dangerous area. At this school were uniformed students who were well fed and well behaved. We hoped this would serve as an example of a well-run school.

Photo 15. Visit to school in Cité Soleil with Rafael Cavada

At the school about 500 young people and several mothers attended job training courses, during which they were taught sewing and design. The school was run by the Mothers of Perpetual Succor — small, thin, fragile nuns. Some of them, such as Mother Santina and Sister Dulcimar, were so loving toward these young people that I was convinced I was witnessing a true miracle.

The first time I visited them was with General Bacellar, who brought them his own radiocassette player, which he had promised them as a classroom aid.

With Chilean journalist Rafael Cavada, we visited them in February 2006. Cavada showed them accurately in a program he prepared for Chilean television (Photo 15).

This school was an oasis of peace in the midst of the violence and, at the same time, a ray of hope and concrete assistance for those living in extreme poverty, especially the women and children.

The problems run deep in Cité Soleil. The missions before ours achieved little there — something that can be explained by the lack of specific programs to help people. Political repression was not the main problem.

The gangs had taken stock of the situation and established a sort of liaison with certain sectors. This sometimes had temporary benefits for Haitians, though in the long run, the gangs could only be a blight on the country. On top of this, the gangs were exploiting the situation by portraying themselves to the international community as victims, which of course they were — but not of MINUSTAH. They were victims of their own society, which had opened to them the path of violence.

During the early days of his presidency, Préval attempted to open a dialogue with the gangs, in the hope of hammering out a peaceful solution so that they would stop abducting and murdering other Haitians and firing on the Blue Helmets. He was right to try this, though perhaps it took him longer than it should have. Meanwhile, the gangs kept shooting at us, and all we could do was try to neutralize them while the talks continued.

The way I saw it, if Préval's government failed to launch a strong aid program, the country's overall security would deteriorate. And that program would have to be linked to stiffer measures against violence in general, and not only through police on the street. As was the case with MINUSTAH, his government will be judged largely by what it achieves with security.

If all possibilities for dialogue are exhausted, sooner rather than later it will make sense to take control of Cité Soleil, following appropriate guidelines. After that, police should be installed to take permanent control of the area, and an effective aid program should be launched for the residents.

The country badly needs a functioning legal system capable of ensuring effective justice that puts criminals where they belong: in secure and appropriately humane prisons.

Haitians should be provided with training, education, and jobs. At the same time, the authorities should take the bull by the horns and establish a rule of law that actually works. They should provide an opportunity for their own people to improve their lives, and they should do this in coordination with MINUSTAH and the rest of the international community.

Notes

1 4ième Recensement Général de la Population et de L'Habitat, Bureau du Recensement, mars 2005, Haiti.

2 UNDP, "Human Development Indicators, Country Fact Sheet." http://www.UNDP.org.

3 CIA, "The World Factbook – Haiti." https://www.cia.gov/.

4 ICG, "A New Chance for Haiti?" Latin America/Caribbean Report no. 10 (Brussels and Port-au-Prince: ICG) November 18, 2004: 7. http://crisisgroup.org/home/.

5 ICG, "Spoiling Security in Haiti," Latin American/Caribbean Report no. 13 (Brussels and Port-au-Prince: ICG), May 31, 2005, 4.

6 Augusto Heleno, "El Componente Militar de la Misión de las Naciones Unidas para la Estabilización de Haití," *Military Review*, January–February 2007: 9.

CHAPTER TEN

The Haitian National Police and the Judicial System

THE HAITIAN POLICE force is another player in this story and sometimes part of the problem rather than the solution.

The PNH, a fairly new organization, started out well under the wing of the international community. On several occasions we tried to organize joint operations. Officers from the PNH and UNPol would pledge to deploy their forces together; then, usually, the PNH officers would fail to show at their assigned places.

If this seems strange, it shouldn't, as General Heleno's experience with this police force demonstrates:

> From the outset, I felt that the PNH authorities failed to submit to the "modus operandi" of the police forces, in other words, they continued acting autonomously.
>
> They hoped for material support from us and when forceful action was required, normally during the initial planning, it was usually poorly executed.[1]

Government officials, the mission chief, senior officers, UNPol officers from MINUSTAH, the Senior National Police Council (CSPN), and I would meet every week at the Primature, the prime minister's house. These meetings, led by the prime minister himself, were attended by various authorities, who

Photo 16. PNH Director General Mario Andressol

normally included Ambassador Valdés, who sometimes had to defend MINUSTAH from accusations that it was soft on crime. More than once I saw the ambassador gently but firmly defend our performance, which made me proud to be his fellow countryman.

These meetings were also attended by Mario Andressol, the PNH Director General (Photo 16), who feigned deafness whenever the PNH was discussed. I used to joke with General Bacellar about who actually understood what PNH Chief Mario Andressol was saying, since when he did speak, he mumbled.

Most of these meetings were conducted in French and dealt with security, but related subjects were also discussed, such as the PNH's uniforms and pensions. I often wondered what I was doing there.

When the Haitian army was dismantled in 1994 during Aristide's presidency, Andressol, a former infantry captain, fled the country to save his skin. He lived in Brooklyn until 2005, when the transitional government offered him the post of PNH Director General.

Andressol struck me as a serious and honest man who genuinely wanted to do things properly. But he sometimes seemed overwhelmed by the circumstances, which exceeded his capabilities and the troops available to him.

During Aristide's second administration, Andressol, Luc Eucher, and Robert (Bob) Manuel worked hard to modernize the PNH. They were soon forced to abandon their posts — indeed, the country — after receiving death threats, many of them from within the PNH itself.

I am sure that Andressol is in for a rough ride, yet I am moderately optimistic that the PNH's situation will improve.

Not until January 2006 were we able to meet with Andressol and UNPol to coordinate operations. This happened due to pressure from the military officers on the provisional authorities and with the support of the UNPol commissioner Richard Graham Muir and subsequently President Préval himself.

The current PNH has a dreadful image: it is poorly structured, equipped, and trained. According to its own sources, about one-third of its policemen are themselves involved in crime, and as a result the population does not trust them.

On August 29, 2005, in the capital, an operation led by PNH Department Director Carlo Lochard during a football game in Martissant led to 16 deaths.

The preliminary investigation revealed errors and serious omissions on the part of the PNH. As a result, those responsible for the operation were arrested, though they were later released.

General Heleno described the problem accurately:

> The breakdown in communication between the mission and the PNH reached its climax in February 2005 on the anniversary of the fall of Aristide, when PNH units shot at a demonstration accompanied by Brazilian troops and reporters from the local and international press.
>
> In addition to causing the deaths of a number of demonstrators, this situation endangered the troops in the PNH's line of fire.
>
> In addition to this, although the PNH leaders insisted that the demonstrators were armed, declarations by both the media and MINUSTAH left no doubt that the PNH had deliberately attacked a peaceful march.[2]

This was exacerbated by the politicians' alleged links with sectors of the police and even with the gangs, whose names were familiar to contingents throughout the country.

Andressol's security detail was provided by French gendarmes, Chilean *carabineros* and UNPol personnel, not his own people. We had also assigned MINUSTAH security personnel to his house to prevent attacks on him and his family.

One of the core problems Andressol faced was how many police to recruit and where to post them. At the time of my posting, the PNH had about 5,800 officers to serve a population of 8.5 million. That was one officer for every 1,400 people. Even in the Port-au-Prince, where security was shakiest, there was little police presence (Photo 17).

In New York, there is one police officer for every 200 people. To achieve New York's standard, at least 25,000 police would have had to be added to the force to ensure the population's safety.

Photo 17. Haiti police at a CP

The first campaign to recruit new police attracted 33,636 applicants. Of these, 578 were chosen, including 27 women.

The PNH presence in the cities was minimal. The situation at the border was even worse. To guard the country's 1,271 km of coast, the PNH had two 40-foot boats and three 30-foot boats in Port-au-Prince. MINUSTAH provided them with 6,000 gallons of fuel per month. For the northern zone, they had one 40-foot boat and three 32-foot boats in Cap Haïtien, which ran on fuel provided by the U.S. Embassy.

It goes without saying that these boat patrols had an extremely limited radius of action. In the 12 months I was there, they would sometimes arrest illegal immigrants, but they never found any weapons or drugs, though it was common knowledge that everything was transported by sea or air.

As I have noted, Cité Soleil was on the coast, yet that sector was not covered by a sea patrol. According to our studies and analyses, most weapons, drugs and ammunition were probably being imported through that part of the coast, or else by light plane. More than once we found the wreckage of light aircraft near a makeshift runway. At least one of these planes had been registered in Venezuela. The relentless gunfire faced by MINUSTAH forces made it clear that the gangs had basically unlimited weapons and ammunition, which was entering the country freely.

It was rumoured that in the Port Salut area in the south and near Port-de-Paix in the northeast, you could hear the sound of light aircraft at night. Our pilots were telling me they were encountering airplanes during their flights over the country.

Haiti was being used by gangs as a drug transshipment point for North America. I often suggested that since the Americans and Canadians did not have troops on the mission, they could at least provide information on planes, boats and movement in general along the country's borders. Nothing ever came of this, which is hard to understand, since these countries are the ones most affected by the drug trade.

To make matters worse, the Haitians had no helicopters or planes, and the mission's aircraft had been earmarked for other purposes.

One day I went to the office of a middle-aged man who identified himself as a former Haitian Army officer. He was very well dressed and formal, and when he introduced himself he saluted, which moved me. He then asked me to have MINUSTAH repair an old UH helicopter that had belonged to the Haitian Army. I had no idea the helicopter existed, but I promised to see what could be done. I warned him, though, that it would be difficult to help, since the technicians we had were for our own equipment.

After inspecting the helicopter, our technicians told me it had not been flown for many years and that only an authorized company could certify it as flightworthy again. Also, we did not have the equipment to repair it. I never saw the ex-officer again.

The border with the Dominican Republic is 360 km long and only nominally controlled. It is physically easy to cross, which made it difficult for us to control who entered and left the country. The border control posts included Ouanaminthe in the north, Balladeer and Malpasse in the centre (including the capital), and Anse-a-Pitre in the southern-central region. These were "virtual" posts, barely manned at all. Everyone knew that the border was a sieve for smuggled goods.

MINUSTAH did not have sufficient forces to control the border effectively in addition to all its other security tasks in the cities and towns. I suggested to President Préval, when he asked for assistance, that he post his own police at the border, with MINUSTAH providing back-up where necessary.

On several occasions when I flew over the border, I would ask the helicopter pilot to fly low so that I could study the two countries side by side. Every time, I noticed just how invisible the border was. There were three or four authorized border crossings, but very few people used them.

The Dominican Republic is much more developed than Haiti, although it too lacks efficient border controls. Whatever the long-run solution, it will have to involve the Dominican Republic. Haiti is not solely to blame.

MINUSTAH had developed various plans to support the PNH, such as police training. When UNPol and the PNH planned a joint operation, the PNH officers rarely turned up at the meeting point. What weapons they brought with them often lacked ammunition. It probably would have been more useful to deploy UNPol police on the ground with the PNH — something that was done only toward the end of my mission.

Most of the police weapons were M14s from the Korean War or the Vietnam War. The officers had few bulletproof vests, let alone proper helmets. Eventually, the U.S. government donated 1,623 weapons. The PNH officers looked almost heroic with their primitive gear.

In the capital you sometimes saw PNH officers trying to direct the chaotic traffic. In Cité Soleil they were nowhere to be seen. Andressol told me how hard it was to find police who were willing to be sent to that zone. The gangs used to threaten their families to dissuade them from going there.

The police stations were in a deplorable state. Nearly all of them had been destroyed. In Cité Soleil they had been burned down. We repeatedly asked President Préval to have them reopened to protect our contingent, but to no avail.

In July 2006 I was in my office when the JOC Operations Officer on duty told me there was a serious problem in Martissant, in the hills south of the city. According to early reports, civilians had been killed early that morning. The first thing I told myself was that Préval's truce had been broken.

I informed General Elito, suggesting that one of us go to the scene of the tragedy. The other should stay in contact with Ambassador Mulet, since the situation would soon enough be noticed by the national and international press, with all the problems that entailed.

He decided that I should go to Martissant, that we should keep in touch by telephone or radio, and that it was vital to determine the scope of the problem in order to advise Ambassador Mulet and take the necessary measures.

Before leaving headquarters, I called Lisbeth Cullity at the Political Affairs Office and Thierry Faggart from the Human Rights Office, whom I asked to accompany me. At 8:30 a.m. I left to see what was happening on the ground, since the information was still patchy.

Martissant is a densely inhabited district with narrow streets and flimsy houses. This zone was being controled by a Sri Lankan company, deployed from Jacmel. It was too small to cover the entire zone. Its actions were limited to sporadic patrols.

On my arrival, I was met by the Sri Lankan troops, who described the situation. While I clambered up the hill through the narrow lanes, I saw rivulets of blood, suggesting that there were dead bodies inside or in the courtyards of these houses (Photo 18).

Photo 18. Inspecting Martissant on the day of the tragedy

Early that morning, 22 people had been brutally murdered, including three children between the ages of 8 and 12. These crimes had been perpetrated by two armed gangs, the Ti Machet army ("Lamè Ti Machet" in Creole), led by Roudy Kernisan, and "Lamè Ti Bwa," led by "Apousan."

The point of this massacre had been to drive out the gang that controlled the area, and also to destabilize Préval, who just two days earlier had persuaded the Senate to formally approve Andressol's appointment as PNH chief. Andressol had been at that post since the days of the transitional government. One of his main tasks, besides strengthening the police force, would be to eliminate those corrupt officers who had generated so much tension both within and outside the PNH.

Yet despite the gravity of the situation, the only PNH officer in the area was a commissioner I had brought along in my own car because I happened to bump into him while leaving my office. Cité Soleil attracts plenty of attention, but unless the structural problems that create violence in Haiti are solved, especially in the capital, Martissant is going to become much more dangerous than Cité Soleil.

It took me a while to accept that in practice, Haiti has no reliable police force. If that is what *I* saw as a foreigner, imagine how utterly defenceless the

Haitians themselves must feel. No wonder they are so reluctant to hand over their weapons. But to be fair to the PNH, they are not the country's only problem, nor are they the only source of its problems.

When people ask me how long MINUSTAH should stay in Haiti, I always tell them, "Until the Haitians can provide their own security." Even in the most optimistic scenario, it will be at least five years before Haiti has a police force strong enough to do so.

I often talked to Préval's advisers about organizing a military force along the lines of the French or Spanish *gendarmes*. Then the police could handle certain tasks while the second force controlled the borders and dealt with other problems. These advisers always replied that they did not want an army, that they had had terrible experiences with the last one. I replied that they should develop another type of force, one that would stay in the barracks. The Haitians will, of course, decide this for themselves.

Once the PNH became answerable to UNPol, the lack of operational coordination became a much thornier problem. Security forces in a particular zone absolutely *must* report to a single command. In Haiti they did not, which made the situation even more complicated. Also, during my time with the mission, the PNH was being trained by police from France, Spain, Canada and the United States (among other countries). One can only wonder whether this is creating a force with a single set of procedures—something that is essential to institutions of this type.

As far as training the new PNH is concerned, the police force of a single country should be used as a model. Chile's Ambassador to Haiti, Marcel Young, lobbied for an international police school in Haiti. That was an interesting idea, but the countries providing the training did not take it up.

In February 2006 an agreement was signed between Haiti's transitional government and the UN that gave MINUSTAH an enormous say in the new PNH's structure. Haitian nationalists frowned on this, seeing it as an infringement of their sovereignty. Because of the discontent generated by this measure, it was not implemented until after Préval came to power. In August 2006 a plan was drafted to increase the police force to 14,000 by 2011.

As early as July 2006 the PNH was increasing its presence on the streets. It still has a long way to go, and its path will not be easy. Whatever the criticisms that have been leveled at them, remember that more than 100 PNH officers have been killed since MINUSTAH began operations.

The judicial system has contributed to the problem of violence in Haiti by encouraging an atmosphere of injustice and lawlessness.

That system is based on antiquated guidelines, some dating from 1835, others hardly more recent. These need updating to reflect the country's present circumstances.

The various UN resolutions assigned MINUSTAH an advisory, supportive role in terms of helping the Haitian authorities carry out legal reforms. This work is ongoing, though little has been achieved so far. For example, senior officers always knew the locations of gang leaders like Amaral and Evans, but arrest warrants were never issued for them.

Worse still, in an attempt to prevent more violence, the government opened a dialogue with these people. During Préval's early days as president, gang leaders were taken to meetings with the authorities in state vehicles, while in the streets our troops continued to be shot at and kidnappings continued. This only heightened Haitians' lack of faith in the judicial system.

Impunity is the acknowledged, brutally accepted norm in Haiti, where the people do not trust their own institutions. Many associate state power with political corruption, pure and simple.

To make matters worse, when a list of candidates for Congress was drawn up, several military officers called to tell us that the list included people known to have taken part in violent acts, who had links with gangs in their areas or with drug trafficking.

During the electoral campaign, candidates had been arrested carrying weapons. Others had been caught with armed companions.

Equally serious was that the Haitians regarded judges as ineffective when it came to investigating crimes and handing out punishments. There was a widely held view that criminals were walking the streets who ought to be in prison and that people in prison were not being offered even minimal legal protections. This discredited the judicial system.

UN Resolution 1542 calls for aid to restore the rule of law in Haiti, including its penal system. Resolutions 1608 and 1702 emphasize MINUSTAH's role in supporting the police and the judicial system. But all those resoluations have had little positive effect.

Some studies suggest that the following should be done to reform the prisons themselves:

1. Deploy international officers to all Haitian prisons to teach national personnel standard procedures.
2. Establish a real budget for penal reform and ensure the commitment of all donors to this reform.
3. Reconstruct and redesign prisons to ensure prisoners' basic human rights.

The easy solution is to earmark aid for new prisons. But this ignores the fact that *the system itself* is what is not working. According to legal experts, the

Photo 19. Prison visit

legal system needs to be overhauled and funded adequately. Only then will it make sense to improve the penal system.

In Haiti, mass prison escapes are not uncommon. The principal reasons are badly trained guards and, of course, corruption. Also, Haitian prisons are dreadful places where prisoners live in subhuman, overcrowded conditions. And the guards are no better off than those they are guarding (Photo 19).

In the central prison in Port-au-Prince, the guards had fewer than fifteen rounds each for their antiquated weapons. During my time as AFC, the presence of the MINUSTAH military force was the only thing preventing mass escapes. A platoon of Jordanian and sometimes Peruvian soldiers watched the perimeter, which was just three blocks from the government buildings.

The day Préval came to power, 300 inmates in Port-au-Prince launched a rebellion, and troops had to surround the prison to prevent them from escaping. On May 20, 2006, troops prevented an escape from the prison at Fort Liberté. (Some did escape that day but were eventually caught and returned to custody.)

There were three times more prisoners than the facilities were built to hold. Toward the end of my mission, 100 petty offenders had to be released to make room for others charged with more serious offences.

In August 2006 about 3,000 prisoners in the Port-au-Prince facility were crowded into an area of 2,500 square metres — less than one square metre per person. All of them were kept in their cells around the clock. Seventeen of the country's 24 prisons were overcrowded and had minimal sanitation. Prisoners were being abused by their fellow inmates; some of the female prisoners were being raped by their guards. Yet 90 percent of these prisoners had yet to be tried — a violation of the basic notion of law.

The police precincts had their own jail cells, where conditions were just as bad, which only strengthened the general belief that Haitians had no effective legal rights.

As of December 2006, 300 prison officers had been taught prison management through a 320-hour course.

According to some who should know, the judicial system is plagued with corruption, political cronyism, and poorly trained judges. Also, staff shortages are chronic. The ICG has submitted excellent reports on policy and security. One of these states that "Haiti's legal system needs to be radically overhauled, which will only be achieved through external assistance." It goes on that the "lack of practice and knowledge" of lawyers and judges is "one of the most persistent problems."

These same experts note that many of those taking part in trials "lack any kind of education," a shortcoming that is especially obvious among justices of the peace, who handle over 80 percent of the cases outside the capital and who undertake the initial investigations of serious crimes. Reports have noted their "extremely poor training."

Because Haiti has no records, it is impossible to know whether the prisoner has committed crimes in the past. As a result, the judicial system has become "an enormous black hole." Also, public prosecutors usually misclassify cases on the basis of a penal code that has barely changed since the Napoleonic era.

According to the report, all of these problems have contributed to one of Haiti's most glaring problems: the high number of people imprisoned without being tried — something that is evident in nearly all the country's prisons, especially the National Penitentiary in Port-au-Prince, where 96 percent of inmates are awaiting trial. And as many as a hundred prisoners there may still be in jail *despite having completed their sentence* because there are no documents to indicate they have paid their debt to society.

In this atmosphere, the fact that judges spend months without being paid goes virtually unnoticed, but it is a factor that contributes to the extensive corruption in the legal community.

The ICG report also points out that the courts and the correctional facilities are both in "deplorable" condition.

All of these problems were aggravated by the civil disorder that broke out after the February 2004 coup, when prisons and courts were vandalized and sometimes destroyed. That was "the final blow to previously weakened institutions since between 1994 and 2000, the countries that provided economic assistance stopped contributing, fearing the lack of stability in Port-au-Prince."[3]

The judicial system's severe problems have made it even harder to reduce the country's violence.

Claudia Mojica—a good friend of mine, who worked in MINUSTAH's Political Affairs Department for several years, and who had been on several missions to the country—told me that the PNH had made some progress in the mid-1990s but had since fallen back.

The last link (or the first, depending on how you look at it) in the security chain should be education. But a quick look at the statistics from the country's last census shows that Haiti's education system is unlikely to improve security in the short term.

In March 2004, former Prime Minister Yvon Neptune was arrested for his alleged role in the violence that had fallen on the city of Saint Marc in February of the same year, during his administration. He was never properly tried, and despite pressure from the international community, he continued to be held under arrest.

Neptune began a hunger strike that almost caused his death. Even that failed to sensitize the transitional government, despite the efforts of Ambassador Valdés. This was a real headache for us, regardless of the ethical issues involved, since if anything happened to Neptune, the situation in the country would deteriorate. If a well-known figure like Neptune could have his rights trampled like this, imagine what ordinary Haitians faced.

He was taken to MINUSTAH's Argentine hospital on two occasions. Only after Préval took office was a solution found to this impasse. Neptune was eventually released and left for the United States.

There are signs that things are beginning to change. A UNSC resolution for Haiti, dated August 2006, called for 16 legal specialists to be sent to Haiti. By December of that year, three of them had arrived. MINUSTAH has a Justice Section, but it isn't large enough to have much impact.

As often happens in Haiti, "systems" and "structures" are adopted that are extremely efficient on paper and conceptually well designed and probably work well in other circumstances, but they are ineffective in the country's particular circumstances. Haiti needs a functioning legal system, but it is years away from having one. It would benefit from being treated like a post-conflict country—that is, from a more active approach by other nations.

Fair laws, an efficient police force, and a functioning judiciary will take a long time to achieve, but a start can be made. Education might well be one key. Another might be the fostering of a society in which citizens accept responsibility for their acts, no one is above the law, and citizens' duties are understood, just as their rights are guaranteed.

Notes

1 Augusto Heleno, "El Componente Militar de la Misión de las Naciones Unidas para la Estabilización de Haití," *Military Review*, January–February 2007: 10.

2 Ibid., 11.

3 Europa Press, "Haiti debe afrontar una reforma total de su sistema judicial para controlar la violencia en el pais." Noticias de América, Lukor.com. Available at http://www.lukor.com/not-mun/america/portada/07020302.htm.

CHAPTER ELEVEN

The Military Force in Action

WE BEGAN the mission with a 6,700-man force, which reached a maximum of 7,500 for the elections and ended with 7,200. In reality, we had only 6,400 in August 2006, since as I have pointed out, it is one thing to determine the number of contingents to be used and quite another for them to actually turn up at the zone where they will be used.

At the UN, the functions and missions for the military force are laid down in a document called the "Directive for the Force Commander," which is drawn up by the DPKO in New York. On the basis of this document, each mission commander draws up his own plan according to his own particular circumstances. In our case, this was known as the MINUSTAH Military Campaign Plan and was submitted to the DPKO for authorization.

General Heleno, the first commander of the mission, had drafted his own plan, which General Bacellar had subsequently modified to suit the new circumstances.

On the basis of this plan, the units deployed throughout the country drafted their own plans, which were submitted to MINUSTAH Headquarters for approval.

Nationwide, units were deployed according to operational needs. On the basis of conversations between the governments that were contributing troops and the DPKO in New York, the characteristics of the units and general zones where they would perform their functions were stipulated.

As I mentioned earlier, our HS was located in the MINUSTAH central building on John Brown Avenue, in what had once been the Hotel Christopher. Around 100 officers from nearly 22 countries worked there. Most of them were assigned to the mission for one year, though some were there for only six months, as in the case of the Americans and Canadians.

This building also housed most of the mission's offices and civil agencies; to these, a series of installations in the sector were added to house MINUSTAH personnel.

The military contingent was distributed throughout the country's major towns as follows:

Cap Haïtien: The Chilean battalion
Fort Liberté: A Spanish military company along with a Moroccan company (which would be replaced by the Uruguayan battalion in March 2006)
Gonaïves: An Argentine battalion (army and marines)
Jacmel: A Sri Lankan battalion
Les Cayes: An Uruguayan battalion
Hinche: A Nepalese battalion
Port-au-Prince: A Brazilian battalion
2 Jordanian battalions (but only 1 from mid-2006 onwards)
Chilean and Argentine Helicopter Units
Two Engineering companies (Brazil and Chile–Ecuador)
1 Guatemalan MP company
1 Philippine company
1 Bolivian company (as of September 2006)
1 Sri Lankan company
1 Nepalese battalion
1 Peruvian Special Forces company
Logistics personnel at the Logbase, near the airport

In the capital, one Brazilian battalion was deployed to the Bel Air zone and two Jordanian battalions to Cité Soleil and the north zone as far as Cabaret, while a Peruvian commando company was detailed to Shodecosa (an industrial port complex near Cité Soleil). A Sri Lankan company was assigned to Martissant and Killick at the south exit from the capital.

This zone would subsequently be reinforced by the transfer of an Uruguayan company from Fort Liberté, another Sri Lankan platoon, and a Chilean platoon from Cap Haïtien. In mid-September an infantry company arrived from Bolivia and joined the forces responsible for Cité Soleil.

To support the operations we had two Puma helicopters from Chile, three UH helicopters from the Chilean Air Force, and two 212 helicopters from the Argentine Air Force.

The UN had a Dash 7 plane with room for about 40 passengers as well as two Russian Mi-8 helicopters for MINUSTAH's use. However, none of these could be used for military operations; in fact, their crews were civilian.

We also had two construction engineers' companies in the capital, one Brazilian and the other combining Chileans and Ecuadorans.

The Philippine company protected the facilities and key personnel on the mission (VIPs), while a Guatemalan unit was used to back up the Military Police.

Through Resolution 1608 of the UN Security Council (February 14, 2006), as a result of the elections 750 soldiers were added to the mission force as a reinforcement and reserve unit. To meet those numbers a second Jordanian battalion was sent to the capital.

Under this same resolution it was decided to create an intermediate command in Port-au-Prince, known as the Sector HQ (SHQ), with a headquarters staff of 50 officers. This command would be responsible for planning and directing the units in the capital under a Jordanian general.

Within HQ we had the Provost Marshal's Office, which investigated delicate issues on the mission and also examined offences and possible crimes or accusations in which our personnel were involved. Its lawyers and military personnel were from the Guatemalan Military Police. The same office oversaw preventive campaigns relating to vehicles, alcohol and drug management, and compliance with the Rules of Engagement (ROEs).

In addition to its everyday activities, this unit investigated traffic accidents involving mission personnel, which were by no means uncommon in a country where the local people drove recklessly and pedestrians jaywalked as a matter of course.

Between 2004 and the time I completed my mission, 403 accidents or situations involving MINUSTAH personnel were investigated. The mission's Human Rights Office would receive complaints from the population, which would subsequently be examined. These complaints usually involved alleged mistreatment by the military force, arrests on suspicion, and delays in handing arrestees over to the PNH.

During the mission's first two years, a single case of sexual abuse involving military personnel was investigated, as well as 134 traffic accidents involving civilians, 39 cases of behaviour that failed to meet UN standards but did not constitute a crime, and two cases of suicide among our personnel. This work included 20 investigations of excessive use of force by the military contingent.

Besides investigating these situations and cooperating with those in charge of them, we consistently encouraged our troops to adhere to UN guidelines, in particular the ROEs. In this respect, MINUSTAH has been one of the least complicated UN missions ever—which may explain why, when General Mehta interviewed me for the job, he told me it was a peaceful mission. I presume he was referring to this aspect rather than to the gangs.

At all times, the mission's senior officers implemented a single, clear policy: truth, transparency, and strict compliance with guidelines.

For each investigation the head of the contingent and the UN in New York were informed. In the event of doubt, it was up to the Code of Conduct Officer, rather than the military, to immediately launch an inquiry. That was why our relationship with the NGOs in the capital was crucial—they had an ear close to the ground and carefully monitored situations where military personnel were involved. They also worked alongside MINUSTAH's Human Rights Office.

Given the size of the military force, personnel problems were few. The behaviour of MINUSTAH personnel was almost always appropriate. There were some disciplinary problems, but only a handful of these occurred in the units, and they were dealt with by the commanders themselves, who repatriated the ones involved according to the procedures of the contingent's home country.

In October we had to deal with an allegation that Jordanian troops had entered a factory near Cité Soleil called Larco. They were accused of mistreating some of the workers. Several MINUSTAH agencies launched an investigation. They found that while lives had not been threatened, the soldiers had used excessive force. As a result, we held meetings to adjust our procedures and had the soldiers themselves return to the factory to win back the people's trust.

On December 1, 2006, an American missionary named Phillip Zinder was kidnapped by a gang on Route #1 and Jordanian troops were accused of standing by while it happened. An investigation found that they had remained inside their vehicles during the abduction. Their only possible excuse was that they were being shot at from all sides whenever they left their vehicles.

Once the investigation was over, I concluded that the matter could definitely have been handled better. The Jordanians' inaction had generated an enormous amount of negative publicity in the United States, which forced us to remind our institutions how to act in difficult situations.

During the time I was on the mission, we repatriated 51 soldiers, 9 as a result of psychiatric problems, 2 for disciplinary reasons, and the rest for personal problems such as a death in the family.

Between September 2004 and August 2006, out of an average force of 7,200 men (25,000 soldiers in all, when rotations are taken into account), we had only 24 cases of dengue fever and malaria, and most of these men had con-

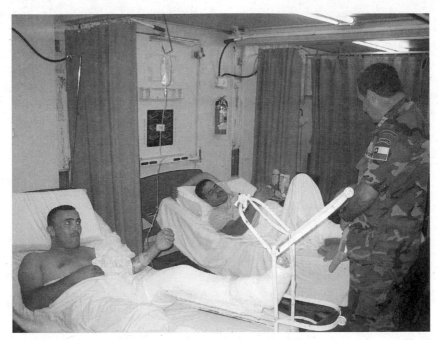

Photo 20. Visiting MINUSTAH soldiers at the Argentine Hospital

tracted these diseases on previous missions elsewhere. This speaks well of the quality of health care we were providing our troops.

Statistics on the medical care provided by the Argentine hospital during this period, and studies carried out at headquarters, indicate that 455 operations were performed. There were 3,336 dental consultations, 948 orthopedic operations, 2,613 X-rays, and 4,961 lab tests. A total of 994 soldiers were admitted to hospital, and 48 ultrasounds were performed. Also, 161 kinesiology treatments were provided, together with 7,481 medical consultations and 7 psychiatric consultations. Finally, 2,068 medical consultations were provided to the Notre Dame orphanage.

On the whole, our contingents' medical needs were well looked after, both at the unit level and at the Argentine hospital, where the personnel were highly professional. In major emergencies, the wounded or sick were transferred to the Dominican Republic. During my time on the mission, there were around 10 such cases (Photo 20).

I often spent time with the Jordanian soldiers in Cité Soleil. I noticed quickly that they were taking most of the mission's casualties. I sympathized with them—they were being shot at all day while doing their best to help a somewhat hostile population. The contingents outside the capital were having a very different experience of the country. They did not often hear gunfire, and when they did it was rarely aimed at them.

Indeed, when they weren't conducting operations — which they did well — the units outside Port-au-Prince lived a normal barracks life, playing sports and visiting nearby places, obviously with a security detail, which provided some semblance of normalcy. The Jordanian soldiers and the units stationed near Cité Soleil had a far more difficult time. A number of false accusations against the Jordanians did not improve relations with the Haitians in their zone.

One day, one of the leading embassies sent senior MINUSTAH officers a report stating that our troops were selling munitions to the gangs. Proof of this crime, submitted by the chargé d'affaires, was a carton of bullets with "UN" (in Cyrillic letters) printed in large letters on the lid. This carton had been handed over by a contact who worked for that embassy.

As soon as I had the background information, I launched an investigation. I suspected that something was fishy, since HQ was relentless about supervising the contingents' ammunition stocks.

The investigation concluded that the accusation was false. Indeed, we had solid proof that it was. The UN does not purchase ammunition — each country brings its own. There was no such thing as an ammunition carton with a UN logo. And in any case, no contingent in Haiti was using Russian-made ammunition.

There were other examples, such as claims that food was being exchanged for sex or money by certain contingents. A transparent investigation was always conducted; these claims were never borne out.

I do not mean that these things did not or could not happen; I am saying that whenever this information came to me, it always turned out to be false. There was a campaign designed to discredit our troops by accusing them of misconduct.

The gangs made good use of disinformation, accusing us of using indiscriminate force and of wounding and killing people every night. Their accusations were always proven false.

The NGOs in Cité Soleil sometimes accused our soldiers of firing at their offices. In one case, the Doctors Without Borders office in Cité Soleil had been shot at. The Military Police made a detailed investigation and proved that the calibre of the ammunition found was not used by the UN forces in the area and that no Blue Helmets had been nearby when the shots were fired. I delivered that information in person to the directors of this NGO, who were satisfied with what I told them.

To be fair, some of our soldiers were not as careful with their weapons as they should have been, but I do not think that all the gunfire these NGOs took came from our personnel, especially during December 2005 and January 2006.

These NGOs, especially Doctors Without Borders, are valuable organizations staffed by wonderful people. I acknowledge their enormous contributions as well as their bravery, even though some people are reluctant to defend them because they find it so difficult to coordinate their activities with the mission.

MINUSTAH had a 6,700-man force, in keeping with the UNSC. Actually, only 6,400 were available, which was fewer than we needed on the ground. From September onwards, we began bringing in units from other zones, such as a Chilean platoon from Cap Haïtien and two Uruguayan platoons from Les Cayes, as well as a Bolivian company, to reinforce our units in Port-au-Prince. We also transferred the Peruvian contingent from Jacmel to Shodecosa on the edge of Cité Soleil.

One must take into account all the personnel on leave, which averaged 250, and also subtract from the operating personnel those serving as guards and security personnel. In practice, nationwide we fielded fewer than 4,000 soldiers on any given day.

These personnel spent most of their time patrolling, escorting columns and authorities, protecting installations, supporting the elections and manning checkpoints, as well as conducting offensive actions when required.

When MINUSTAH began its mission, a Brazilian brigade was assigned to the capital in Bel Air, while a Jordanian battalion was stationed in the northern zone, in Hinche and Saint Marc. By late 2004 the senior officers realized there were not enough Brazilian soldiers to cover the entire capital and requested the reassignment of the Jordanian battalion, which was scheduled to arrive and begin work in the capital. That battalion arrived in November of that year.

When the mission began, Bel Air was a more challenging neighbourhood than Cité Soleil. In other words, the Jordanian troops were not initially assigned to the hardest part of the mission.

To get a firmer grip on the situation, the first step our contingents took was to work determinedly and professionally in the area of responsibility (AOR), all the while complying with the ROEs. The second step was to initiate programs to bring the troops closer to the civilian population.

According to our reports, in 2005 clean drinking water was delivered to 59,501 people. By August 2006 a further 37,867 people were receiving it. Also, the contingents' military doctors treated 16,368 Haitian civilians in 2006. In 2005 and 2006 our soldiers conducted 175 operations to clean the streets and canals of the towns and cities. Those same years the contingents delivered school supplies to 26,342 children.

Our military contingents were doing far more than simply guaranteeing the country's safety, but none of this was publicized. I asked MINUSTAH's

Press Office to highlight this outreach, but in vain — it seems the newspapers did not care.

As a whole, the troops were extremely professional. Some of them had taken part in previous missions with well-trained senior officers. The language issue was rather complicated since not all the officials had a good command of English, one of the official UN languages that we used for giving orders during emergencies. In any case, one of the necessary qualifications for the contingents' senior officers was that they be able to speak English.

None of the soldiers who came to Haiti spoke Creole. Some spoke French — for example, some of the UNPol police. Most of them spoke Spanish or Portuguese. The UN provided local people to interpret for us. The idea was that in every operating unit there would be a local person who spoke Creole.

Often on Route #1 or in Cité Soleil, when I tried to talk to the soldiers on the streets, they would reply in a language I did not understand. I would show them the rank on my collar, repeating "Deputy Force Commander, General" several times, which elicited no response other than a smile. I would ask them to call for an officer, and once he arrived, he would smile like the rest and usually say, "No English, no English."

The language problem was sometimes intractable. The troops were supposed to win the people's support. Unfortunately, not all the patrols took an interpreter with them, which meant they could not establish contact with the locals.

Some contingents had an extremely poor command of English, which was not even spoken by most of the officers. Thus I found that our own army's idea of promoting knowledge of English as a professional requirement had been the right one.

Some of the contingents had light weapons, which were usually suitable. I noticed that some wore fibre helmets while others had out-of-date steel models, as well as bulletproof vests made from thin cloth. It is unthinkable for soldiers to participate in missions like this without protective gear.

Some contingents had been poorly trained for urban operations, which was what they mostly had to conduct in Haiti. So they were required to take training in this.

After October the situation in Cité Soleil began to deteriorate; the gunfire our troops received increased steadily. Our mission in that sector was to patrol the streets and ensure that people could walk freely through the area. We were also responsible for keeping Route #1 clear and for ensuring overall security. To these ends we deployed fixed patrols at the CPs to check vehicles and prevent abductions.

Our personnel found the absence of even minimal government services perplexing. The government should have been doing humanitarian work and creating jobs or simply keeping the streets clean, cutting down the undergrowth, depositing rubbish in appropriate places, eliminating rats and ensuring hygiene. In short, engaging in activities that would have helped us separate honest citizens from criminals.

The Haitian provisional government was doing none of this, and the international community was doing very little. Our troops quite rightly complained, since they were doing a great deal in all these respects. Yet at all the meetings I attended with the transitional government, we would hear the complaint that we were failing to ensure people's safety.

At one of the meetings I attended at the Primature, the prime minister expressed annoyance that our soldiers were failing to protect the garbage trucks. I reminded him that this was not in the mandate and that we could guarantee their safety only to the extent of keeping the routes safe. It was unthinkable for me to assign a military patrol to each vehicle, which elicited a certain amount of ill feeling against me at the meeting.

I never heard the transitional government authorities acknowledge what we had done to benefit the country, or refer to the calm outside the capital, where everything was peaceful thanks to MINUSTAH.

We soldiers were on our own, assisted by a few NGOs. But this was not enough to neutralize the gangs, and our demands that the authorities do what was needed fell on deaf ears. In post-conflict situations such as these, the relevant players must understand that many things must be done to bring about security.

Nationwide, the security level maintained by MINUSTAH was always acceptable. But perceptions are often more important than reality. Unfortunately, Cité Soleil was regarded as a reflection of the whole country, and MINUSTAH was judged according to the situation in that one place.

One thing that depleted our contingents was guard duty. There were certain critical points — prisons, VIPs' homes, and so on — that should have been covered by the PNH or by the UNPol Police Unit (FPU). They were not, and this sort of work reduced our capacity to carry out our principal duties.

Another difficult area in the capital was Cité Militaire, where the Brazilians started doing what they had long been doing in Bel Air: steadily increasing their control and winning over the people. By August 2006 the only neighbourhoods not under their control were Simón and Pele, where the gang leader was Ti Blanc.

Plans were drawn up for these sectors, which were only partly carried out. Either the forces that had been assigned failed to turn up, or the military, UNPol, and the PNH failed to achieve coordination. In the case of UNPol, we kept asking for operations to be coordinated under a single command. Not until July 2006 did we finally begin to act together on the ground.

We were aware of the PNH's shortcomings and always tried to support them, to no avail. Problems were compounded by the government's failure to ensure a greater police presence on the streets. The PNH officers lacked the necessary quantity and quality of personnel, and they had already suffered more than 100 casualties, so they were not overly keen to involve themselves in operations.

In October 2006, gunfire in Cité Soleil and along Route #1 steadily increased, especially against our soldiers, who were practically besieged inside CP16. Some people asked us yet again why we were not taking firmer action against the gangs. I was beginning to understand, with General Bacellar, that we were virtually on our own as far as security was concerned and that we could not count on the PNH. I started to get a little worried, since the situation was highly complex.

One of the main challenges for me as a military commander was to stay focused on my actions and on the mission that had been entrusted to me and not to get carried away with particular events.

Around this time — from October 2005 to January 2006 — we were under heavy pressure to go into Cité Soleil and clean up the gangs. We knew that the civilians would take more casualties than the gangs if we did this. And civilian casualties could have a devastating impact on our mission, given that the international press was reporting solely on Cité Soleil.

In Port-au-Prince we received a visit from a top official of an important country, who attended a meeting with the highest authorities in the transitional government at the Primature, which I also attended. After discussing various issues, this official took me aside and asked, "General, when are you going into Cité Soleil?"

There was a sudden silence. Mustering all my resolve, I stuck my hand in my pocket and pulled out the casing of a 5.56 bullet I had picked up in Cité Soleil. I showed it to him and said, "Do you think this is how we're going to solve the problem of crime in this country? You're wrong — it's not bullets they need, it's work, education, health, respect for human rights, in short, other instruments. I'm by no means unwilling to use force — if it's used the right way, it may be necessary — but we will *not* solve this problem just with soldiers and bullets."

I added that his country could certainly help with intelligence and logistics to ensure that our mission achieved the goals laid out for us by the international community. My words were met with stony silence.

This tells you how frustrated so many of us were on the mission, as a result of some people's extreme simplification regarding what was wrong with Haiti and how to fix it. The solution seemed so *simple* from the outside: apply force and develop tourism.

In December, in the middle of the electoral process, the press exaggerated the danger on the streets and criticisms came in from all sides that the military contingents were doing nothing about it. A more nuanced reading of the situation was that there were people in Haiti who had no interest in holding elections or in bringing law and order back to the country.

Ambassador Valdés and I used to meet every day to analyze events. He was a man accustomed to pressure, and he stayed calm. Yet I could not help sensing a subtle sort of pressure to do more.

Our strategy was to control the zones, isolate Cité Soleil, and adhere to the rules of engagement. Often, at the endless meetings with MINUSTAH and with the DPKO authorities who flew in from New York to evaluate the mission, I would stress that the situation in the country would not be solved by bullets and that there were deeper problems, such as widespread poverty and a crippled state apparatus. I told them of my meeting with that top official who had visited the country.

Because the gangs used women and children as human shields, if we invaded Cité Soleil most of the casualties we inflicted would be women and children. No UN mission could survive a day like that.

I based my decision not to go into Cité Soleil or to arrest the gang leaders on the shortage of information on the gangs, which was partly due to the lack of a police force to provide it to us and partly due to the lack of such information within MINUSTAH itself. Operating without sufficient intelligence would cost many lives, not only of our contingent but also of innocent civilians.

Our soldiers would have liked nothing better than to attack the people who had shot at and killed our troops. But a commander must be cautious and wise in his decisions and not lose sight of the mission.

The UN authorities understood all of this, since I sent them daily briefings. They were hardly surprised by what I said, but their conversations revealed a certain understandable impatience with the security situation.

At various times, General Bacellar and I had told the UN of our apprehension about the situation and how the new command system—the one with the SHQ as an intermediate command—was not the best way to improve security. A bad decision to use force would damage the political process—something a general must recognize.

In December I talked to General Bacellar about the inadvisability of launching a military operation as we were being asked to do. I told him we should keep on doing what we were doing: gradually gaining ground and slowly achieving a more advantageous position so that when we had reliable information, we would be able to conduct surgical operations with our commandos.

In August 2006, a month before I returned to Chile, Ambassador Mulet and other MINUSTAH staff, including me, met with a top official of the

Préval government. He demanded that we use a firm hand in Cité Soleil. I heard him out, and then I told him, politely but firmly, that he was part of a legitimately established government because the military forces had acted calmly and responsibly when everyone had pressured us to act more harshly.

Regarding his insistence that I move troops into Cité Soleil and implement harsher measures, I told him told we knew where the criminals were but had avoided going in after them, since we knew that they hid behind innocent women and children. If we acted the way he was demanding now, we would cause enormous collateral damage. That would be bad for the elections and work counter to the UN mandate and, therefore, for Haiti's future.

I stressed that this was why we had drawn up an incrementalist strategy that would eventually enable us to achieve effective control of all the zones in Cité Soleil. And I reminded him that what he was asking me to do was precisely what certain businessmen had wanted us to do before the elections and that we had refused.

And I reminded him that the legal system was doing little to deal with these criminals and that the PNH was nowhere to be seen in the most dangerous areas, which is exactly where he was asking me to send in the military.

I explained that we had avoided the use of force so that President Préval would be able to assume his post without any unnecessary deaths. And I pointed out that during the first two months of his government, the president himself had asked us to abstain from force in Cité Soleil, since he had opened a dialogue with the gangs to persuade them to lay down their weapons.

I reminded him that on several occasions the gang leaders had been taken in the government's own limousines to the president's office to talk to the president while gang members had continued attacking our Blue Helmets.

I told him that I had seen no sign of the Haitian government in Cité Soleil— no sign that the government was doing anything to benefit that community— and that I was still awaiting arrest orders for the gang leaders.

I said that if he wanted to help us, he should get his own government to take actions that would encourage the local people to support us and to overcome their fear of the gangs. And that so far, the Préval government had done nothing to help the people of Cité Soleil and its surroundings. So it was hardly fair for him to ask us to take firm measures.

Ambassador Mulet, who was listening to the conversation, watched me as I talked, nodding away.

The meeting ended on a friendly note, but I needed to be clear and categorical about my position, since four members of our contingent had been killed and several wounded. Besides, I was sure I was right.

I later told President Préval himself that he should not only rely on our security measures to control the violence but that he should make a special effort to implement measures to support the population, especially in Cité Soleil, since I had been waiting for four months but seen no results.

MINUSTAH typically assigned mid-level officers to each area of responsibility (AOR). Those officers usually acted independently. Given the lack of reliable intelligence and the likelihood of collateral damage, we had decided not to launch mass operations but rather carefully targeted actions with Special Forces. These were known as "surgical operations" because of the accuracy required to avoid collateral damage.

This strategy worked well at the national level. We hardly ever received reports of confrontations outside the capital, since our military forces tended to do police work.

This cautious approach made it possible for us to fulfill the UN mandate. It also propped up the transitional government until elections could be held and paved the way for Préval to assume the presidency. I believe that had we given in to the temptation to use force, none of what now exists — a government, a Parliament and relative peace — would have been possible.

The UN had assigned our forces three missions: to support the transitional government; to protect human rights; and to support the electoral process. The mission's officers were quite clear that force would not solve the problem of acute poverty or the absence of a properly functioning state.

Later we realized that in order to design a strategy, we needed to analyze what was happening in the country as a whole separately from what was happening in the capital. We had the countryside under control as far as security was concerned. Unfortunately, that was no good to us in the face of domestic and international public opinion, which was judging us on the basis of what happened in Port-au-Prince. I often told Ambassador Valdés that any use of force in Cité Soleil would strongly affect the elections and the mandate itself. He always gave his total support of this view and was our strongest bulwark against the pressure we faced.

Convinced that we should adhere to the UN mandate over our natural inclination to use force, we deployed our soldiers in the capital so as to isolate Cité Soleil and keep Route #1 open to traffic and free of kidnappers. We achieved this in July 2006. We also set up checkpoints throughout the city to control traffic but above all to impede the transfer of kidnap victims to Cité Soleil. The idea was to gradually and safely increase our control of the zones run by the gangs.

Since the elections were a strategic objective for the mission, we made every effort to ensure that our operations did not negatively affect this process.

For a number of reasons, the elections were delayed — first until December, then until January, and finally until February 2006. This had a tremendous impact on security, since we had to put off any major actions so as not to affect the elections. Also, the elections would only pass the transparency test if the people of Cité Soleil took part in them.

Once again, the military forces were compelled to wait, which was a problem for General Bacellar and me, especially when we visited the military units, which wanted to move against the gangs. It took a lot of explaining. On February 7 the elections were finally held. I do not think they would have been possible had MINUSTAH's political and military officers not stuck to their earlier decisions. Key roles were played in all of this not only by Ambassador Valdés but also by General Elito, who had been in Haiti for less than a month.

Some hoped that once the elections were over, we would finally be able to move against the gangs, but I had my doubts. It turned out that I was right. After the elections, President-Elect Préval tried to arrange an escape hatch for the gangs. The government told us quite clearly that while he tried to do that we were not to conduct operations in Cité Soleil.

Our conversations at headquarters revolved around the fact that we had previously held back so that the elections could be held and that now we were holding back to support Préval's efforts to make a deal with the criminals. Despite our doubts, we had no choice but to support him.

The relative tranquility in the capital between February and May 2006 was due mainly to the fact that the gangs in Cité Soleil and elsewhere had supported the electoral process and had stopped behaving quite so violently toward us. This took a lot of explaining during our meetings with the officers of the various units.

We knew full well that the threat was still present, and I did not think that Préval's approach was going to work, since crime was extremely profitable and not all the gangs would be willing to abandon it.

Once Préval was elected, we moved on to another stage, the new government's "honeymoon" with the gangs. It would last until July 7, when the massacre in Martissant took place.

We had thrown our support behind the transitional government, we had ensured that elections were held, and now it was up to us to support Préval and the government in this attempt to make peace with the criminals. Once again, we were unable to take full control of the ganglands. The results of that speak for themselves.

Looking back, if we had chosen to heed those who urged us to take a firm hand, Préval would not be president today.

Political and electoral factors influenced military operations. So did our problems with our own military structure.

Operationally, our forces in the capital were controlled through Tasking Orders, meaning that we were answerable to the Sector Commander, General Al Husban, who was responsible for security in the capital. Despite this, after we had dealt with the operating documents, General Bacellar and I still found time to control the units on the ground.

General Al Husban often pointed out that while he was on the ground, he never saw anyone from the government or the police. He was fully aware that his own soldiers' presence alone would do nothing to solve the problems in the capital.

Most of the confrontations with the gangs, and most of our casualties, involved the two Jordanian contingents. This made the general reluctant to use units from his own country for offensive operations. I saw his point, but I explained that we had a mission to accomplish — the fact that the others were not pulling their weight was no excuse for us not to do so.

At one point, I ordered an offensive in one area of the capital, and the commander of the battalion in charge of carrying this out, who had suffered a number of casualties, gestured to me in front of his officers that Cité Soleil was a dangerous area.

I told him to have an officer translate my words to his officers. I then explained that we were in Haiti acting under Chapter VII of the UN charter and that it was precisely because of the danger that we were here, and that his soldiers were expected to act in accordance. I then asked him to tell me quite clearly if they thought otherwise.

As I told General Mehta, the problem was that the mission's structure was not allowing me to act like a commander. The problem was not the sector commander but rather the fact that the mission's structure did not allow us to deal with the situation at hand.

In December, I assumed the post of commander while General Bacellar was on leave. (I would take a few days in March to celebrate my birthday in Chile with my family.)

The security situation was worsening, especially in the capital, where according to the reports on our troops' ammunition consumption, we were firing as many as 5,000 rounds every 24 hours, mainly at night. This figure sometimes spiked to 10,000, especially in Cité Soleil and Cité Militaire.

At the various meetings I attended, it was often suggested that armed groups — such as the Dessalines Army, with 300 men — were operating in the north of the country. So we sent Argentine and Chilean patrols by helicopter and by land to look for any signs of these groups' existence, since they were being mentioned at every information meeting at HQ. No proof of their existence was ever found.

It intrigued me that the Intelligence Officer, an American, was always talking to me about the Dessalines Army. I kept telling him to prove to me it existed. Likewise, the ex-FAd'Hs never proved to be a problem for the military force. Clearly, our intelligence program was still in its infancy, which left us susceptible to rumours.

In the capital, by late 2005 kidnappings had risen to an average of 60 per month; by mid-December shootings were up to 250 per month. Eighty-five percent of those shot were Haitians, and 15 percent were foreigners (including Haitians visiting from abroad).

Ninety-three percent of the kidnappings in Haiti were taking place in Port-au-Prince and only 7 percent outside the city. This did not match the information the outside world was getting, according to which the entire country had been plunged into chaos. The only exception to this was Chile, where the people knew our contingent was helping the people — though they knew little about the more negative aspects of the mission.

According to our reports, kidnappings in the capital were happening in the following areas: 32 percent within the city itself, 18 percent near the airport, 14 percent in Delmas, 10 percent in Cité Militaire, 9 percent in Carrefour, 8.3 percent in Cité Soleil, 0.6 percent in Martissant, 0.6 percent in Fantamara, 6 percent in Routes des Dalles, 3 percent in Bel Air, 2 percent in Routes des Frères, and 2 percent in Centre Ville. Thirty-seven per cent of those abducted were male and 63 percent female; 43 percent were adults, 35 percent teenagers, and 22 percent children. Also, most of these crimes took place between 6 a.m. and 2 p.m. They rarely happened at night.

The initial ransom demands ranged between US$20,000 and US$300,000. By the time ransoms were actually paid, these figures had usually fallen to US$1,900 to US$30,000. The ransom was usually paid inside Cité Soleil.

These gangs tended to run in groups of no more than six. Some of them operated from the tap-taps and used small firearms. Coordinating their actions by mobile phone, they would approach a vehicle and threaten the driver until he opened the door. They would then seize their victim and carry him or her somewhere inside Cité Soleil.

The situation in December 2005 was extremely tense. General Bacellar attended several meetings with political sectors and the provisional government, who were pressuring us to get tougher in the capital. So we increased our presence on the ground. Meanwhile, we were spending hours in meetings with the government and the police authorities to discuss ways to control the violence. Yet we were unable to go directly to where we knew the problem was. All we could do was bring the fever down; we could not cure the illness.

We also deployed joint control posts of Blue Helmets with UNPol and the PNH, but it was difficult to get either to show up in the more dangerous areas. And the presence of Sector Command only lengthened the chain of command and control.

All of this changed in June 2006. We launched Operation Siege, which for the first time allowed us to have fixed patrols on Toussaint L'Ouverture Avenue, Industry Avenue and Route #1. From then on there was a sharp reduction in kidnappings.

When I was in Chile in October, our army's Commander-in-Chief, General Juan Emilio Cheyre, told me he planned to spend Christmas with our forces in Haiti. This was confirmed over the next few days, and on December 23, while I was AFC, he flew to Haiti in an army plane, accompanied by his wife, María Isabel Forestier.

His Christmas visit was important to our contingent. Still, visits like that have their ups and downs. We had to coordinate a great deal before his arrival, which was complicated because of all the new ideas we kept thinking up.

When he and his wife arrived in Port-au-Prince, their first stop was MINUS-TAH HQ, where the general was briefed on the situation and greeted the Chilean officers. After that, we headed for the Chilean units in Port-au-Prince.

The next day, we had lunch with Ambassador Young. In the afternoon, Major Díaz took María Isabel on a tour of the city, with all necessary protection.

At about 3 p.m. we set off for the Engineer's Unit. I told the CIC that the Peruvian military bishop was on a visit to Haiti and was with the Peruvians, who were located in the same direction we were heading. I thought it would be good for the two to meet. He liked the idea. My vehicle was not armour-plated, but never mind. We set off for Shodecosa, with "The Rat" carrying a Galil, ready to deal with any problems, since we were going to drive past Cité Soleil and Route #1.

About five minutes out from the Peruvian unit, I heard gunfire. The radio warned us that the situation was difficult and that one of our men had been wounded. I told the CIC we had better head to the Engineers' Unit instead. He immediately agreed. While we were driving there, the radio fed us more details. A Jordanian officer had been shot dead at CP15, 300 yards from the Peruvians.

This was not the time to tempt fate, and my presence as a commander was required, so I left the CIC at the Engineers' Unit, where our men had gathered in the courtyard. After greeting them, the CIC ordered them to remove their hats and caps and requested a minute's silence for the recently slain officer. After that, I donned my bulletproof vest and helmet and set off for the area where the Jordanian had died. The CIC continued his visit with the engineers. When I returned, I found him playing volleyball with the men.

At CP15 I learned what had happened. Captain Yousef Mubarak Alfith — a thirty-one-year-old father of three — and 10 or so soldiers had been handing out buckets of water to the local people. He sat down in an armoured vehicle

Photo 21. Captain Mubarak with the pail seconds away from his death

to rest, leaving the door open. As soon as he sat down, he was shot in the head (Photo 21).

The previous October I had attended the funeral of another Jordanian soldier, Abd Almharat Muhammed, who had also been shot at CP15.

When I arrived at the Jordanian unit, less than an hour after Mubarak's death, I found total desolation. Colonel Mohammed Al Sabayleh, the Jordanian commander, had gathered all the officers in a lounge full of pictures of the King of Jordan. On my arrival I offered them my condolences. Without a word, he showed me a projection on the wall of the photo that had been taken of the captain a few minutes before his death—the same one that is in this book. There were no words to express the sadness and anger we all felt about his death. After spending some time with them, I went to HQ to start the paperwork. Then to the Argentine hospital, where Mubarak's body had been taken, and then back to collect the CIC.

In the evening we had a Christmas dinner with the Engineering and Helicopter Units. The Chilean personnel at HQ were also there, and so were Ambassador Young and his wife. All things considered, it was a pleasant celebration, but clearly, I did not have as happy a night as I had wanted.

María Isabel had brought videos with greetings from the families of our mission personnel, which had been recorded by our army. These showed the wives and children of our personnel sending their best wishes to their fathers and husbands. There were several tears shed that night while we watched the videos. After that, General Cheyre handed out gifts for the staff. All of this was undoubtedly an important gesture of support from the military family to our soldiers.

The next day, we flew with General Cheyre to Cap Haïtien. It was a good visit and enabled the CIC to meet our people, to each of whom he gave a present. They played the previous night's video again, with similar results.

We returned to the capital, and General Cheyre continued on to the Dominican Republic. Most of the senior officers in the capital saw him off at the airport.

The day after Christmas, I led the funeral ceremony for Captain Muburak and said a few words on behalf of the military force. Much to my surprise, no one from the Haitian government was present. They had sent someone to all the previous ceremonies. This was totally incomprehensible both to me and to all the other military men on the mission. But it would not be the last time.

On 27 December a DPKO delegation arrived led by Ambassador Hedi Annabi, Assistant Secretary General DPKO, who was accompanied by General Mehta and Lieutenant Colonel Pessora, an officer from the Brazilian Army.

The first thing that surprised me was the timing of this visit — General Bacellar and I had been expecting them since the second week of December. The visit had been postponed for a number of reasons, which had caused General Bacellar a number of problems, because he kept having to change his ticket to Brazil, where he was going to spend the Christmas holidays. Besides, if you want to review a mission, obviously you should make sure the FC will be there, not his replacement. Apparently this does not occur to these organizations.

We had several working meetings with this delegation. One of these was very important to me and to the mission as a whole.

General Mehta walked into my office as soon as he arrived from the airport, and we discussed the security issue. He began by saying that he was extremely worried about the situation in the country, since the elections had been indefinitely postponed, thus compromising the success of the mission. Also, he was concerned that violence was on the rise.

The information they were receiving from Haiti only mentioned problems, abductions and deaths. They could not help but have a negative view of the situation in the entire country. Clearly, at least to me, he had fallen into the trap of equating Cité Soleil with the whole of Haiti.

During my first conversations with General Mehta, I told him what we were doing and said that the country was calm and under our control. As far as the capital was concerned, I told him we planned to control the kidnappings and mentioned the problems we were having with certain contingents. I told

Photo 22. Captain Mubarak's funeral

him I had devised a strategy that included training, as a response to the short-comings of the mission's structure and the problems that New York had caused by setting up a Sector Command.

I began by giving him an overview of the country and by pointing out that certain measures and structures were hampering our ability to command. In order to make the right decisions, Ambassador Valdés needed quick answers and up-to-date information about what was going on. I also mentioned the incompetence of the Haitian government — in particular, the absence of a functioning police force and of effective programs to help the people. General Bacellar and I felt that the solution had to start with a change of structure, one that would enable us to take direct charge in the capital.

It seems that General Mehta had been considering the same idea. At one point in the conversation, he gave me the perfect opening for that discussion.

"What is going on in Cité Soleil?" he asked. "When are we going to take control of Route #1?"

"General," I asked, "could you come to the window of my office?" I had a large, west-facing window that overlooked much of the city. "Do you see those houses over there?"

"I can," he replied.

"Well," I continued, "that is Cité Soleil, and instead of helping me control the situation, you have established an intermediate command between that place and the Mission Command, which has made the problem worse. *You know as well as I do that command should focus on the point that will determine the success or failure of the mission.* That is precisely what Cité Soleil means for MINUSTAH."

He replied that he had done this so that the Force Commander would not lose sight of the strategic vision of the mission and turn the capital over to a lower-ranking commander.

Perhaps I sounded a little arrogant, but it was necessary at that moment.

"General," I said, "when I taught strategy to my students at the War Academy, I always told them that of all the duties that concerned the commander, there was one he could not neglect, which was to be present at the point where the fate of the manoeuvre was determined. Cité Soleil is the strategic point of this mission, meaning that the commander must keep a close eye on it. Yet you've given me an intermediate command that only prevents me from acting. In a straight line, less than 5 kilometres from this office, is where this mission will be determined, for better or for worse, yet you're asking General Bacellar or me to wait to see what another commander decides. That goes against what we need to cope with the issue of insecurity, so I ask you to reconsider. And that is not only my position, but above all that of my commander."

We left the office to visit some units. He did not say much on the journey. We started with Sector Command, where General Al Husban was waiting for us. General Mehta asked several questions and called for a firmer hand in the most dangerous parts of the capital. Next we stopped at the First Jordanian unit, which four days earlier had lost an officer. One of General Mehta's advisers asked the Jordanian commander to explain why joint actions had not been carried out with the PNH. Then he asked why the checkpoints on Route #1, one of them adjoining UNPol, were not operating, and continued with several other questions, which together amounted to harsh criticisms of this commander.

I, too, had my doubts, but I also understood how hard it was to spend 24 hours a day being shot at in a place where people were being offered so little hope by their own government. And I thought it unwise for an outsider who had only just arrived to criticize my men in this way, especially considering that they had recently suffered a death.

I calmly told General Mehta that I would not allow him to ask questions in this way, since I felt it was disrespectful. I added that he made it sound as though we were incompetent, and I pointed out that so far no one had thought of any solutions to the problems posed by his adviser.

At that moment, I stood up, as did the entire delegation, effectively ending the visit. While we were leaving, the Jordanian commander took my arm and thanked me for supporting his men.

The next day, I stayed in my office, because I had a lot of paperwork to catch up on. General Mehta went off to visit the units with Sector Commander General Al Husban, telling him he wanted to see Route #1 and CP16. When General Mehta returned in the afternoon, he seemed upset and I asked him what the matter was.

He said that General Al Husban had refused to take him to these places, explaining that they were very dangerous. To this he had replied that he had come from New York precisely to see the problems and that we should not worry about him.

General Mehta later told me that he was prepared to visit these places in a civilian vehicle, but that he preferred not to upset the Sector Commander. He was extremely annoyed about the situation, but in the long run it was a good thing in terms of what we hoped to achieve.

Before the delegation returned to New York, we convened in Ambassador Valdés's office to exchange views. In the presence of Ambassador Valdés I turned to Annabi and Mehta and gave them a detailed explanation of the security issue, during which I mentioned the issue of the sector I had referred to earlier and added two further points.

The first was that UNPol needed to remain under the operational command of the military force when the two were acting jointly. The second was that MINUSTAH needed to improve its capacity for analyzing data, since JMAC, our intelligence organization, had failed to provide our soldiers with useful information. I ended by saying that the issues in Haiti were not strictly military and that stronger efforts were required from the provisional government, which was scarcely visible on the ground.

The meeting was rather tense, but I felt that my views had been supported by Ambassador Valdés. After the meeting, Annabi and Mehta were extremely friendly toward me and expressed their confidence in my command. Then they returned to New York.

After this, I divided my time between meetings with the transitional government authorities, meetings with the MINUSTAH authorities, duties at the mission's HQ, and my visits to the contingents. I had several working meetings with Colonel Horacio Sánchez to examine possible courses of action to deal with the security problem, which boiled down to one thing: Cité Soleil.

While I was in command, I issued several operating orders in an effort to solve the problem of insecurity on the streets. These generally involved mixed patrols with UNPol and the PNH in certain districts of the capital. But I always saw the same result: the streets were patrolled only by our soldiers. UNPol and the PNH would fail to turn up.

General Mehta and the UN people were well aware of this, and I know how hard General Bacellar was trying to change the situation. I felt I had to do something to encourage the troops to leave their vehicles, so I made what was perhaps an unwise decision.

I went with Major Díaz, NCO Leiva, and the Philippine guards I had under my command to CP15, where the captain had been killed a few days earlier. Leaving our vehicle behind, we walked with Major Díaz, NCO Leiva, and Sergeant Ortiz from Route #1 to CP13, where the Peruvian soldiers were. The soldiers were astonished to see us making this dangerous journey on foot.

The atmosphere was extremely tense. I thought about my children and wife with every step, but I was also telling myself that this was an example I had to set. Perhaps it was reckless of me, but later events would prove I had done the right thing. The commander should not always be first on the line, but sometimes he does have to do what his soldiers are doing. The impact on the troops can be enormous.

In late December and early January, the security situation in the capital became even more complex. Then on January 12, while I was in charge of the mission (FC), since a new commander had not yet been appointed, we faced a tense situation in Ouanaminthe, across the border from the Dominican town of Dajabon.

Ouanaminthe is a town of about 77,000 whose people make their living from agriculture and trade. The two countries had made a strong effort to improve their border controls, but corruption, the lack of national ID documents, and the absence of government officials to control the entry and exit of people and vehicles meant they virtually didn't exist. Since 1999 there had been an agreement between the two countries to ensure effective border control, but it had failed to change things much.

The PNH station was about 400 metres from the Ouanaminthe bridge on the River Massacre, which marks the border between the two countries. Basically, people were crossing back and forth without controls. The Dominican side was just as open as the Haitian side.

Every month between 1,500 and 2,000 Haitians were being deported from the Dominican Republic, where they had gone to seek better lives. This was also a site of human trafficking, especially of children, who were being sold to foreigners. While I was in Ouanaminthe, I often saw white couples with very young Haitian children, who would stay for a couple of days and then disappear. It is likely that weapons and drugs were also entering Haiti by this bridge.

We had deployed a Spanish platoon nearby at Fort Liberté. That force was coordinated with the nearby Chileans in event of emergencies.

On the day I am describing, the corpses of 24 Haitians were being returned to their country. They had suffocated while trying to enter the Dominican Republic illegally and were going to be buried in a mass grave in Ouanaminthe.

The moment the truck reached the cemetery, a crowd rushed the vehicle, trying to remove the dead bodies.

This situation had not been coordinated with the Haitian authorities, let alone with MINUSTAH, and havoc ensued (Photo 23). The few PNH officers were quickly overwhelmed and fled the scene. When the Spanish unit tried to restore order, the demonstrators attacked them. They also attacked the Spanish barracks with guns and stones and even Molotov cocktails.

The Spanish requested help from a neighbouring unit, which provided two armoured vehicles. Also available were personnel who were in the area to greet their fellow countrymen as they returned from leave in the Dominican Republic.

It all could have gotten much worse, and in the end only one person—a Haitian—died. Ten Blue Helmets were wounded. The Haitian corpses were sent back to the Dominican Republic.

It has generally been assumed that La Base 52, the gang in control of the sector, took part in this action. In fact, it seems to have been a frantic reaction by Haitians trying to recover the bodies of their kin.

The incident was handled well by Colonel Luis Flores, who led the Spanish unit. But just in case, I ordered that a unit be ready to fly by helicopter into the affected area. In the end this proved unnecessary.

Then again, the situation pointed to a prominent underlying issue: the incident could have been prevented if there had been a functioning state, an efficient police corps and better coordination with the Dominican authorities.

I have no doubt that lax border controls worsened the problem of safety in Port-au-Prince, where the gangs had both weapons and ammunition, which had to come from somewhere. There were mobile patrols on the roads, yet the gangs had no trouble dodging these.

Yet for all the country's poverty, some initiatives provided a ray of hope. The European Union was rehabilitating 67 km of the Haïtien–Ouanaminthe–Dajabon road and 5 km of the Fort Liberté–Milot road. These projects included a new bridge north of the existing one at Ouanaminthe as well as a regional marketplace at Dajabon. An Italian corporation had won the bid to undertake this project. Even so, until action is taken to deal with the border problem, it will continue to fester.

At the time of General Bacellar's death, which I will discuss further later, on January 6, 2006, while I was AFC, attacks on the MINUSTAH soldiers were increasing. Only one zone was creating problems—Cité Soleil. I decided that on January 17 we would launch an operation along Route #1 to take control of that zone.

General Al Husban, who still headed Sector Command, was instructed to take charge of the mission. Our goal was to prevent the gangs from using the streets and to keep traffic flowing on Route #1.

Photo 23. Riots in Ouanaminthe

Brazilian soldiers would occupy the cemetery on the eastern side of Route #1 while the Jordanians entered the CP2 sector on a house-by-house basis. Once we were in control of the checkpoint on the north of Route #1, we would advance south.

The Jordanian unit commander and I inspected the most dangerous place. I told him what I expected and gave him instructions, which he was to carry out in coordination with Sector Command. On January 17, at about 6 a.m., Operation Beachhead began.

I had already instructed the Sector Commander, by means of orders issued on January 5, and I had received and approved the plans that he had drawn up to accomplish the mission. His plan was to gain effective control of Route #1 and establish CPs along it so Haitians, the PNH and UNPol could all travel on it safely.

This operation required elaborate planning, which I supervised. Every minute counted, and every movement had to be according to plan.

The day before, members of the Chilean Engineering Corps, commanded by Lieutenant Colonel Iturriaga and Captain Enrique Olivares, had installed containers and cement blocks at CP2 to provide protection for our men in the high-risk zone. Though our engineers performed their duties superbly, showing the high quality of our army specialists, this was another example of the risk that troops in the capital were being forced to confront.

As always, and remembering that elections were approaching, we tried to proceed in such a way that collateral casualties would be minimized and that our own forces would not be needlessly endangered.

By early morning, our helicopters were flying at 2,500 feet and sending us information on ground movements. The danger we faced was from the gangs near CP2, which, using some empty houses, had been preying on our soldiers in the sector known as Carrefour Drouillard.

According to later unconfirmed reports, about 25 gang members died during this operation. As usual, we never found a single body. It seemed that it was part of gang culture not to leave behind the bodies of gang members who died during clashes. We seldom found bodies, except those of men who died when gangs fought one another.

At headquarters, Colonel Sánchez and intelligence personnel closely monitored the ongoing operation. At 10 a.m. I was informed that while inspecting some houses in front of CP2, Captain Tariq Abed Alfattah Aljaafreh and Sergeant Rabi Jalal Marei Aldlaifi had been shot dead by gangs just a few metres from where our engineers had set up the safety post.

When the news arrived, I was at headquarters following the operation. At the same time, I was informed that General Al Husban had decided to cancel the operation. This contradicted the orders that had been issued and frustrated our plans to gain control of the zone.

My instinct was to order that the operation continue, but my advisers told me not to insist. A general had decided against continuing an operation, and that left me with a simple choice: relieve him of his command, or accept his decision. Reluctantly, I chose the latter course.

The Jordanian troops' morale was severely affected by this tragedy. Once again, I visited them at the zone of operations and then at their barracks, where the air was heavy with grief. That day, I did something that is not included in any textbook but that I felt was important to our men's morale, especially that of the Jordanians.

I asked the commander to summon his men. In their presence, using an interpreter, I told them why we were on this mission. I told them that it was I who had ordered an operation that had taken the lives of two of their officers. I added that I was there, facing them, so they could look me in the eye and see that I shared their grief.

I said that I would continue to do what had to be done, because this was the mandate our countries and Haitian society had given us. We would not betray that trust, because our martyrs were expecting us to fulfill the mission they had sacrificed their lives for, and that the great majority of Haitians trusted us and supported our work. My words were received with widespread applause, together with cheering and singing.

The fact that I had often been in Cité Soleil, where I had accompanied those men in high-risk situations, came in handy at this point.

On the day of the funeral, a valedictory ceremony was held at the Argentine hospital. Once again, this was not attended by a single representative of the Haitian government. I expressed my annoyance to Ambassador Valdés, who agreed that this showed a lack of consideration and respect. A *New York Times* journalist approached me and pointed out their absence, which I admitted annoyed me.

As AFC, I had to bid farewell to our comrades. This is part of the address I gave:

I have said so before, there is nothing that can deter us from making this country a safe, stable environment where their citizens can live peacefully. Nothing will stop us from contributing to the enforcement of human rights, while we contribute to holding elections that will ensure the road to stability, order and development.

How joyfully these soldiers came here to assume this charge, and how joyfully did their kin say their farewells, how many dreams and hopes they carried in their hearts that will not be fulfilled.

One thing I can assure you is that the mission for which you gave your lives will be honoured. You can rest assured that that is what we are working for and what we will achieve, regardless of the cost.

It is in circumstances like these that I am saddened to see that the thousands of voices that call for the support of the MINUSTAH soldiers are silenced by minor criticisms from certain people that do not and will not understand our mission.

Nor do they understand the tremendous respect that our men feel towards the Haitian population, nor how fully the Blue Berets are committed to observing human rights and following procedures that are ultimately based on respecting the dignity of every human being.

It would seem that there are people for whom stability and order is not a course they wish to follow.

To that minority I say the MINUSTAH soldiers will do everything that is necessary, everything which lies within their power, to fulfill the United Nations mandate.

We soldiers, though we love life, are not afraid of challenge, especially not when it demands sacrifice for a good cause, such as Haiti and its people.

Despite their grief, overcoming rage over their loss, in spite of the lack of understanding of those who will not help their own country take the path it should, everywhere in this country every MINUSTAH soldier will follow his duty, duly but with the firmness befitting a person who holds justice and prudence in his hands and, in his mind, is convinced that peace and democracy are the only possible scenario where development may be attained, and to that we will pledge all our endeavours.

We are fulfilling the dreams of these fallen soldiers, so now rest in peace, comrades-in-arms, for we will carry on the mission, and rest assured that we will never falter.

Photo 24. Jordanian officers' funeral

When General Elito took over as FC at the end of January 2006, after hold-ing talks both with me and with headquarters, he invited General Al Husban to have a word with him in his apartment. They had a frank meeting at which Elito declared that he intended to assume more direct command over the units in the capital.

As the days went by, the new FC realized the gravity of the security issue in the run-up to the February elections. Thus his first decision was to assume full command of all the forces so that we could cope successfully with an event that was crucial to our mandate.

General Al Husban was always a serious, hard-working officer. He was not the issue — rather, the issue was a chain of command that did not allow us to be as efficient as the situation required.

On February 1, General Elito sent the DPKO a document in which he requested that Sector Command be dissolved, that General Mahmoud Al Husban be relieved of his duties and that Sector HQ cease its functions. He argued that for the sake of the upcoming elections, orders to these units must come from the MINUSTAH commander without any mediation.

Ambassador Guéhenno, second in command at the DPKO in New York, was already aware of the situation, for we had discussed it with him and General Mehta in December during their visit to Haiti. We felt that it was the only feasible way to exercise effective control over the capital.

We did not have to wait long for an answer. On February 3, the DPKO accepted our argument, while also pointing out that the existing chain of command had been established by Resolution 1608 of the UNSC. Therefore it was up to that organization to formalize the change. Also, it would be advisable to inform the Jordanian representative at the UN of the decision.

That same day, General Al Husban was informed of the situation. The day after that, he requested permission to travel to his country. He never returned to the mission.

The officers of SHQ were reassigned to various departments of MINUS-TAH Headquarters. The same day, the MINUSTAH commanders were called to a meeting, during which General Elito assumed direct control of all units. After that, operative control became easier for commanders.

The entire situation could have been avoided had the views of those in Haiti been consulted beforehand.

Things were far from easy for those of us on the mission at the time, though the quality of the training we had received in the army enabled us to deal with these challenges.

The military strategy devised by Bacellar and Elito yielded good results. Their plan—to advance cautiously without surrendering the terrain won back from the gangs—enabled UNPol and the PNH to gradually join our operations. This in turn helped us achieve better control over security in the capital.

First, we reorganized the command in the capital, which involved reviewing how our units were deployed. Second, in cooperation with a more solid and confident JMAC, we organized the GHQ information system.

The arrival of a Brazilian battalion in Cité Soleil provided a welcome dose of enthusiasm for our operation. In August we finally managed to increase the pressure on Cité Militaire. For the first time ever, we were able to effectively control the strategic safety perimeter around the capital—the square formed by Toussaint L'Ouverture Avenue, Industry Avenue and Route #1. To achieve that control, at General Elito's command we launched Operation Enclosure, to which I will refer later on.

During this operation, the Peruvian, Uruguayan, Bolivian and Chilean units achieved outstanding results amidst great danger by deploying a platoon in the zone from July 2006 onwards. The Sri Lankan personnel at Martissant also performed well.

I have no doubt that, if things should become more difficult, the military commanders will need to deploy more soldiers, drawing them from contingents in areas where safety is not an issue. These will surely include Chilean soldiers.

I still contend that unless we use the global strategy I have described — including concerted action by the Haitian government and MINUSTAH and, of course, continued international aid — Haiti's problems will never be solved.

But at the same time, I contend that military force will never be enough to succeed in the mission.

A massacre was avoided in 2004. The transition government found support. The first freely democratic elections in the history of the country were held. A new government was elected. The military supported several initiatives they were asked to implement. Then, going beyond their mandate, they undertook numerous civic and humanitarian initiatives across the country for the benefit of the Haitian people. The Chileans' actions have set an example of how to proceed so as to earn popular support.

Given the situation that confronted them, the military behaved in an exemplary fashion. Whenever justice and discipline had to be enforced, senior officers did so with no hesitation.

It was my task to welcome and see off several contingents that arrived and subsequently left the mission. When they left with UN decorations on their chest, even when I could tell that they had wanted to achieve more, I could see how proud they felt of what they had done. They knew that we were doing all we could, and more.

CHAPTER TWELVE

Parliamentary and Presidential Elections

HAITIANS TAKE GREAT pride in two things: their country was the second in the Western Hemisphere to achieve independence (in 1804); and it was the first "black" country to do so.

A key section of the UNSC's Resolution 1542 concerning Haiti made it clear to MINUSTAH that municipal, parliamentary, and presidential elections were to be carried out as quickly as possible. A subsequent resolution, 1576, encouraged the transitional government to explore all possible avenues for including in the voting process all those who remained outside the transitional government and who had rejected violence.

The Provisional Electoral Council (CEP) was tasked with organizing the elections, which were to be carried out within the framework of Haiti's Constitution (1987). All political parties and the Haitian people were invited to participate in the elections, which would create — so I expected before beginning my assignment — a starting point for the solution to Haiti's crisis, which at times had seemed almost permanent.

Voting was to be based on the French system, which included a second round for the presidential and legislative elections. The schedule initially included a registration period for voters for the November 2005 elections. In practice this was difficult, as Haitians were not provided with identity cards (four attempts at issuing them had failed) and the vast majority of them lived a long way from any town.

The first idea had been to hold the municipal elections on October 9, 2005, and the first round of presidential and parliamentary elections on November 13. The second round would be held on December 18. Congress would be established on January 9, 2006, and the president sworn in on February 7. With all this in mind, the PEC decided to conduct the registration from April to August 2005. Jacques Bernard, a Haitian American, had been hired to direct this activity, with assistance from the OAS and MINUSTAH.

Colonel Barry MacLeod, a Canadian officer who had once been MINUSTAH Chief of Staff, was brought back to the mission to oversee the election's security and logistics. Around the same time, MINUSTAH brought in Gerard Le Chevalier of El Salvador, a good friend of mine and an outstanding professional with long experience in events like these. Chevalier would be supported by Martín Landi and Colonel Edmundo Kearney, two Argentines who along with Le Chevallier would be crucial to the success of the elections. Another important step was the creation of the Voting Guards (Agents de Securité Èlèctorale), a 3,600-strong force that would provide security during the elections.

According to the 2003 census, there were approximately 4,250,000 voters in 10 districts and 140 municipalities throughout the country. Those voters would be able to register at 424 voting centres, 165 of them permanent, the other 259 temporary.

To organize this event, 11 district and 155 community offices were established. For the election itself there would be 802 voting centres with a total of 9,203 voting booths employing some 50,000 officials. To count the votes, district centres would be organized, which would feed their results to a computerized centre at SONAPI, in the capital near Cité Soleil.

The first challenge we faced was security. At first we were asked to deploy all our military forces throughout the country to every polling booth. We considered this inadvisable. Instead, General Elito decided to deploy our military according to their areas of responsibility (AORs) and to coordinate MINUSTAH's local contingents with those of the Force Commander's reserve in the capital. Because of the country's current security conditions, he thought better of deploying all his forces at once. Instead, the focus would be on our ability to react (with the use of helicopters) and on maintaining sufficient presence in the most troubled areas.

The plans were for a president, 30 senators, 99 delegates and about 10,000 local officials to be elected. To understand the complexity of all this, consider who was being elected just at the municipal level. Voters would be electing 140 mayors as well as 280 deputy mayors (i.e., two for each mayor). They would also be voting for 1,717 councillors, 5,048 in other municipal positions, and

483 municipal delegates — an unusually high number for such a poor country. "Second degree" elections were also being prepared — that is, indirect elections for municipal and district assemblies. There were about 2,500 such posts to be filled indirectly.

I realized that something was amiss with this system as soon as I grasped Haiti's main problem: the state's institutions are terribly weak. In addition, the two-round electoral system makes elections more expensive. Add to that, Haiti's constitution provides for an enormous number of elected officials who must be paid state salaries despite the country's very weak finances.

Haiti probably has more elected officials per capita than any other country. The resulting problems are only compounded by a feeble political culture and undisciplined political parties.

And there were other problems that affected MINUSTAH's election planning. While the political parties were choosing their candidates, the PEC had to ratify the voting places, prepare the voter lists, and print the ballots (this last step was done abroad). On top of that, it had to distribute voting cards as well as information on where to vote (which sometimes changed at the last minute).

The PEC soon fell far behind in its work. This weakened Haitians' trust in the process, which threatened to provoke violence.

The process was costing around US$79 million, US$61 million of that for the national elections. The municipal and local ones still hadn't been held by the time I finished my assignment in December 2006. If all of these elections had been held simultaneously, more than US$10 million might have been saved.

For the elections to be regarded as fair, Cité Soleil — which rightly or not was everyone's bellwether for progress in Haiti — would have to participate in the voting and be seen to be participating. This was no minor challenge, since it was the most violent place in the country.

The registration process generated a voter list of 3.2 million — a record for Haiti. Many Haitians received voting cards for the first time ever. Fifty-three percent of those authorized to vote registered with a birth certificate, 21 percent through witnesses, and only 26 percent by means of photo ID. In a country where only a handful of people had ID cards, this was no mean achievement. The success of the voting process can be attributed to the OAS, which with MINUSTAH's assistance developed an ID system for Haiti that included the latest available technology.

An ID card — such a simple thing — was hugely appreciated by Haitians. At a downtown school that operated as a polling booth, Ambassador Valdés was approached by people who showed him their ID cards and thanked him for them (Photo 25).

Thirty-four presidential candidates and 36 political parties were registered for and participated in this election. To me, this shows how hard it is for

Photo 25. At a polling booth with Ambassador Valdés

Photo 26. Chilean helicopters transporting voting equipment

Haitians to reach a consensus. To overcome all their severe problems, they will have to learn how.

For these elections, 130 tons of voting equipment were transported (Photo 26). Military assistance was crucial not only to securing the polling booths but also to transporting voting materials to places that could not be reached by road (a Uruguayan patrol once took eight hours to reach its destination).

The elections had to be postponed because of delays in publishing the lists and frequent changes in polling booth locations. Thus, November 20 gave way to December 7 and then to January and finally to February 7 — the date decreed by the constitution for swearing in the president. That date, coincidentally, would mark the twentieth anniversary of Baby Doc Duvalier's ousting as dictator. Had the elections been delayed any further, the transitional government probably would have fallen.

This delay affected the country's security, as borne out by the number of kidnappings and murders during this period. It also affected our plans to take more decisive military action against the gangs.

René Préval was leading in all polls; some of them placed him between 55 to 60 percent. Other candidates like Leslie Manigat and Charlito Baker were far behind.

MINUSTAH had set up a complicated system to monitor the elections. It had also met with the contingent commanders, with whom it had developed response plans for certain situations. The military contingents had carried out various deployments and drills as preparation for any problems that might arise. All of this preparation would be crucial to the success of the election.

February 7 arrived. Military forces had been deployed to the designated areas two days earlier. At about 6 a.m., General Elito and I left with Ambassador Valdés to inspect some of the polling booths.

Like the rest of the Chilean contingent, I had participated as a member of the military during voting in Chile, so I had some idea of what to expect that day. The most unusual thing I saw at such an early hour was the long lines of Haitians waiting for the polling booths to open, in tight queues with everyone pressed against the person in front. The polling booths were packed, but all was orderly and peaceful (Photo 27).

Ambassador Valdés told me that this was not the first time he had been in the middle of a crowd like this. I joked that because of his experiences during the protests against the Chilean military government, it was probably the first time he had stood next to a soldier who was protecting him. He laughed heartily.

With some trepidation, Ambassador Valdés told some international observers that they should remember they were in Haiti, not Luxembourg, and that they should understand the scenario before venturing any comments.

Photo 27. Election day at a polling booth

Photo 28. Ambassador Valdés and José Miguel Insulza, Secretary General of the OAS

We knew it would take at least three days for the marked ballots to travel from the polling booths to the community centres. From there they would be sent to the districts and eventually to the final counting location at SONAPI in Port-au-Prince.

The voters showed an unprecedented degree of calm. On election day, three people died in the country as a result of criminal acts, but only one of those deaths happened near a polling booth. Another was caused by a collapsing wall. On the whole, it was a peaceful day.

On the morning of the elections, the OAS Secretary General, former Chilean minister José Miguel Insulza, arrived from Washington (Photo 28). He was flown over the city in a helicopter, seated next to Ambassador Valdés. Afterwards we all met up at the Chilean Helicopter Unit. Insulza and Ambassador Valdés were old friends, and it was always a pleasure to spend time with them both.

Between February 6 and 8, MINUSTAH forces were deployed all over the country. At headquarters we worked 24 hours a day, which meant that I had to take over from General Elito every couple of hours. At GHQ we would hold all-night meetings with representatives of the various MINUSTAH agencies in order to analyze the situation, which was growing more complex as time passed.

At some of the booths, ballot boxes were stolen, but by and large things went well. The only truly disturbing event took place in the north, at Grande Saline, where a polling booth was attacked by a crowd. I sent Argentine troops from Gonaïves to restore order, and in case the situation got worse, I prepared to dispatch an UNPol unit. But this proved not to be necessary.

That night I went to the place where the votes at ONAPI were being counted with the help of Colonel Kearney, who was doing a great job with Martín Lundi.

General Elito, who had been FC for less than a month, was a wonderful commander with a superb work ethic. The success of the elections would be due mainly to his leadership.

We knew that because of how the votes were being counted, the results would not be announced until at least three days after the elections — in other words, no sooner than February 10. We also knew that people would be anxious to know who their new leaders would be, more so as the days went by. But there was little the military could do except speed up the patrols carrying the voting equipment. We placed our buses and helicopters at their disposal. The actual counting was in the hands of the CEP.

The press contingent was based in the Hotel Montana, where the CEP had installed a communications centre, which held news conferences at different times for national and international reporters.

We had deployed Jordanian and Brazilian troops to the capital's main roads. At the same time, we had held back a Peruvian platoon as a reserve that could be transported by land or by helicopter to wherever its presence was necessary. These soldiers had been training with the Chilean Helicopter Unit in "fast rope" — that is, descending quickly by rope from a helicopter. I went to visit them at the place where they were bunked — the airplane we had fitted out as a lounge.

Everybody assumed that the Provisional Electoral Council would take three days to call the elections. We were sure they would result in a victory by Préval and that calm would descend on the capital.

After a five-day wait, on February 12, the CEP informed the country that Préval's lead had slipped to under 50 percent. If that figure held, a second round of voting would be necessary. This announcement triggered the first protests in the capital. It was a mistake to provide information piecemeal — it only heightened the tension. There were some street disturbances, but on the whole, "tense calm" would be a good description of the mood in the capital. It helped that we had tightened security at the airport and on the main roads.

On February 13, six days after voting day, as arranged with General Elito and according to UN procedures, I took some post-election days off. By then, the CEP still had not delivered the vote count. The protesters on the streets of the capital were behaving peacefully; even so, they were clamouring to know the results.

That same day the Hotel Montana, where the international press were headquartered, was invaded by protesters. No activities had been scheduled at the press centre, and it was not a UN site, so security there was in the hands of the PNH and UNPol.

Around 9 a.m. the UNPol officers at the Montana informed MINUSTAH Headquarters that people were gathering outside on John Brown Street, where they were putting up barricades and blocking traffic. A UNPol Unit from Nigeria was dispatched to the hotel; it would arrive around 11 a.m.

At 9:40 a.m. the Joint Operations Centre was informed that the situation was getting out of hand, with the crowd threatening to invade the hotel, and that something had to be done since there were government officials inside. At 9:45 a.m. a Philippine crowd-control unit was sent to block the hotel entrance from protesters.

The use of air units had to be authorized by Steven Smith of the Aviation Unit, a civilian who could neither leave his house nor communicate by telephone. Because the situation was deteriorating, Colonel Rodrigo Bisbal, commander of the Chilean Helicopter Unit, made arrangements to airlift 20 Guatemalan soldiers to the hotel.

On the direct orders of General Elito, and with Amassador Valdés's guidance, at 12 p.m. a Jordanian UNPol Unit was taken by helicopter from the police academy to the hotel, arriving at 1 p.m. Also, René Préval was airlifted to the hotel by an Argentine helicopter in the hope he would be able to calm the crowd.

At 1:30 p.m., in the midst of all these complexities, Ambassador Valdés and the American, Canadian, French and Brazilian Ambassadors were transferred from the tennis courts at Pétionville to the Chilean Helicopter Unit. There, they met with Préval. At 4:50 p.m. they were all airlifted by Puma helicopters to the Parliament building to speak with the transitional government authorities about calming the situation. At 5:10 p.m. the authorities were transported back to the tennis courts in Pétionville.

In all, there were 24 flights that day, using two Puma helicopters from the army, three helicopters of the Chilean Air Force and two Bell 212s of the Argentine Air Force. This use of helicopters would have repercussions at the UN. It took us a lot of time to explain to the UN in New York that except for Bisbal's initiative, things would have gotten much worse.

This was one more indication that military helicopters must be directed by the FC, not the civilian adviser.

The hotel owners later complained to MINUSTAH about the disturbance. It helped that South African bishop Desmond Tutu was visiting the country at the time; his calls for peace were welcomed.

On February 15, after two days of negotiations, the CEP, on the recommendation of election observers, decided to divide up the blank votes, which accounted for 4.36 percent of the total.

This division allowed René Préval to win 51.21 percent of the vote, Leslie Manigat 12%, and Charlito Baker 8.24%. René Préval had cleared the 50 percent-plus-one hurdle and was now president elect. After that, things began to settle down.

This was the most transparent election in Haiti's history, and the one with the greatest participation. More than 63 percent of registered voters cast a ballot.

On April 21 the second round of voting was carried out. Nationwide, the participation rate was lower than for the first round. Only 1 million citizens participated—just over 30 percent of those who had registered. In any case, the second round was only a formality—the real election had been on February 7.

Under Haiti's bizarrely complicated system, Préval's government will have to spend more than US$105 million to conduct all the elections it is required to hold. By some analyses, Haiti will be holding 11 different elections at a cost of about US$196 million by the end of 2011. Common sense tells us that something is wrong here.

Préval was supposed to take office in February, and he could have done so once he was declared winner. But he refused to take office until there was a functioning Congress. That came about on May 9, after the results of the second round of voting had been announced. He took office as president on May 14, 2006.

On February 17, MINUSTAH accomplished one of the three pillars of its mandate: it had helped conduct elections in Haiti. But our task was far from over.

Soon enough, I started hearing Haitians telling us it was time for the soldiers to leave Haiti and that their presence was no longer necessary. I felt more ashamed than angry about these comments. Had we listened to them, tragedy surely would have ensued. The elections had been important, but even a glance at the situation suggests that the country's work is just beginning and that the presence of the Blue Helmets and other instruments will be important for some time.

CHAPTER THIRTEEN

A Wrongful Accusation

FROM THE TIME I began the mission, one of the first things I did on arriving at my office every morning was ascertain the security situation through the MINUSTAH centre of operations. After that, I would spend some time reading the Chilean newspapers on the Internet. Also, the army issued a daily news bulletin with a press summary and distributed it on the Internet to all overseas personnel.

In late September 2005 I read an article in a Santiago newspaper with this heading: "General Aldunate, second in command of the UN in Haiti, was part of the Mulchén brigade of the National Intelligence Operation (DINA) and could be involved in the murder of Carmelo Soria."

The article suggested that a former agent of this intelligence organization, a retired sergeant major, had stated that "in that unit [the Mulchén brigade] there had been a man named Aldunate Herman who was a Lieutenant." The same article included background information that that unit had been involved in the death of a former officer of the Economic Commission for Latin America and the Caribbean (CEPAL) in Chile.

I immediately thought this was absurd—I had never been in that organization, so my army file would defeat the accusation. However, I was surprised that the information had been released while I was on a UN mission.

I had led a public life, especially during my years as a professor and when I headed the Field Department of the Army War Academy, where my tasks included organizing (with other officers) various seminars that had national consequences. I had also taken part with other officials in several academic events with social and political activists involved in civilian–military relations. And I had published articles in the national press.

I had even more questions about the timing of this situation — that is, while I was abroad on an international mission — since I had previously been commander of a regiment as well as head of both the Paratrooper School and Special Forces. That is why I had appeared many times in the press. I had been a public figure who could be reached at any time.

After my commission abroad, I had been promoted to general. Because of the issues I handled at the Office for National Mobilization — I was the country's authority on arms control and military service, among other things — I was constantly in the media.

The newspaper indicated that my possible link with DINA had appeared in an extrajudicial statement made in 1993 by the retired sergeant major. In this statement, which was more than 12 pages long, he mentioned my name in only one line.

"Why is this coming out now?" I wondered. "Why me?" But at the same time, I was sure that because the suggestion was so absurd, it would be cleared up quickly. I was wrong.

The issue made it into the news in early October and became headlines when the daughter of the person affected by this incident launched an active publicity campaign, which some politicians and civil rights activists joined.

Knowing this, I left for Ambassador Valdés's office and told him what was happening. I remember that morning well, and what I said to him: "Ambassador, this accusation is false and unfair. I am not responsible for the charges being made against me and I am willing to appear before the Supreme Court of my country to clarify the situation."

Looking steadily at me, he replied, "General, I believe you, don't worry".

But I *was* worried, so I went to the Chilean Embassy to speak to Ambassador Young. I explained the situation, which he already knew about. Again I stated my absolute innocence, but at the same time I expressed how unfair and serious this accusation was for a person who was representing his country on a delicate mission. I told him what I told Ambassador Valdés — that I was willing to immediately appear before the court in my country to clarify matters.

As the days went by the accusation found wings. At MINUSTAH headquarters, rumours were spreading. Ambassador Valdés asked me for a written statement on the situation, which he sent to UN Headquarters in New York.

That same afternoon we had a meeting with the staff, and I asked General Bacellar for an opportunity to speak so that I could clear up any doubts about the matter. Which I did. At the end of the meeting, and without going into too much detail, I pointed out that the accusation was utterly false and that I had

Photo 29. Press conference with Chilean media via videoconference

resolved to face justice in my country as soon as possible. When I was finished, all the officers expressed their support.

The incident made headlines in the international press as well. I was in every newspaper, and for two weeks I gave no fewer than five interviews a day on this subject — for the radio, for television, and for the print media. I always expressed my respect for Mrs. Soria but at the same time expressed my doubts regarding whether this was the best way for her to cope with the loss of her father.

I did not refuse any interviews, and I expressed my absolute conviction that the situation would be cleared up. I never ceased to carry out my duties, since at the time our men were under daily attack from the gangs.

I stated my willingness to testify wherever I might be asked to do so, insisting that the rule of law imposes obligations on all of us. Yet I sensed that in this particular case I would not receive fair treatment.

Because of the uproar in Chile, a videoconference was held between the media and the Communications Department of the Army at an Air Force Unit in Santiago. I spent about an hour with journalists fielding all their questions (Photo 29).

After that, I thought it essential to return to Chile. I asked for special leave to do so, which was granted. Back home, I appeared before the Army. It is interesting that there had been no petition for me to appear before any court.

Even so, I arranged to appear before the judge who had conducted the trial in this case. He immediately told me that the sergeant major who had involved me in this had taken back that part of his testimony where he stated I had been a member of that unit.

That interview lasted about three hours. When it was over, and at my request, the magistrate handed me a document stating that according to the information he had, I was not involved in the events he was investigating.

Meanwhile, in New York, several calls for my resignation had been submitted to the UN.

The Commander-in-Chief of the Army and the Minister of National Defence, Jaime Ravinet, had offered me all their support, backed by my record and by the absence of any evidence that I had taken part in any unlawful incidents. As the days went by, many Chilean politicians began to express their support for me, except for some whom I contend were misinformed.

When I returned to Haiti, I showed Ambassador Valdés a copy of the document that the magistrate had given me, along with a statement from me to be sent to New York. I met with Ambassador Young and his wife Isabel to describe my activities during my visit to Chile. Once again they gave me their wholehearted support, the memory of which I will always cherish.

A few days after my return to Haiti, a meeting between various ambassadors and the Core Group was convened to analyze the situation in Haiti. Ambassador Valdés said that he wanted to read a statement since he thought it appropriate to inform the ambassadors about the situation. Before entering the conference room, he handed me a document so that I would be aware of its contents, which he would be reading to the diplomats.

At the end of the meeting, and after analyzing the issues on the mission agenda, Ambassador Valdés read the statement. After that, various ambassadors — from the United States, Brazil and Argentina — came up to me to express their support.

After that, Thierry Faggart approached me. He was in charge of MINUS-TAH's Human Rights Department, a man with whom I had a good relationship. He asked me what I thought of the statement, and I told him it was a good one. He told me he had written it, which I took as a statement of support.

I thought the accusation against me, and the media process that resulted, had been unfair. The Sorias have every right to seek justice for the death of their father. But my public reputation did not deserve to be ruined, which is something that deeply affected my family. That accusation also cast a shadow on Chile's reputation — and all because someone without any solid evidence had mentioned extrajudicially that I had supposedly belonged to a particular unit.

When an accusation like that reaches the media, the damage is almost irreparable. The fact that I had been exonerated did not appear as prominently as that fact that I had been accused.

Months later, the UN, through Under-Secretary Annabi, requested that I remain with the mission for one more year. In that unpleasant situation, the fact that Ambassador Mulet had asked me to stay past the end of my term was the strongest vote of confidence I could have hoped for.

When the UN Secretary General arrived in Haiti for a visit and shook my hand in front of everyone; when I received the UN Medal for my work on the mission; and when President Préval himself asked me to extend my assignment for another year, I was able to find closure for a thankless chapter of my mission.

Some time later, while I was talking to my wife about the situation, she told me how she had coped with the accusation. One Sunday while she was home, since she was not getting any news from me, the children told her to check the Internet, where there would be news about Haiti. She typed my name into the Web browser and was surprised to see that I had made the headlines, charged with that terrible accusation.

She mentioned that even though it was night time, she had called General Javier Urbina at home, who told her that the matter was being dealt with by the army, which was staying in contact with me. Meanwhile, he suggested she remain calm.

I would later find out that General Bacellar told the UN that if I were taken off the mission, he would resign his post. This speaks of his enormous understanding and his loyalty to me as commander.

CHAPTER FOURTEEN

A Terrible Blow: The Death of General Bacellar

ONCE I ARRIVED on the mission and had taken up my post, I needed to plan my leaves. I had to coordinate those with General Bacellar so that one of us would always be present on the mission. We agreed that he would take the last two weeks of December—during which I would be in charge as Acting Force Commander—and that I would go to Chile in March for my birthday.

Which was exactly what happened. He flew to Brazil on leave in December and would be back in Port-au-Prince by the end of the month.

General Bacellar and I had developed a system whereby he devoted himself to political matters, including meetings with the authorities. I focused on military matters, though when operations were launched he was always present and made the important decisions. In his absence, I attended political meetings in his place.

General Bacellar was a very cheerful and easygoing person, besides being open to the suggestions of his personnel (Photo 30).

At the time he took his December leave, the situation in Port-au-Prince was extremely tense because of the rising numbers of kidnappings and murders. At every meeting he attended, he was blamed for the dangerous environment and pressured strongly to apply "a firm hand" against crime. Put simply, they wanted our soldiers to go into Cité Soleil and crush the gangs.

Photo 30. General Bacellar at the Argentine Hospital

After every one of these meetings, he and I would agree that the problem would not be solved by sending our soldiers in against the criminals. The huge social problems that Haiti faced would not be solved by force, especially while the provisional government was doing little or nothing to address them. We also knew that any military operation would affect the political process, and we were being careful to ensure that did not happen.

In this respect, we always remembered the advice of General Bacellar's predecessor, General Heleno. According to him, there was another solution: help the population, build the country's institutions, and use military force only when absolutely necessary. I would also recall General Urbina's advice to always be careful.

Things were not easy for the mission's senior officers. The pressure on us was enormous, but Ambassador Valdés always supported us. I believe that his political sense told him that a tactical win could bring about a strategic disaster.

In November, General Bacellar took a few days off and went to the Dominican Republic with his wife, where he rested and went diving. This caused a minor respiratory problem. The commanders at headquarters teased him by asking what a paratrooper was doing scuba diving.

When he returned to Haiti, his wife Grazia came with him to spend a few days in Port-au-Prince. One day, with the Chilean patrol, we had lunch at his house. We had a very good time and talked about everything, including one topic that, in view of what happened later, would hold special significance for me. Grazia asked me how had I been chosen for this mission.

I told her how I had been chosen, and that I had wanted this mission, and that I was glad for the challenges I was facing. Chilean soldiers were here, and I had wanted to serve beside them. She said nothing, but her silence spoke volumes.

That night they told us about their plans to visit the United States, where their children lived, and that they would do so at the end of the general's posting in August 2006.

In December 2005, in the days leading up to his departure for Brazil, I noticed that General Bacellar was very quiet. I called Major Dutra and told him I was worried, because during lunch General Bacellar had said practically nothing and seemed distant.

We all thought it was because he missed his wife deeply and that everything would be all right once he returned to Brazil. We also felt that the pressures of the mission were another cause.

When he came back from leave in early January 2006, lunches and meetings were no longer the same. He was quiet, and those closest to him noticed it, though I believed his mood would lift with time.

On Friday, January 6, he attended a meeting with the businessmen of Port-au-Prince. After the meeting, he told me they had treated him with harshness and disrespect, accusing him of encouraging the violence.

His apartment was next to mine at the Montana. That Friday night we got together in the parking lot of the hotel, and he explained in detail the situation he had faced. I told him I would not attend any one of those meetings where he had been treated rudely, since everyone in this country knew about the link between the gangs and certain businessmen.

We spoke for about twenty minutes that night, and after promising to meet the following day, I went to bed at around 10 p.m., since I had work the following day.

I learned later that after speaking to me he went to the Brazilian battalion, where he had dinner with the personnel. I also learned that he rang Grazia that night.

At our hotel there was a division of Haitian security guards. General Bacellar and I had agreed not to deploy soldiers for this. We did not want to use them for something we felt was not that important.

Both General Bacellar and I relied on a security detail from the Philippine Company. Every morning they would pick us up at around 6:30 a.m. and accompany us all day. They would leave the hotel after we went to our rooms. I had included Sergeant Major Leiva in my security detail.

On the morning of Saturday, January 7, at about 6:15 a.m., I heard a gunshot very close to my room. I did not give it a second thought, since I could hear gunfire from my room every night and there were normally quite a few gunshots at this time.

I dozed off again until I heard someone pounding on my door. I got up, opened the door and found Sergeant Ortiz, a Filipino from my security detail, yelling, "The Force Commander is dead!"

I left my room in the shorts I was wearing and saw that the door to his apartment was closed.

Sergeant Ortiz took my arm and led me to the stairs, where you could see General Bacellar's apartment. I saw him lying on the floor wearing a T-shirt and shorts with his gun next to him; his head was bleeding.

I returned to my apartment, picked up the radio and called Major Díaz, who was just setting off for his office. I explained what was going on and told him to phone headquarters so that an ambulance and the Military Police could come.

I also ordered him to notify the mission's security detail of what was happening and to inform Major Dutra, who must come to the hotel immediately.

I arranged for Sergeant Ortiz to remain in front of the door to the general's apartment until I returned. In the meantime, I got dressed and called Ambassador Valdés to tell him what had happened.

About half an hour later, security personnel began arriving at my apartment. At that point, no one had entered the general's apartment.

When I saw the general from the stairs, I had thought of entering his apartment to see how he was, but from what I had seen from the terrace, I knew instantly that nothing could be done. Because of the investigation that would follow, it would be better not to disturb the scene.

As personnel began to arrive at my apartment, I organized work teams. I met with the security people and the investigators to begin the initial inquiries.

My room had become the centre of operations. About fifty people had arrived, including the ambassadors of Chile, Argentina and Brazil, as well as Ambassador Valdés, who had come over right away and taken control of the situation.

At that time, I received many calls from the contingents. I continued to give them orders despite the situation.

Phone calls came in from all over the world on our cellphones.

The atmosphere was quiet. In the midst of this, an ambassador said that this death had been caused by the brutal meeting with the businessmen the previous day.

I heard him and immediately called him to the terrace in front of everyone and told him that I did not accept what he was saying. I added that neither

General Bacellar nor his country deserved this and that the only decent thing one could say at such a moment was that he had been a great commander and a great person and that we all regretted what had happened.

The truth is that I was very harsh on that ambassador, but General Bacellar deserved better than an oversimplification like that. Moreover, as commander in charge of the mission I had made it my task to protect his image — what he meant to us and to his army and his country.

At that moment, I received a call from New York from General Mehta and Under Secretary Annabi. Both of them expressed their sincere condolences and offered me their support. They added that they trusted me completely in my new position as mission commander. They were well aware that General Bacellar's death had come at a difficult moment for Haiti and that the responsibility now thrust on me would be difficult to handle.

In between the conversations and the organization of the work teams in my apartment, I asked Major Díaz to check the Internet and see what was being said in the press about this incident. I was furious to learn that a Chilean newspaper had published an article that said something along these lines: "General accused of human rights offenses takes over as force commander of MINUSTAH due to death of Brazilian General." I cannot express the anger and hurt I felt at the moment.

I was faced with a complex situation. Next to me was the dead Force Commander. My soldiers were being shot at by criminal gangs. I was in charge, representing my country, and having to suffer the indignity of this remark by a Chilean newspaper. It was all a bit much.

As already noted, my alleged human rights violation had been cleared more than two months earlier in the Chilean courts and at the UN itself.

I phoned General Cheyre in Santiago and informed him about the situation concerning General Bacellar and expressed the sadness and pain regarding the situation with the press at such a difficult moment, as well as the rage I felt that a newspaper from my country had taken advantage of the situation.

He registered my complaint, and a couple of hours later I saw on the Internet that the headline for this article had changed and now referred solely to General Bacellar's death.

At that moment, Major Dutra arrived at the apartment.

The friendship between my assistant and Marcelo Dutra was essential. We had to speak to the family, and Marcelo was very good at that, remaining calm at all times. It was a very difficult moment but we had to pull through.

As the hours went by, the investigation followed its course. At about 10 a.m., those in charge of security as well as UNPol entered the apartment.

Outside the hotel, journalists had gathered. I ordered the Guatemalan Military Police to seal off the area and prevent anyone from taking pictures of the scene, and certainly not of the general, to safeguard his dignity. But a photographer went to a floor above the apartment and took his picture.

Once the UNPol technicians had done their job, we had to transport the general's remains to the Argentine hospital. I asked the investigating team for permission to bring in a priest before his body was removed. To this they agreed.

In the afternoon a Brazilian priest arrived. Just before we moved the general's body from his apartment, we prayed for him. The other soldiers and I personally carried his remains to the vehicle that would carry him to the Argentine hospital.

At those difficult moments for all of us, and despite all the pain I felt, I knew I could not break down. There were 7,500 soldiers under my command at a time when security problems were at their worst, and they expected me to encourage them and direct them well.

When people talk about loneliness at the top, this is what they mean, and this was the moment when I realized it most clearly. Being a commander is a harsh and often thankless profession, but it is also what we are trained for.

After removing the general's body from the apartment, we had to deal with much paperwork. The first thing I did was meet with headquarters to describe what had happened. The atmosphere was very sad, since General Bacellar had been well liked by everyone. I began by saying that he was still here with us in spirit and that he would have wanted us to carry on, and that we must redouble our efforts for his sake.

Colonel Horacio Sánchez Mariño and Colonel Carlos Lorente from the Uruguayan Army were crucial factors during this crisis. That night we all met with Major Dutra and Carlos Díaz at my apartment to plan what was to come, which we all knew would be very difficult.

Many tears were shed that night. We pledged to preserve the general's good name: he had been a wonderful commander for us. Since this terrible incident was going to raise difficult public relations issues, I thought it best to be as open as possible about our investigations. That became our objective.

Haiti is a country that thrives on rumours. Stories began to spread that General Bacellar had been murdered by the gangs, who had killed him with a rifle with a telescopic sight. There was even talk that South African mercenaries had taken his life.

Our duty was not to judge him. It was to sympathize with the general and his family.

The following day I received more phone calls from New York expressing their support for my command. I thanked them for their support and said that this unfortunate situation would not stop us.

During this period, security in the capital continued to deteriorate, with some 260 kidnappings in a month.

As a gesture of comradeship, the Peruvian commander offered to assign me a security detail in case I needed it. This was not necessary, but I deeply appreciated the gesture.

The farewell ceremony for General Bacellar was held on Thursday of that week (Photo 31). It fell to me and to Ambassador Valdés to say some words. This is what I said:

> On behalf of all the military personnel of MINUSTAH, I bid farewell to Lieutenant General Urano Texeira da Matta Bacellar, our Force Commander, who carried out his duty with honour, professionalism, courage and wisdom from September 2005 until last Saturday.
>
> His wisdom, leadership qualities and intelligence were the instruments through which General Bacellar carried out his duty. I believe that these will be his legacy for us: his great humanity as a professional soldier with an exceptional career serving his country, which he embraced with the same responsibility and dedication as always as Commander of MINUSTAH.
>
> I had the honour and privilege to serve under his command as Deputy Force Commander, and I can assure you that he always strove to accomplish the mission with proper security for our troops.
>
> He was determined not to fall into the temptation of improvising since he knew that this would not only damage the mission but also be harmful for the soldiers.
>
> As a parachutist, he knew the risks of our profession very well and gave proof of this and of his courage.
>
> General Bacellar's commitment to following the UN's orders of providing security for the Republic of Haiti is something I strongly and calmly uphold today before his casket.
>
> All around the country, Haitian citizens express their gratitude to MINUSTAH every day despite the opposition of some people, who will not defeat us.
>
> My General, rest assured that we will continue carrying out the mission. The best proof of our loyalty and gratitude toward you will be that peace and security will reach every corner of this country, where law and respect for human rights will be clearly exercised.
>
> General, thank you for everything. We will always remember you fondly.
>
> You lead, guide and pave the way for us.
>
> General Bacellar, rest in peace.
>
> May God bless you.

That day, a Hercules C-130 arrived from Brazil with a delegation of generals and officers to escort General Bacellar's remains back to his country. I asked them when they returned to Brazil to take some of our Military Police, who would complete the investigation in Brazil. They agreed to this. Marcelo Dutra would escort the casket on behalf of the mission. What lay ahead for

Photo 31. General Bacellar's funeral, with Ambassador Valdés

Photo 32. General Bacellar being transported to Brazil

him in Brazil would not be easy: being with the general's wife and attending to her at such a sad moment.

At night, with the Brazilian Ambassador, I helped carry the general's casket up the Hercules' ramp past a long line of soldiers (Photo 32). We all saw his body off with great sadness.

I do not think anyone knows what goes on in the mind of someone who decides to act as he did. I only know that my deep respect for him is untarnished. I feel thankful to have met him and to have been able to serve under him.

Other people, faced with a situation like his, would have succumbed to the temptation to apply military force. Bacellar never forgot that though we were soldiers, we would not help this country by inflicting death. He was adamant that he would follow the UN's mandate and remember the trust his own country had placed in him. That had always been his resolve, and as his successor it would be mine.

Later, General Elito renamed Camp Bravo — where the Brazilian battalion was deployed at Port-au-Prince — General Bacellar Base. Haiti owes a great deal to that soldier.

CHAPTER FIFTEEN

The First Few Months of Préval's Government

AFTER GENERAL BACELLAR'S sad return to Brazil, wrapped in his country's flag, I became Acting Force Commander and was quickly brought back to reality by violent events that allowed me no time to mourn his loss.

During one of the times I called New York, I told General Mehta that it would be a good idea to name General Bacellar's replacement as soon as possible, since the morale of the Brazilian troops would be strengthened by having their own general.

I must add here that the Brazilians' performance was exemplary at all times and I felt comfortable being in command of them. Indeed, when I visited the Brazilian battalion soon after General Bacellar's death, I saw the depth of their grief, but I also saw their tenacity and their will to carry on with the mission. They were model soldiers.

Mehta replied that my leadership was trusted at the DPKO and that the UN would be taking its time to name a replacement. Which meant that during the three most crucial weeks of the mission, fate had left me in command of the MINUSTAH forces.

The third week of January, we were told that the UN had appointed General Elito Siqueira Carvalho as General Bacellar's replacement. On January 22, a delegation headed by General Albuquerque, Commander-in-Chief of the

Brazilian Army, arrived in Port-au-Prince along with other officers. Among them was my new commander.

General Elito came from the same Military School group as Generals Heleno and Bacellar. All three had been close friends. The new Force Commander was a small, well-built 58-year-old, and from the moment he arrived I knew we would get along fine. The first thing he told me was that he was a serious athlete and he hoped so was I. As it turned out, we would form an unbeatable pair in volleyball.

Elito had served in the Special Forces and was a paratrooper like Bacellar. We began referring to our work team as a patrol, which lent a special sense of unity to our command group. Our conversations were always laced with references to the commandos.

The next day, the Brazilian delegation had a surprise for me. The Brazilian government had awarded me the *Duque de Caxias*, the Peacemaker's Medal, which I received at a ceremony accompanied by Ambassador Young. General Albuquerque, Commander-in-Chief of the Brazilian Army, presented me with the award. He was joined by the Brazilian Ambassador to Haiti, Paulo de Cordeiro de Andrade Pinto.

Elito's first days on the mission proved that he was up to speed about events not only in the country but also within MINUSTAH. He told me he had held several conversations with General Heleno about me and had detailed information on what was going on.

From the start he expressed a great deal of confidence in me and an equal amount of goodwill. He always asked for my opinion when faced with a decision, realizing that I had been on the ground there longer. He would retain this humility throughout his time as my commander. Until my last day, he was deferential when hearing me out.

The first thing General Elito did when he visited his office—which still held some of General Bacellar's personal effects—was ask for a priest from the Brazilian Unit to bless all our offices.

He moved into General Bacellar's old apartment in the Montana, which told me he had great inner strength.

Just as I had done at the beginning, he expressed a wish to meet all the units, so we organized visits to all the contingents, bearing in mind that we were less than two weeks from elections. The country was reaching its highest level of violence, especially in the capital.

The first decision Elito made was to take control of the elections at a national level. The second was to take direct control of all units in the capital. I had been asking New York for this authority from the start, always in vain. MINUSTAH Headquarters had long been calling for both courses of action.

Elito was smart enough to realize that these two issues were the most important ones of the many we had outlined for him.

It was clear from the outset that the new FC's leadership would be highly tactical — in other words, he would be strongly hands-on. And for that to work, he had to make those two decisions.

After the elections, Ambassador Valdés and General Elito held meetings with President-Elect Préval. During those meetings, where several MINUS-TAH advisers were always present, various matters were discussed. These included security, which was also discussed with some of Préval's advisers, including Robert (Bob) Manuel, who would later become the president's main adviser. Manuel understood the current situation perfectly, having been Secretary of Public Security in a previous government.

At these meetings with the president-elect, what Elito wanted to know — as did everyone — was what Préval's policy on violence and the gangs would be.

I met Bob Manuel at a dinner at Ambassador Young's house. There, I grasped soon enough that he had a clear idea of what he had to do. He also realized that the new government and MINUSTAH would have to advance cautiously toward solutions to Haiti's many problems. After that, I would hold various meetings with him, and we would often talk on the phone to coordinate our actions.

At that time, in Cité Soleil and in the capital generally, the gangs had scaled back their violence and kidnappings. They believed that under Préval, whom many of them had supported, their situation would improve.

For example, General Toutou, a gang leader, announced that his followers would hand in their arms and support Préval. Amaral Duclona, the most wanted gang leader in Haiti, said that his followers wanted peace and that his willingness to disarm would depend on how the new government implemented its program.

Early on, Bob Manuel asked us not to launch operations in Cité Soleil, since the government was communicating with the gang leaders in the hope of finding a peaceful solution.

And that is what we did; while Préval met with Amaral, Ti Blanc, Evans, and others, we were convinced this was a dubious venture.

One morning when I arrived at the Parliament building, Bob Manuel told me these gang leaders had just left a meeting with Préval. I confirmed this information with the soldiers in Cité Soleil. They told me that a presidential car had arrived earlier that day to pick up the criminals and had returned later to drop them off.

The violence had decreased, but that did not mean that the threat of it had disappeared or that the gangs had stopped firing at our soldiers. I complained about this to Bob Manuel more than once. I contended that when it came to the MINUSTAH soldiers, the gangs were taking advantage of their truce with the Haitian government.

During the election campaign, Préval had stated that the issue of violence could not be solved by military means and that he was going to focus on addressing the economic plight of the poorest citizens. Meanwhile, the political parties closest to him declared that their aims were to support development projects and seek peaceful solutions to the problem of violence.

There is no question that the gang leaders had supported the voter registration process. Their motives included a not-so-secret desire to obtain a general amnesty and to be granted passports so that they could leave the country. As it turned out, Amaral would find shelter in the Disarmament Demobilization and Reintegration Program (DDR) by handing over some of his weapons. Jean Eody, a lieutenant of Amaral's from Belony, would surrender to the authorities. As a result, people were able to travel freely through Cité Soleil as of July 2007.

Ambassador Valdés had pledged to remain on the mission until elections were held. He had been working for two long, exhausting years as Special Representative of the UN Secretary General, and he believed he had fulfilled his duty of helping establish a new government. Now that the country had an elected president, he wanted to move on.

But he had one personal task left to accomplish—a visit to Habitation Leclerc. This old hotel was at the top of Martissant, the same district in the southern part of the Port-au-Prince where I had found 22 bodies murdered by a gang in July 2006.

This hotel had been the home of General Leclerc and his wife Paulina Bonaparte and had a beautiful view of the sea. It had lodged people from the international jet set such as Richard Burton and Elizabeth Taylor. At one point, it had also lodged Ambassador Valdés's father, the distinguished public figure Gabriel Valdés Subercaseaux.

He had insisted that his son visit this place before leaving Haiti, something that Ambassador Valdés had not been able to do because of the limited free time available to him and also because the hotel was in a very dangerous area.

Juan Gabriel told me about all this, and I told him I would arrange security.

I did some research, and there were some problems, but by adopting proper security measures, it could be done.

Juan Gabriel, his wife Antonia, and Pablo Piñera, DG-Administrator of the Foreign Ministry, went with me to visit this place that had once been beautiful. We found that everything had been destroyed and abandoned and that some poor families were living in the rooms, with no electricity or running water. It was difficult to imagine what it had been like before, when movie stars had stayed here.

Photo 33. Award from Brazil, presented by Ambassador Valdés

At the end of April the Brazilian government decided to award Ambassador Valdés and me the Order of Military Merit, with the grades of Great Officer and Knight Commander respectively (Photo 33).

In May, for the inauguration ceremony of President Préval, Chile sent a delegation headed by the Minister of National Defense, Vivianne Blanlot. She arrived with Senator Mariano Ruiz Esquide and Patricio Hales as well as Pablo Piñera from the Foreign Ministry.

I had known Mariano for a long time. He represented Chile's VIII Region and lived in Antuco. I had worked with him when I served as regimental commander in that city.

I also knew Patricio, because of weapons control and military service. I had been the national authority on both files when he was Vice President of the House of Representatives. He was also a former cadet at the Military School.

The delegation that attended the president's inauguration visited MINUS-TAH Headquarters, where a thorough briefing of the situation was provided. They took the opportunity to visit our troops in the capital and in Cap Haïtien. This allowed them to see the complexity of the mission at first hand.

Among other things, Minister Blanlot visited President-Elect Préval at his home. At the end of that visit, she held a press conference with Haitian journalists. She told them that Chile could help their country in many ways. One was to investigate whether part of Chile's copper-generated surplus could be used to help their country in the form of soft loans. (Copper, an important Chilean export, was getting an excellent price at the time.)

This suggestion made the headlines in Chile, but I sense that her remarks were based more on wishful thinking than on a concrete plan. Even so, and regrettably for her, the matter caused her some grief.

The day before her return to Chile, the minister invited Ambassador Valdés, Ambassador Young, the delegation, and the Chilean commanders to lunch at a restaurant in Pétionville. After lunch, several members of the delegation spoke, as did the minister. They emphasized the importance of our presence there and of the job our soldiers were carrying out.

That night we held a farewell party for Ambassador Valdés at his residence. President-Elect Préval and the highest authorities of the transitional government along with the ambassadors of most of the countries represented in Haiti were present.

At the party, several people expressed their gratitude to Valdés for all his work. Everyone present thanked him for the enormous contribution he had made during his two years with the mission.

When Préval arrived at the party, he asked the authorities of the transitional government to stand next to him. He then called for unity and urged people to work together for the good of Haiti. This brought a moment of hope to all of us, for we well knew that problems lay ahead. But we also knew that Préval's close relations with the Haitian people could well reduce the tension and violence.

That afternoon, Minister Blanlot took part in Préval's investiture at the Haitian Congress—a small space for the number of officials present. Afterwards, the delegation returned to Chile.

Préval took office on May 14. The first thing he did was call for dialogue to lead the country to stability. He acknowledged MINUSTAH's contribution to Haiti as well as the support of the international community, but he added that the country's problems could only be solved by the Haitians themselves.

At a session with the UN Security Council, Préval expressed his hope that MINUSTAH's mandate would adjusted to support reforms to the judicial and police systems.

Préval chose Jacques Édouard Alexis as prime minister. His 18-member government was drawn from seven political groups that had supported him during the election. Five of these people had been ministers in previous governments.

At that time, the situation was calm, especially in the capital. But I insisted on pointing out that this was a fragile peace, given that the gangs still had weapons as well as areas under their control.

In the meantime, the UN still had not decided who would replace Valdés. Several candidates were being discussed, including a Peruvian, an Argentine, a Uruguayan, and a Guatemalan.

Larry Rossin, a U.S. State Department official who had been Valdés's second-in-command, stood in temporarily. At one time he had served as Ronald Reagan's civil delegate during the military operation in Grenada. Rossin was well versed in the political complexities of the MINUSTAH mission. We got along well at work, but I must add he did not get along well with everyone else. He was criticized by some for his "Anglo-Saxon" attitude, in the sense that he expected everything to turn out as planned.

During his time as Valdés's replacement, Rossin invited me to accompany him to Préval's house for a meeting between General Elito and the mission's political advisers.

There had already been meetings between General Elito and Préval and his advisers. On the basis of those, we realized that Préval did not have a clear idea of how to deal with the gangs. All he had were vague notions, and the foremost among these was that the violence could be ended through dialogue. He wanted to give the gangs an opportunity to end the violence voluntarily.

When we arrived at Préval's residence, Casa Rosada — an impressive mansion owned by the Haitian Ministry of Foreign Affairs — we encountered tight security measures that forced us to leave our weapons in our vehicles.

We stepped onto a beautiful terrace overlooking the city and waited for Préval. Soon enough, we saw him come out, dressed casually in a T-shirt, jeans, and moccasins with no socks. He greeted us warmly, after which we sat at a table and he began to ask us for our views about the situation. While he asked questions, General Elito summarized the security issues. I kept silent, since it was up to my commander to speak for us both.

The meeting was almost over when Préval pointed at me and asked for my opinion.

This was the first time I ever spoke to him, and I let him know what I thought. From that point on we developed excellent rapport.

I told him that a truce with the gangs was well and good, but all of us knew how fragile and how temporary it was. I told him that we needed to know what he planned to do about the gangs: grant their leaders amnesty? deport them? fight them with the rule of law? That last one would be the right way.

And I told him that there were several issues related to the gang violence, such as the absence of police, dysfunctional judicial and penal systems, and the fact that the state had stopped helping its citizens. In a climate like that, I continued, you could not ask MINUSTAH to take specific action.

Préval studied me in silence while I gave him my views. When I was done,

Rossin gave his own, followed by Lisbeth from MINUSTAH Political Affairs and by Bob Manuel, who was also there.

Préval then replied that he wanted to give the gangs the chance to become part of a system of peace and disarmament and that he would do everything he could for that to happen. He added that he had developed relations with some of the gang leaders and that he would strive for a peaceful solution.

When he was finished, I told him that as members of MINUSTAH, we were required to follow the mandate the UN had assigned us. And the UN had called on us to provide a safe, stable environment for Haitians and that if, in trying to do so, we were shot at, we would have to respond in accordance with the guidelines the UN had set for us.

The meeting ended a few minutes later. We took some pictures as keepsakes. Préval was extremely gracious throughout. I left the president's home with the sense that Préval had inherited a highly complex situation in a country with many needs and few resources. He also faced profound structural issues. Yet I also sensed that he was an honest man who was trying to help his country and that it was our duty to help him succeed.

The day before he took office, Jeffrey Sachs, a noted American economist, paid him a visit. He offered Préval his views on what had to be done to improve Haiti's economy and overall situation.

I later heard that at the end of that meeting, Préval had looked hard at him and replied: "Look, you are absolutely right, but tomorrow morning when I take office, the teachers, the policemen and all the people in Haiti are going to ask me to pay them their salaries and I" — he put his hands in his pockets — "have no money at all."

That was the real situation in the country — a situation that would no doubt only cause problems for the new government.

I would have several subsequent meetings with President Préval. I always saw him as a good man with good intentions. But the weakness of Haiti's institutions and the poverty of its people has made it exceedingly difficult to solve the country's problems except perhaps in the very long term. And I am not sure the international community will have the stamina for that.

In any case, those of us present in Haiti at the time felt that he was one of the few people who might get a start on finding solutions for Haiti.

During the presidential campaign, some people had suggested that Préval was running for office simply to pave the way for Aristide's return. This had alarmed some elements of Haitian society, but especially some sectors of the international community. But when he took office, Préval would say only that the constitution allowed all citizens to freely enter and leave the country.

It did not help that from South Africa, Aristide was saying that the election results showed that Haitians wanted him to come home. In the event, he did not return, which has helped maintain peace in the country. His return would have led to disorder — something that I am sure Préval does not want. But unless the situation improves, even the thought that Aristide might return will threaten peace in Haiti. And I would point out that a number of the people who brought Haiti to its present state are also outside the country, and would also harm the country if they returned.

Préval's government contacted the gang leaders to try to persuade them to give up violence. We began receiving a trickle of information that the gangs were going to lay down their arms and that the violence would cease, but it never happened. Our patrols were still being fired on, and kidnappings were still occurring, albeit fewer of them.

I continued to believe that despite Préval's efforts, there were gangs that would never give up violence — it was simply too profitable.

Préval's stand toward the gangs began to harden. While still keeping his door open to their leaders, he began to urge us to take more action against them.

Once, while visiting the Parliament Building, the Minister of the Interior, Chief of Police Andressol, Ambassador Mulet, Commissioner Muir from UNPol, and I were at a meeting with Préval. The president spread out a map of the capital and began to say where and how he would like our troops deployed, detailing where he wanted our armoured cars to be located. He looked at me and said: "General Aldunate does not agree with me."

The others remained silent, waiting to hear me out. I calmly replied: "Mr. President, the safety and location or use of the soldiers is my responsibility. I am concerned that there still is no one from the Haitian state in Cité Soleil, that nothing has been done to help those people, and that there are still no Haitian police with us. To make matters worse, Mr. President, we are fighting the gangs while you are sending your car so that they can come and talk to you. This situation requires a decision on your side because it's inconceivable for my soldiers and untenable as a strategy for bringing peace to the country."

After a long silence, he said he would continue to seek a peaceful solution. If the gangs would not help him find one, he would be willing to support much more aggressive MINUSTAH action, even if this meant the loss of lives.

We left that meeting with the sense that we would be dealing with gang violence for a long time yet.

In July, President Préval invited me to his house along with Rossin (Photo 34). Whenever we met, the president would stand at attention and call me "general" in a relaxed, friendly tone. At that meeting, after a long conversation, to which Bob Manuel also contributed, the president asked us to step up our military actions in Cité Soleil.

I told him we were already doing that. Resorting to a Haitian proverb, I told him: "Mr. President, *piti piti swazo fè nich*," which in Creole means, "Little by

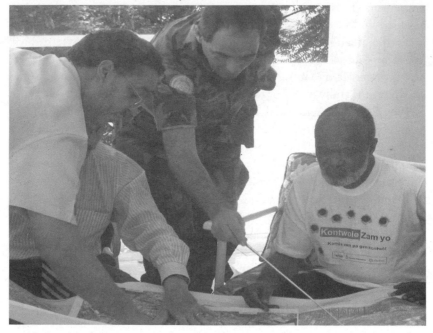

Photo 34. President Préval at a coordination meeting at his house

little, the bird makes its nest." He laughed heartily at my use of that proverb. And he saw my point, which was: we were gradually gaining control of Cité Soleil but there was no magic spell available to us. I pointed out that 12 of our Blue Helmets had been killed by the gangs and almost 90 wounded. That was why we were doing things in a professional, sensible way.

Noticing his positive, relaxed mood, I said, "Mr. President, I would like to ask you a favour."

"General, ask away."

I pointed out that guns on their own would not solve the violence in Cité Soleil, or elsewhere. I asked him to reopen the school in Cité Soleil and to assign Haitian police to the neighbourhood. It was important to win over the hearts and minds of the people who lived there, to get them on our side and isolate them from the criminals.

I told him once again that it was wrong not to have any Haitian police there, however difficult it might be to send them in. I also made it quite clear that the MINUSTAH forces could not succeed in Cité Soleil unless the government—especially the PNH—cooperated with them. He agreed with me and said he would work out how to make it happen.

Rossin suggested later that I might have been too harsh with the president. I replied that I was looking out for my soldiers, who were the only authorities present in Cité Soleil. As AFC, my duty was first to the mission and then to my troops' safety. I had told the president what I thought he needed to hear.

I thought it unfair and inappropriate when people called on MINUSTAH to use its sticks without offering any carrots. It occurred to me that past missions had failed for just that reason.

From July onward, Préval began to make more decisions against the gangs. This encouraged us to develop new operational proposals at headquarters. At a snail's pace—which is the speed at which things are done in Haiti, where there is only a present and no future—the help I insisted on getting began trickling in.

In late June we received a delegation from a Brazilian organization whose members had been soldiers in the Brazilian battalion that had taken part in the Suez War in the 1950s. This group, besides keeping alive the memory of those who had taken part in that event, sought to distinguish those who had excelled in humanitarian missions, especially Brazilian personnel who had taken part in peace missions.

General Elito told me that this organization had decided to award its medal to Lieutenant Colonel Carlos Díaz, Sergeant Major Alex Leiva, and me. An emotional ceremony was held at the General Bacellar Base. Present was the Brazilian Ambassador and all of his country's military personnel. It was yet another demonstration of friendship and appreciation from the Brazilian community.

In early July, Santiago informed us that we would receiving a visit from General Óscar Izurieta, the new Commander-in-Chief of the Chilean Army, and that a few days later President Michelle Bachelet would arrive with a delegation.

On July 20 the Army Commander-in-Chief arrived. We accompanied him to all our units in the capital and in Cap Haïtien. This was very important to everyone: it allowed our men to talk to him, and it allowed him to see first-hand what our troops were doing.

President Bachelet then flew in from Jamaica. She was already familiar with Haiti. When she was Minister of Defense, she had strongly encouraged the involvement of our Armed Forces in the mission. On Friday we attended a reception with her at the Parliament Building in a very relaxed atmosphere. She and President Préval danced together.

From there we all went to Cap Haïtien. This was followed by a presentation at MINUSTAH Headquarters, during which I expressed to our president my views on security in the country and the role the military were playing. Also president was Alejandro Foxley, the Chilean Foreign Minister. So was General Elito, who with his usual courtesy asked me to describe the events of the mission (Photos 35 and 36).

Photo 35. President Préval, General Izurieta, and I in Port-au-Prince

Photo 36. Greeting President Bachelet in Port-au-Prince

On Saturday afternoon the Chilean delegation returned home. Our president's visit was proof that Chile was committed to helping Haiti—a commitment greatly appreciated by all, especially by our troops.

Around that time I was summoned yet again, along with Larry Rossin, to appear before Préval. The president told us he wanted to visit Cité Soleil as soon as possible. He wanted to show people that their president was standing with them and that violence had no future.

That was a good idea but also too risky. I told him I could not guarantee his safety, so it could not be done. He replied that in that case, he wanted to go to Cité Militaire.

I thought that could be done without too much risk. There was always the threat of snipers, but we could arrange a less dangerous scenario.

Rossin told me to work out the details. I agreed, on one condition—that President Préval abide by our rules. We agreed that in two days, the president would be able to visit the area.

That same day I met with headquarters to plan security for him, since Cité Militaire was next to Cité Soleil.

The afternoon before Préval's visit, Rossin called to say that Préval was coming to our office to see how the arrangements for his visit were coming along. Within minutes, he arrived at headquarters.

Without any protocol, I invited him into my office. There I explained what we were going to do for his visit.

At one point, I let Préval know the limits of his visit in terms of what he could and should do and that he could only be in areas where we could ensure a reasonable level of safety. Also, that if I sensed any kind of danger, I would let the president know it was time to leave.

In a fit of pique, and in front of Préval, Rossin said, "General, as leader of the mission, that is something I will decide."

Calmly but firmly I answered that that was something that I, as the highest military authority, would decide and that there were no two ways about it.

There was an awkward silence. Then I approached Rossin to ask him if he was aware of the enormous problem we would have on our hands if Préval were hurt or killed. He did not reply, and I could tell that he had accepted my point.

For this event, which could have strategic consequences, Préval's security detail included Brazilian soldiers as well as officers from UNPol and the PNH. Once again, Colonel Sánchez showed strong initiative in planning and organizing this visit. This included placing snipers on rooftops in case they were necessary to drive off a gang attack.

I was with Préval while he visited Cité Militaire (Photo 37). At one point during his visit, in front of a crowd, which began to gather in great numbers

Photo 37. President Préval's visit to Cité Militaire

once people realized he was among them, and in front of the assembled press, he declared that those who had and used guns would be killed if they did not hand them over, so they had better stop doing violence. I believe that moment was vital to the mission, for the Haitian president had at last stated his resolve publicly and on the gangs' own turf.

Préval tried to advance beyond the area where our troops were providing security, but the crowd had grown and the ground was becoming dangerous. We no longer had good cover of some of the buildings, so I told him: "Mr. President, this is as far as we can go, we must turn back now." He accepted this without hesitation. That ended his visit, which I believe had many positive aspects. One of these was simply that he had been present in a dangerous zone where MINUSTAH was active. Another was his message of support for our work, to which he added that those who chose violence would find themselves confronted, so they had better lay down their weapons now.

A few days later, I got a call from Bob Manuel. He asked me to come to the Parliament, because he had heard that some gangs wanted to surrender their weapons in front of him. He read me the list of weapons, most of which I knew were no longer being used by the gangs, if they ever were. But he vouched for the accuracy of the list, which had been delivered to him that morning.

THE FIRST FEW MONTHS OF PRÉVAL'S GOVERNMENT **203**

So I went to the Parliament, hoping his list was accurate, though I doubted it. As it turned out, those weapons were never delivered. Even so, it was a clear sign that even though the government still maintained contact with the gangs, it wanted us to take a firm hand with them.

In August, Manuel called me again to tell me that a member of the Evans Ti Couteau gang wanted to surrender. He asked us for help with this, because the surrender would put a dent in the gang and might result in plenty of useful intelligence.

Since General Elito was on leave, I decided to support Manuel even though I wondered how useful this surrender would be. I arranged for this gang member to be taken to the Bacellar Base, where the Brazilians were stationed. I also drew up a complex system for his delivery and custody as well as a method for processing and evaluating any information he provided.

We found ourselves dealing with Ti Henry, a 25-year-old who could have been mistaken for a rap singer. He introduced himself, though, as Raoul Dentiste. According to our mandate, we could not hold him in custody in our barracks, so we took him in as a government "guest." To buttress that, I asked the Haitian authorities to send us a written document requesting this assistance.

As it happened, the information he gave us was unreliable and of little use. I do not doubt he was hoping for a plane ticket out of the country for himself and his family. Eventually, we handed him over to the Haitian authorities.

Around that time, another incident caused further worry at MINUSTAH Headquarters. We heard from Chile that our Puma helicopters were going to be withdrawn from the mission because of technical problems.

This was a serious blow to the mission. Those Pumas were the only aircraft we had with enough space to carry 12 men equipped for operations. The remaining helicopters, the Chilean UH-1Hs and the Argentine Bells, had less room, which would limit our forces' effectiveness.

Ambassador Young understood very well the impact the loss of those machines would have on the mission. He also worried that Chile's presence in Haiti would be diminished as a result.

But there no argument we could make to keep them. Those aircraft had to undergo maintenance, the amount depending on age and hours flown. How long we would be without them would depend on how much work they needed. At the end of July, they would be transported back to Chile for an indefinite period.

Their loss undoubtedly affected our performance, but with the support of our Helicopter Unit and the Argentine contingent, we adjusted as best we could. We also asked other countries to send helicopters. At the time my assignment ended, Brazil seemed likely to do so.

In August, Kofi Annan, the UN Secretary General, paid us a visit. During his 36 hours in Haiti, he held a meeting with the MINUSTAH personnel. He then asked for a meeting with the military personnel only. This was held in a large warehouse at the Logistics Base by the airport. At that meeting, he recalled that before rising to the UN's top job, he had worked at the DPKO. That meant he was well aware of the tasks that military contingents faced.

Before that meeting, Hedi Annabi, the second-in-command of the DPKO, who was visiting with Annan and would later replace Edmond Mulet as the mission's leader, invited me to chat in an office while we waited for his boss. Annabi told me that he knew my mission would end in a couple more months. Then he asked me to stay at my post for another year. He added that Ambassador Mulet had asked him to ask me and that the people in New York supported the request he was making.

I thanked him for his faith in me. Then I told him it was for my government and the Chilean Army to decide whether I stayed, and that if my government extended my assignment, I would remain in Haiti.

After the Secretary General returned to New York, many people on the mission, including Ayaka Suzuki and Ambassador Young, asked me to consider prolonging my assignment. My answer was always the same: that it was for my country to decide, and I would do what my country told me to do. Also, that in the Chilean Armed Forces, extensions of assignments are frowned upon — which is something I completely agree with.

As the days went by, Port-au-Prince remained peaceful, except of course, in Cité Soleil. By now the business community was pressuring Préval, and I think they were right to do so. The kidnapping rate might be lower, but the streets were still not safe.

We planned and carried out Operation Siege. This was intended to strengthen our control of Industry Avenue and Toussaint L'Ouverture, where most of the big commercial enterprises in Port-au-Prince are located. This was part of our general plan to advance toward Cité Soleil.

Operation Siege involved all the forces we had in the capital and produced excellent results. For the first time, we were able to rely on the daily presence of the PNH in that sector alongside our soldiers.

Our strategy, as planned at headquarters, was to exert steady pressure while advancing along every street and through every sector in Cité Militaire. The Blue Helmets would not get ahead of the UNPol and PNH officers. The government would have time to talk to the gangs while we were besieging Cité Soleil.

Our operations were no longer hampered by the elections. We were concerned, however, that more "open" operations might result in civilian casualties, so we intended to proceed gradually.

Cité Militaire and Cité Soleil were separated by Route #1, and the gangs travelled freely from one sector to the other. It was clear there should be only one command unit for both neighbourhoods, which were after all a single operating area. For that reason, General Elito sensibly changed the contingents' areas of operations.

The Brazilian battalion that had been responsible for Bel Air and Cité Militaire now expanded its zone to include Cité Soleil. That meant changing the AOR of the Jordanian unit, which was now assigned the route north up to the Cabaret district. The Jordanians also expanded their scope of action toward the border with the Dominican Republic, where they guarded the convoys taking aid to Haitian civilians.

The Brazilians were now in both Cité Militaire and Cité Soleil, the toughest areas of the capital, though Martissant, where the Sri Lankans were, was in the same league.

All of these decisions demonstrated General Elito's leadership skills. The mission's senior officers now had direct control over the most dangerous area.

In the early morning, the transfer of responsibilities was carried out in Cité Soleil. The arrival and departure of the new troops at CP16, which was inside that zone, had to be carried out methodically so as not to endanger our men.

For the first time we saw permanent FPU patrols from Senegal, China, Jordan and Pakistan on the streets of Cité Soleil and small PNH units doing what we had requested for so long: setting up police controls in conjunction with our troops. We finally had a suitable structure for carrying out our missions, even though our intelligence was still weak.

In addition, mobile patrols were deployed along these routes, which allowed us to keep the roads free so that citizens could travel, which in turn dramatically reduced the number of kidnappings. Meanwhile, we considered increasing the pace at which Brazilian troops were advancing inside Cité Militaire. All of this was sending the gangs in Cité Soleil a clear message: "You will be next after Cité Militaire. Either you stop the violence or we come and get you wherever you are."

Cité Militaire was under the control of Ti Blanc, whose gang members moved among various safe houses. Almost every day, we were receiving messages from that gang that its leaders wanted to surrender or that Ti Blanc was in some location or another. Rumours were part and parcel of Haitian life.

The Brazilian troops under Colonel Paulo Humberto continued to extend their control over Pele and Simón, two neighbourhoods in Cité Militaire. The gangs' gunfire and ambushes failed to halt their progress. In Cité Soleil, progress was slower, as we had expected.

We maintained the contingent at Checkpoint 16. Now, however, we launched a well-planned operation to gain the support of the people there through soldiers helping the community. To start with, the Brazilians painted and refurbished the plaza in front of their security post. For this, they hired some of the local people, who were eager for work. Soon enough, they had transformed the plaza into a leisure area and handed it back to the local people.

During this work, I paid them a visit. The gangs were still a threat, but no longer in front of CP16. Even so, we always had snipers on our roof, scanning the surrounding area with binoculars and alert to any situation.

The Brazilians were planning to install electricity in the plaza. Someone who knew the country well had told us that if the plaza was illuminated, safety problems would diminish. Unfortunately, by the end of my mission, this had still not been done. I hope it will be soon.

Soleil Street 9 crossed Cité Soleil from north to south, running in front of CP16. It marked the boundary between the Evans and Amaral gangs, Boston and Bellecou. This street was mostly dirt, which meant that every time it rained, it was impassable. Brazilian and Chilean engineers paved part of this road, which contributed greatly to people's living conditions besides improving our mobility.

Programs like these were a huge success. Perhaps one day the resources available for quick-impact projects will be channeled to military units.

Beccause Cité Soleil was still dangerous, as part of "Operation Siege" we increased our forces at CPs 18, 21 and 23. In particular, CP21 at Bois Neuf allowed us to protect this complicated area far more effectively than before.

During this operation, Peruvian troops patrolled Route #1 while the PNH and UNPol manned control points throughout the area.

Now we had a permanent presence in the entire sector, which made for better security. For the first time ever, we had a fully functioning security force.

The birthday of former President Aristide was on July 14, 2006. Despite all precautions, three Brazilian soldiers were wounded during gang attacks in the area between Boston and CP21.

As the days went by, we realized we were going to need more troops in the capital. Thus I ordered the redeployment of some contingents. An Uruguayan company and a Chilean platoon were brought in from Fort Liberté and Cap Haïtien respectively and assigned to Cité Soleil and Cité Militaire, under the commander of the Brazilian battalion, who was in charge of this AOR. We also deployed a Nepalese platoon and expanded the Sri Lankan unit's operating area to the north of Martissant.

All of this helped us sustain and quicken our advance in Cité Militaire. It also signaled that we intended to achieve complete control of Cité Soleil.

When the Chilean platoon — which was a Marine unit — arrived, I went to see them at the Helicopter Unit. There I explained to them what their mission was.

One day, I invited Ambassador Young to greet the soldiers who had arrived in the capital from Cap Haïtien, and we shared some moments with them. He told them how proud he was of them and how much faith he had in them. This platoon would rotate in and out of the neighbourhood with army personnel assigned to Cap Haïtien. All of them performed superbly while I was on the mission.

During this operation, I met with President Préval to explain the plan to him. Once again, I pressed him to support our efforts by reopening the school in Cité Soleil, which the local children needed so badly. Unfortunately, he did not do this, at least while I was on the mission. I also asked him to set up a PNH post in the neighbourhood, which I assured him we would protect. This did not happen either.

By now we were strengthening our control of the area with each passing day. This, despite complaints from some politicians and even from the gangs, who were blaming *us* for the violence. Their allegations were never proved, and the results of our work continued to show promise.

President Préval visited the area of operations and later phoned us to share his positive impressions. I told Ambassador Mulet and Préval himself that the zone of operationas should be left to us, the military commanders, and that thè president should devote his time to his own duties. But I also realized that his enthusiasm was crucial to our own success.

My days were packed with visits to the checkpoints and to the units outside the capital. There were also constant MINUSTAH meetings to attend. General Elito had adopted the same policy as General Bacellar: he represented us at these meetings; I devoted myself to activities with the troops. Unless, of course, he was on leave or away from the capital.

At the beginning of September, Ambassador Mulet summoned me to his office and again asked me to extend my mission for another year. I thanked him for his faith in me but told him I had been sent for a year and that whoever replaced me would no doubt perform his duties efficiently. I added that if the Chilean Army and government decided I should stay, I would do so.

Ambassador Young told me he was doing everything he could to convince the Chilean Foreign Ministry to extend my mission.

I was getting phone calls from New York asking me to stay on, and people from the mission were asking the same. I had to tell all of them the same thing: that the decision was my government's to make and that I would do what my country asked me to do.

At the end of a meeting with President Préval at the Parliament, he took my arm and said, "General, as long as the problem of safety is not resolved, you cannot leave Haiti. If need be, I will speak to President Bachelet."

I thanked him for that but reminded him that the decision was not mine.

Bob Manuel called me on my cellphone and told me that if necessary, his president would call Chile to request an extension of my mission. I told him that Chilean institutions had their own procedures and that he should allow them to play out in the normal way, without interference.

During this period, the matter of choosing my replacement was at a standstill in New York because they were waiting for a decision from Santiago about my future.

I was honoured that they all wanted me to stay. At the same time, doing so would have a personal cost to me, even though my family had always supported me on this mission.

Few qualified people in my profession ever have the chance to practise their leadership skills in circumstances like this. Even so, my feelings about staying on were mixed. On the one hand, this was an exciting and deeply fulfilling mission. The military action, in addition to the political work and social interaction, was deeply satisfying and made me proud to be wearing the Chilean flag. On the other, I sincerely believed that it was for my country to decide what it wanted of me.

I told General Izurieta that I was willing to accept whatever decision our country made: I would stay if it asked. But we both knew that Chile's best interests had to be considered. Moreover, other countries in the region had a right to participate in MINUSTAH.

A few weeks before my assignment ended, I was asked through official channels to extend my stay for two more months. I told New York and the army itself that they were the ones who had to decide and that my only duty was to follow orders.

At times like these, I remembered my first conversations with General Lugani and General Heleno. They had told me this could only be a one-year mission owing to the tremendous pressure it involved.

In early September, Chile decided that my mission would end in September 2006 as had been established. Now the process of seeking a replacement began in earnest.

It was decided that General Raúl Gloodtdofsky of Uruguay would replace me. I began to pack.

CHAPTER SIXTEEN

Putting My Backpack Away

FOLLOWING THE DECISION that my mission would end — my final day would be September 30, 2006 — I began the checking-out process.

I sent my military equipment back to Chile on the contingents' transfer flights. With Carlos Díaz I drew up a detailed list of things I had left to do. Those included saying farewell to the contingents. We made plans for me to visit all the units in the country over a period of two weeks. Which I did.

I visited all the battalions, companies and facilities, where I received warm displays of affection from the personnel. It was gratifying to hear the soldiers themselves tell me that our mission had been accomplished and our objectives realized.

At each of these meetings, after the military ceremonies, the soldiers gave me souvenirs. The Nepalese gave me a *kukri*, the famous Gurkha knife, which is a wonderful weapon very similar to our own curved blade, the *corvo*.

All the soldiers were very pleasant and full of goodwill toward me, but the Peruvian units had a surprise in store. One day their commander invited me to inaugurate a firing range, so I headed to Ambassador Young's quarters next to Cité Soleil.

When we arrived, we witnessed a shooting drill that began with snipers emerging from holes that had been dug only a few metres from where I was standing. They appeared suddenly, shooting at targets about 15 metres from us, using live rounds and hitting all their targets.

Photo 38. Farewell from President Préval at the Parliamentary Building

At the end of this display, I was invited to step onto the shooting range myself. Fortunately, I managed to hit all the targets.

After this, we had lunch with all the members of the unit. They gave me a bust of Colonel Bolognesi, a hero of the Pacific War, as well as a beret from the Peruvian unit, which filled me with pride. It was proof of how closely we had bonded. Considering past relations between our countries, that was no small accomplishment.

Then I went with General Elito and Ambassador Mulet to visit President Préval, who met us in his office at the Parliament along with Robert Manuel (Photo 38).

At that meeting, Préval thanked me for all I had done for his country and recalled the difficult moments we had faced and the good relations the two of us had developed. He admitted that the present peace in Haiti was largely a result of MINUSTAH's efforts. He told me he had wanted me to stay on, but that he understood why the Chilean government had made the decision to bring me home.

As a memento, I gave him a Chilean *corvo* knife and told him that Haiti would always be a part of my life and that I would continue to try to help his country.

By the end of September my replacement, General Raúl Gloodtdofsky, had arrived. As soon as he did we carried out an intense program of handing over responsibilities, which included various working meetings and visits to the units.

MINUSTAH's official goodbye to me was hosted by the Brazilians at the General Bacellar Barracks. All of the commanders of the contingents were present; so were most of the ambassadors of countries with troops in Haiti, along with other authorities. At that ceremony I was awarded the UN Medal, which I accepted with pride. The importance of this medal is reflected in the fact that the Blue Helmets have won the Nobel Prize for Peace. When I was given the medal, I could not stop thinking about the soldiers who died while I was on the mission. I recalled especially General Bacellar (Photos 39 and 40).

At MINUSTAH Headquarters, General Elito hosted an emotional farewell party for me. During that session, which all the HQ personnel attended, he expressed some moving thoughts concerning my departure from the mission and gave me a present—a UN insignia that I keep in my office to this day.

Later, Ambassador Young hosted a luncheon at his home in my honour at which personnel from the national contingents as well as some Haitian officials and guests were present. He and his wife Isabel showered me with affection.

Departure day finally came, and a delegation of the national units and officers from MINUSTAH Headquarters went to the airport to see me off. My mission in Haiti had ended.

On the plane, I spent a long time thinking about all I had seen and done over the past year and realized that my experience had exceeded my expectations in every way.

I felt that I had accomplished my goals as commander. I was proud of the relationships I had built with the various contingents and with the civilians I had worked beside.

On the plane, while I gazed down on the country's topography, I wondered what would happen to its people next. Would they be able to overcome their situation? How many more Haitians would succumb to violence and poverty before their country stood on its feet?

As we flew to Miami, I knew that this country's people and their culture and all the things I had experienced during that year would forever remain in my heart and memories. My duty now was to convey these experiences and visions to my superiors and to anyone who wanted to know more about what goes on in Haiti. I considered this a moral obligation. In particular, there were many experiences I felt I needed to pass on to our personnel.

As the island disappeared from the airplane window, I thought about how different and unfair Haiti's situation is compared to that of a world less than a two-hour flight away.

I remembered the faces of the children who went to school so neatly dressed and with so much hope in their eyes.

The reality they experienced every day was in sharp contrast to those trite speeches on globalization and modernization. But at least we had given them hope for a better future and made a dignified and fulfilling life more conceivable.

Photo 39. General Elito presenting the UN Award

Photo 40. Ambassador Edmond Mulet, Representative of the UN Secretary General in Haiti

Once back in Chile, I called on the Army Commander-in-Chief and the Minister of Defence and gave them a brief account of my mission and of the overall situation at MINUSTAH. I told the Minister of Defence that a number of issues concerning Haiti should be dealt with differently.

It seems that many people thought that my one-year stay in the Caribbean tropics was a bit of a well-paid holiday for me. Chileans know next to nothing about the true nature of the mission — of what really goes on in Haiti or the state of violence, poverty and despair one has to face without losing heart.

Days after my arrival in Santiago, I met with many authorities with whom I shared my impressions and misgivings regarding our country's involvement in MINUSTAH.

I told them that Chile was benefiting greatly from the mission, for it was demonstrating the abilities of our armed forces as well as our commitment to helping a sister nation in our region. Furthermore, our troops were setting a high standard of discipline and expertise, which is something all the other national contingents acknowledged. I also believed that as representatives of our country, we were winning the hearts of the Haitians.

I also told them that a mission such as this, ruled by Chapter VII, was dangerous by definition and that it might well result in Chilean casualties. I wasn't sure that Chilean society was prepared to accept soldiers' deaths as part of the commitment we had assumed. If we ever sent one of our soldiers home in a casket, a difficult domestic situation might well be created, and this had to be anticipated.

I also expressed my concern about the politics of the mission, stressing the frailty of the security that had been achieved and the need to move forward in much steadier ways to solve Haiti's structural problems — ways that did not rely solely on the military.

I added that it was necessary to conduct a much deeper analysis of the existing threats before even considering whether to send or withdraw troops or police. I pointed out that Haiti continued to face huge problems and was going to need long-term commitments from other countries and that the international community must not jeopardize all the gains that had been made by pulling out too soon.

There are many excellent lessons to be learned from Chile's (and my own) experience in MINUSTAH. The first is that the Chilean forces (including me) had received excellent training that prepared them to cope with the challenges they faced in Haiti.

Second, all Chileans on the mission were benefiting from an extraordinary chance to interact with humanitarian, social, international and press agencies as well as politicians and officials. For my part, the mission had involved me in a variety of fields where I worked with a multitude of fascinating people.

One of the advantages of this type of mission is that senior officers must constantly engage with politicians, humanitarian officials, human rights advocates and the press — with all the people who make it possible for such missions to succeed.

I must stress the importance of our professional training, which compelled us to remember the goals of the UN resolutions — goals that I relied on as guides when so many people were demanding that we forget our mandate and resort to rash force.

It is also important to mention the leadership training provided by our military schools and academies. Those institutions emphasize that personal conduct and moderation are vital to strong leadership. I saw this validated in the extreme circumstances we encountered in Haiti: a commander must always be with his troops at crucial moments. Leadership is something that must be practiced, not just preached.

I believe that the situation in Haiti was better than when I arrived and that MINUSTAH can be thanked for that. I also believe that this mission faces two significant threats.

The first of these threats is the pessimism of those who think that progress is too slow and that there is no overall solution for Haiti. With that, I certainly do not agree. The second and perhaps more dangerous threat is that many people think the job is done and that it is time to withdraw.

I know our military cannot stay in Haiti forever, but I hope that a proper evaluation will be carried out before a decision is made. I believe that the situation in East Timor, where the UN withdrew too soon, is a good example of what not to do.

I think we must work toward a stronger contingent of civilian advisers, but I would not dare suggest how much longer the military contingents should stay. I do hope that any analysis of the situation takes into account the country's actual problems.

Sometimes I wonder if we are truly aware of how big a problem we would face if this mission failed. Because of its current insecurity and weak state institutions, Haiti is an excellent transshipment point for drug traffickers in the Western Hemisphere.

It is also important to remember the suffering that Haitians would face and the disappointment they would feel if the UN mission failed. Their lives are still precarious, but at least they are better than before, and the people have entrusted their future progress to the Blue Helmets.

I am grateful for the opportunity my country offered me to serve on an international mission. I was able to work alongside many civilians, agencies and NGOs and to see how valuable their work is. I encountered many men and women who worked in difficult circumstances in the pursuit of an ideal.

Photo 41. With young schoolchildren in Port-au-Prince

I must also say how satisfying it was to have commanded so many officers and NCOs from the countries taking part in MINUSTAH. They were thorough professionals who respected the UN's mandate, their international counterparts, and the Haitian people. Their blood and sweat has not been in vain.

For missions to be more successful, a more complete discussion of everything involved will be required so that participating nations can achieve their goals more effectively. This will mean taking responsibility for the costs and strongly supporting those who participate. It will also mean avoiding the temptation to confuse state policies with domestic politics, because soldiers on the front lines risking their lives — and for that matter, the families of those soldiers — deserve all of our society's support.

Today, those of us who were on this mission value the simple things in life more. We MINUSTAH veterans eventually got used to Haiti's reality, but none of us can fully understand how a country can exist for centuries without functioning institutions and without a government capable of providing its citizens with their most basic needs: running water, electricity, respect for the law, a competent and respected police force.

We talk a lot about the twenty-first century, but it is worth remembering that many countries are still only on the threshold of the *twentieth* century.

In a globalized world, science and technology sometimes overwhelm us with their rapid impact on our lives. This mission reminds us that besides the Einsteins and Steve Jobs there are also Don Quixotes — which is excellent news for those, like me, who believe that many people let themselves be guided by feelings and ideals. There are more people like that than you might imagine. And that group includes the Blue Helmets.

Haiti's future will depend largely on its own people's capacity to develop durable institutions. Nothing could be worse than letting Haiti fall back into chaos, and I believe we should support that nation until President Préval's democratic government finds its feet.

There is no doubt, as I told President Préval when I said goodbye to him, that Haiti will always be with me alongside my memories of the soldiers who served with me there.

The first thing I did when I was promoted to my new post was to put my backpack in my office, because one never knows when it might come in handy.

What I had with me in my backpack was a lot of hope. I believe we delivered this and that we will continue to do so whenever we are required.

Index

Note: Page numbers in italics refer to illustrations. For abbreviations used in the index, please consult the List of Abbreviations, page xv.

Books in the Studies in International Governance Series

Eduardo Aldunate, translated by Alma Flores
Backpacks Full of Hope: The UN Mission in Haiti / 2010 / xx + 232 pp. /
ISBN 978-1-55458-155-9

Alan S. Alexandroff, editor
Can the World Be Governed? Possibilities for Effective Multilateralism / 2008 /
ISBN 978-1-55458-041-5

Hany Besada, editor
*From Civil Strife to Peace Building: Examining Private Sector Involvement in West African
Reconstruction* / forthcoming 2009 / ISBN 978-55458-052-1

Jennifer Clapp and Marc J. Cohen, editors
The Global Food Crisis: Governance Challenges and Opportunities / 2009 / xviii + 270 pp. /
ISBN 978-1-55458-192-4

Andrew F. Cooper and Agata Antkiewicz, editors
Emerging Powers in Global Governance: Lessons from the Heiligendamm Process / 2008 /
xxii + 370 pp. / ISBN 978-1-55458-057-6

Jeremy de Beer, editor
Implementing WIPO's Development Agenda / 2009 / xvi + 188 pp. /
ISBN 978-1-55458-154-2

Geoffrey Hayes and Mark Sedra, editors
Afghanistan: Transition under Threat / 2008 / xxxiv + 314 pp. /
ISBN-13: 978-1-55458-011-8 / ISBN-10: 1-55458-011-1

Paul Heinbecker and Patricia Goff, editors
Irrelevant or Indispensable? The United Nations in the 21st Century / 2005 / xii + 196 pp. /
ISBN 0-88920-493-4

Paul Heinbecker and Bessma Momani, editors
Canada and the Middle East: In Theory and Practice / 2007 / ix + 232 pp. /
ISBN-13: 978-1-55458-024-8 / ISBN-10: 1-55458-024-2

Mokhtar Lamani and Bessma Momani, editors
From Desolation to Reconstruction: Iraq's Troubled Journey / forthcoming 2010 / 226 pp. /
ISBN 978-1-55458-229-7

Yasmine Shamsie and Andrew S. Thompson, editors
Haiti: Hope for a Fragile State / 2006 / xvi + 131 pp. / ISBN-13: 978-0-88920-510-9 /
ISBN-10: 0-88920-510-8

Debra P. Steger, editor
Redesigning the World Trade Organization for the Twenty-first Century / 2009 /
ISBN 978-1-55458-156-6

James W. St.G. Walker and Andrew S. Thompson, editors
Critical Mass: The Emergence of Global Civil Society / 2008 / xxviii + 302 /
ISBN-13: 978-1-55458-022-4 / ISBN-10: 1-55458-022-6

Jennifer Welsh and Ngaire Woods, editors
Exporting Good Governance: Temptations and Challenges in Canada's Aid Program / 2007 /
xx + 343 pp. / ISBN-13: 978-1-55458-029-3 / ISBN-10: 1-55458-029-3